VIEW ON THE RIO MOTAGUA.

[*Frontispiece.*]   [See page 414.]

SUMMERLAND SKETCHES,

OR

RAMBLES IN THE BACKWOODS

OF

MEXICO AND CENTRAL AMERICA.

"Man's gardens blossom in the north,
But Nature's in the south."—CAMOENS.

BY

FELIX L. OSWALD.

WITH NUMEROUS ILLUSTRATIONS

BY H F. FARNY AND HERMANN FABER

PHILADELPHIA:

J. B. LIPPINCOTT & CO.

1880.

PREFACE.

In the winter of 1867 I was stationed at Medellin, near Vera Cruz, as director of an overcrowded military lazaretto. With accommodations for sixty men we had to take charge of two hundred, besides feeding and nursing a considerable number of destitute civilians, both Indians and whites, who had been quartered in the loft of a neighboring cotton-press. Our white charity patients were neither charitable nor patient; they clamored for the expulsion of their Indian countrymen, denounced the French steward as an Oriental .barbarian, and bemoaned the departed glory of the Republic when I stopped their rations of smoking-tobacco. The scum of the Guachinangos, or homeless Creoles of the adjacent seaport-town, they were a lot of graceless scamps, with the apparent exception of a heroic old 'longshoreman who had been brought in an ambulance by a detachment of the harbor police, having nearly bled to death from two wounds which looked very much like French bayonet stabs.

But the supposed exception confirmed the rule when our hero turned out to be a Tabasco indigo planter who had been forced to join Rion's guerillas, and after the defeat of his corps and the confiscation of his property had made his way to Vera Cruz, wounded and penniless, in the hope of gaining admission to the City Hospital. His recovery was slow, but from first to last he behaved with a fortitude that won him the respect of his military nurses, and by and by the sympathy of our city visitors. A Vera Cruz merchant

5

-ent him a fine saddle-horse, and before I discharged him
we collected money enough to help him over the first six
months, or across the ocean if he should prefer to leave the
country. He was a native of Reus in Western Catalonia.
Mexico was on the eve of a general revolution, and the
State of Tabasco was still under martial law, but the
ranchero decided to stay.

"Twelve years ago I crossed the ocean of my own accord,
and I do not repent it even now," he said, when he mounted
his horse at the hospital gate. "Mexico is the freest country
on earth, after all. They may blockade the valleys, and
change their President for a Sultan, for all I care; but there
is freedom in the mountains, and I know a place of refuge
where neither monarchs nor demagogues will bother me."

After the restoration I transferred my medical apparatus
to the Vera Cruz City Dispensary, and the health officer of
the quarantine having tendered his resignation, the foreign
residents recommended me as his successor, with a view of
testing the efficacy of a system of sanitary precautions,
whose adoption I had urged for many years. But the fal-
lacy of that system was demonstrated, to my personal satisfaction at least, by the collapse of my own health. Neither
surf-baths nor dietetic sacrifices would avail me, the climate
refuted the most cogent pathological axioms; and I was on
the point of embarking for a less paradoxical latitude, when
I remembered the man of Reus and his solution of a similar dilemma. Learning that there was a junta of inspecting
officers at the fort, I called upon a former colleague, now
Surgeon-General and member of the Government Immi-
gration Committee. Soon after his return to the capital I
received a communication from the Department of the Interior, and on the same day I exchanged a sea-water proof
trunk for a Mexican pack-saddle. The coast range was

shrouded with the mists of the rainy season, and my countrymen dismissed me with sore misgivings, and gave me
up for lost when they learned that a congestive chill had
arrested my progress at Puebla, but my next letter reassured
them.

"Mexico is the healthiest country on earth, after all,"
I wrote from Tacubaya, the Montmartre of the Mexican
capital; "the fever may blockade your seaports and terror-
ize the lowlands from Matamoros to Yucatan, but in the
mountains is freedom, and I have found a place of refuge
where miasmi and mosquitoes will never bother me."

In the course of the next eight years I explored the highlands of Jalisco, Oaxaca, Colima, and Vera Paz, for the
benefit of my own health or that of my employers, but like
the Catalan farmer, I found more than I had sought. Independence, in the political sense, and a healthy climate
might be found in the mountains of Scotland, and even of
old Spain; but the New Spanish sierras can boast of a
virgin soil with primeval forests which offer a sanitarium to
all who seek refuge from the malady of our anti-natural
civilization, from the old *marasmus* which has spread from
the Syrian desert to the abandoned cotton-fields of Georgia
and Alabama.

We vaunt our proficiency in the art of subjugating nature, but in the Old World the same ambition has led to a
very dear-bought victory, which the countries of the East
have paid with the loss of their forests, and the Eastern
nations with the loss of their manhood; their wild woodlands have been tamed into deserts, and their wild freemen
into slaves; the curse of the blighted land has recoiled upon
its devastators. In our eagerness to wrest the sceptre from
our Mother Earth we have invaded her domain with fire and
sword, and instead of increasing the interest of our heritage

we have devoured the principal; the brilliant progress of the vain god of earth is tracked by a lengthening shadow, the day-star of our empire is approaching the western horizon.

Where shall it end? Mould, sandy loam, and sand is Liebig's degeneration-scale of treeless countries; the American soil may pass through the same phases, and what then? Will the sun-set in the west be followed by a new eastern sunrise? Shall Asia, the mother of religions, give birth to an earth-regenerating Messiah, whose gospel shall teach us to recognize the physical laws of God? Or shall the gloaming fade into the night of the Buddhistic Nirvana, the final extinction of organic life on this planet? It is not much of a consolation to think that in the latter case the nations of the higher latitudes might count upon a protracted twilight. The westward spread of the landblight will drive the famished millions of the Old World upon our remaining woodlands, but the resources of the last Oasis will probably be husbanded with Scotch canniness and Prussian systematism, and before we share the fate of the Eastern nations we may see the dawn of the bureaucratic millennium, when all our fields shall be fenced in with brick walls, all rivers with irrigation-dykes, and all functions of our domestic life with official laws and by-laws. My trust in the eternal mercy of Providence lets me expect another deluge before that time, but the recuperative agencies of unaided nature seem powerless against the greatest of all earthly evils. National and territorial marasmus are incurable diseases; the historical records of the Eastern continents, at least, prove nothing to the contrary. The coast-lands of the Mediterranean were the pleasure-gardens of the Juventus Mundi, the Elysian Fields whose inhabitants celebrated life as a festival; and now? Spain, Southern Italy, Turkey, Greece, and Persia have been wasted to a shadow of their former self, ghouls and afrits haunt the burial-places of the North African empires; and no invocation can break the death-slumber of Asia Minor. Acorns perish in the soil which once nourished the oaks of Bashan; outraged nature refuses to be reconciled. With the glory of the Orbis Romanus the spring-time of our earth has departed, and what America mistakes for the prime of a new year is but the lingering mildness of an Indian summer.

The career whose swiftness is our national boast has led us upon a road which has never been far pursued with impunity; the rapidity of our tree and game destruction is far more unparalleled than the growth of our cities; the misery of the Old World has not taught us to avoid its causes, and the history of the effects will not fail to repeat itself. On the frozen shores of Lake Winnepeg and the inaccessible heights of the central Rocky Mountains a few remnants of the old forests will probably survive, but the great East American Sylvania is already doomed; if we persist in our present course our last timber-States, Maine, Michigan, and North Carolina, will be as bald as Northern Italy in fifty years from now, and our last game will soon retreat to the festering swamps of Southern Florida.

The temperate zone of America will soon be the treeless zone, with a single exception. In the sierras of Southern Mexico large tracts of land still combine a generous climate with a rich arboreal vegetation. Mexico, like our own Republic, has her backwoods States, but their security from the inroads of the destroyer is guaranteed by better safeguards than their remoteness from the great commercial centres. The ruggedness of the surrounding sierras, the supposed or real scarcity of precious metals, and the independent character of the aboriginal population, all conspire to make the *alturas* or mountain forests as unattractive to the imperious Spaniards as they are inviting to freedom-loving visitors from the North.

To my rambles and adventures in these *alturas*, to their scenic charms, their strange fauna and vegetable wonders, I have devoted this volume; but I have rarely touched upon the mineral and agricultural resources of a region which should remain consecrate to the Hamadryads and their worshippers. The cities of the intervening "civilized" districts, too, I have only mentioned as wayside stations for the benefit of non-pedestrian tourists. New Spain makes no exception from the general rule that the nations of Europe have transformed their American dependencies after the image of their mother-countries, and only he who leaves the cities far behind can forget that Mexico was colonized under the auspices of St. Jago and Ximenes.

This collection of "Summerland Sketches" is therefore neither a record of a pilgrimage to the shrines and cathedrals of Spanish America, nor a bid for the patronage of Southwestern land-agencies, but rather a guide-book to one of the few remaining regions of earth that may give us an idea of the tree-land eastward in Eden which the Creator intended for the abode of mankind. In the terrace-lands of Western Colima and Oaxaca, near the head-waters of the Rio Lerma and the mountain lakes of Jalisco, and in the lonely highlands of Vera Paz, we may yet see forests that have never been desecrated by an axe, and free fellow-creatures which have not yet learned to flee from man as from a fiend.

Let us make the best of that last chance, for the time may be near when princes and sages shall envy those who have managed to get a glimpse of Paradise before the gates were closed forever.

FELIX L. OSWALD.

CINCINNATI, *March* 1880.

CONTENTS.

CHAPTER I.

SONORA

CHAPTER II.

COLIMA.

CHAPTER III

THE LAKE-REGION OF JALISCO

CHAPTER V.

THE SIERRA MADRE.

CHAPTER VI

LA TIERRA FRIA

CHAPTER VII

THE VALLEY OF OAXACA

CHAPTER VIII

THE DELTA OF THE SUMASINTA RIVER

CHAPTER IX

RAMBLES IN YUCATAN

CHAPTER X.

THE AMERICAN POMPEII

CHAPTER XI.

THE BACKWOODS OF GUATEMALA.

CHAPTER XII

THE VIRGIN WOODS OF THE SIERRA NEGRA

LIST OF ILLUSTRATIONS.

SUMMERLAND SKETCHES.

CHAPTER I.

SONORA.

Mi pays y los montes me llaman,
Los montes aιιosos del Sιι.—MANUEL VILLÉGAS

OUR boat had left Fort Yuma on a cold October morning, and a little before sunset we entered the Gulf of California. Either the weather had moderated during the afternoon, or the first ten hours of our voyage had brought us to a latitude where October is still a summer month, for some of my fellow-passengers appeared on deck in their shirt-sleeves, and even the Mexican sailors had folded their *ponchos* into pillows and slept or smoked under the lee of the caboose.

Before the twilight disappeared from the mountain-summits of the Californian peninsula I had spread my couch on the pilot-deck, and tried to remember what omens a professional augur would have found in the swarms of migratory birds that accompanied our vessel on her way to the South, when the evening stillness was broken by that ingenious instrument whose sound combines the harmonies of a fog-horn and a steam slate-factory—a genuine Chinese gong.

"Those things will be safe enough up here," I told the cabin-boy, who had just brought my overcoat and a

2

travelling cushion: "I shall be back in ten or fifteen minutes."

The passenger-list of the Gila City included some characteristic specimens of an ethnological class who, in reference to their behavior, can hardly be described as Pacific Americans. There were two excited Sacramento politicians, hot from a ratification-meeting; a troop of miners, on their way to the Sonora diggings, who swore that they were "flush enough to afford it," and threatened to treat all round; there was a commercial traveller, who insisted on talking ungrammatical Spanish; and a little lawyer from San Bernardino County, whose anecdotes would have been interesting contributions to the border chronicle of Southern California if he had been sober; and when a deep-mouthed butcher from Los Angeles became vocal under the influence of the *vino de mezcal,* I stole away to my cabin, got a couple of blankets, and returned to my freehold on the pilot-deck. I wanted to enjoy the luxuries of silence, especially a feeling of growing exultation which my spirit somehow evolved from the consciousness that every hour brought me ten or twelve miles nearer to a land of perennial summer. Are there any germs or remnants of the bird-of-passage instinct in the human soul? I think the phenomenon admits of a different explanation.

This earth of ours is at present ruled by a race of valiant Northmen, and some fur-clad philosophers have assured us that not only valor, but civilization and science, as well as virtue—and consequently happiness—are plants which can only thrive in the snow. It would be more correct to say that science and civilization, which flourished in open air during the golden age of the Mediterranean nations, have become hot-house plants in the nineteenth century. The ripening of their fruits still depends upon a certain amount of caloric, only with this difference,—that the maturative warmth which once emanated from the central body of the solar system has now to be paid for in the form of sea-coal and kindling-wood. But happiness, and that physical beatitude of which health is only the principal condition, have never prospered in the atmosphere of the conservatory. Sunlight cannot be entirely superseded by coal-gas. In the intervals of our noisy Northern factory-life there are moments when echoes from the land of our forefathers become audible in the human soul ; and I think that at such times many of my European and North American fellowmen become conscious of a feeling which I might describe as a Southern homesickness. For man is a native of the tropics, and, like the shell that still murmurs its dreams of the sea, the spirit of the exiled human race has never ceased to yearn for our lost garden-home in the South. In his essay on the hereditary instincts of the human animal, Herbert Spencer remarks that the strange charm of what we call a romantic landscape—*i.e.*, a wild chaos of rocks and forests, the more savage the better—probably dates from a time when that emotion had a practical significance and filled the souls of our woodcrafty ancestors with visions of hidden game and a successful chase. In a similar way, our Paradise traditions, the myth of the Elysian Gardens, the evergreen meadows of the Talmud, as also the Northern saga of a land without winter sorrows, have probably been transmitted from a time when all mankind enjoyed such privileges of the blest on this side of the grave. We may never know if the cradle of our primogenitor stood on the banks of the Indus or in Southern Armenia, or, as Maupertuis tells us, in the mountain-gardens of Arabia Felix ; but all historical and mythological indications point to the South, as well as all tenable theories *a priori*. What imagination

could locate the Garden of Eden in a Russian peat-bog or
in a Manitoba beaver-swamp? Neither Adam and Eve
nor Darwin's four-handed ancestor could have survived a
Canadian winter, and even the Saturnian age of the first
agricultural nations could hardly be reconciled with the
climate of Old or New England. With all the calorific
artifices which the experience of the last hundred generations has transmitted to our century, with well-warmed
workhouses and hospitals for consumptives, the burghers of
Manchester and Boston may manage to counteract the worst
effects of a low temperature, but the nations who "celebrated
life as a festival" have inhabited a different latitude.

"*Los montes airosos del Sur*"—"the airy mountains of
the South"—imparted the same charm to the crusades of
the Knights Templar as to those of the Conquistadores;
the migration of the wild Asiatic hordes carried them to
the Southwest; the New England tourist departs for the
Southeast; and the Italian hegiras of the British poets, the
châteaux d'Espagne of the French romancers, and the old
lament of the children of Israel for their lost Promised
Land, are not inspired by a predilection for any special
country, as much as by an undefined Southern homesickness. "Every mile toward the noonday sun," says the
returning exile in the *Mega Dhuta*, "brings us nearer to
the home of our fathers, the land of sweet tree-fruits and
everlasting summer."

The cabin of the Gila City was much infested with
cockroaches and cocktail odors, and the pilot-deck was too
damp to be altogether lovely; but I remembered that
every revolution of the paddle-wheels diminished the degree of Northern latitude, and the starry hours have not
often brought me happier dreams than those in that October night on the Gulf of California.

The sea-coast of Sonora, with its rocky promontories, abounds in coves and natural breakwaters where the feluccas of the Mexican fishermen may find shelter in any kind of weather. The unrivalled seaport of Acapulco alone excepted, the mouth of the Rio del Toro, near Guaymas, is

PUERTO DE GUAYMAS.

probably the finest harbor of the Northern Pacific, but the trade of the mountainous province is nearly monopolized by an inland market, and the little seaport-town has not much improved since the Spaniards fortified the Boca del Rio in 1685. There are only three *posadas* or hostelries where the traveller can find lodging as well as food, and I had no difficulty in ascertaining the rendezvous of the Morgan teamsters.

The "Morgan Trade and Transport Company" of San Francisco sends a monthly caravan of "prairie-schooners" from Guaymas to San Luis Potosi, and their east-bound freight is generally landed six days in advance of its departure from the sea-coast. As the captain of the Gila

City informed me that his boat had delivered the last cargo a week ago, I lost no time in making my way to the caravansary. Several mules, ready harnessed and saddled, were hitched to the gate of the corral, and the bustle and hubbub in the wagon-shed admonished me to prepare for immediate marching orders.

"How are you, señor?" the company's little clerk hailed me from one of the tent-wagons. "You are our passenger for San Luis, are you not? Can you tell me if there is any mail for us on the Gila?"

"The mail-boy was inquiring for you at the hotel," I replied. "How's Boss Davis, the wagonmaster? He's nearly done loading, it seems?"

"He's not done swearing yet," said the youngster: "I think I hear him back there in that second shed. He inquired for you at different times."

"Glad to see you, doctor!" cried the "Boss," jumping to terra firma from a pile of swaying dry-goods boxes. "I was just going to send for a good interpreter: it takes a dozen curses of sixteen syllables apiece to start a Mexican muleteer, and I was near the end of my vocabulary. Let me get the axle-grease off my fingers before we shake hands. You are just in time: I am going to fix you a seat in my own wagon, unless you prefer otherwise. There will be plenty of room. Do you know that old Fatty Heninger left us last month?"

"I thought so. It seems you've got a brand-new clerk since I saw you at headquarters?"

"Yes, quite a boy: he can ride in my lunch-basket or anywhere. But did you let him weigh your baggage?"

"No: my things are at the posada. Shall I get them right now?"

"You will be left if you don't," said the Boss: "we

shall start in half an hour. I want to get across the Vega before night."

"BOSS DAVIS."

The terrace-land of Western Sonora is divided by a rampart of steep hills into two well-defined regions,—the Vega, or coast-plain proper, a marshy jungle diversified with open lagoons and occasional banana-plantations; and the Encinal (literally "oakland"), the park-like plateau that extends beyond the southern border of Sinaloa and rises in the east toward the foot-hills of the Sierra Madre.   There had been no heavy rains for a couple of weeks, and the ground was so dry that we managed to pull through twenty miles of bottom-land in less than eight hours, and sighted the Yaqui River a good while before sunset.   We entered the ford in single file, and in spite of the colossal blasphemies uttered *in transitu* our teamsters reached the opposite bank in good order, and wheeled in succession to the right into their first camp, an open live-oak grove at the riverside, where each *carretero* was permitted to pick his own camping-ground within a very liberal circuit; we were still in the *tierra mansa*, the country of the tame Indians, where horse-thieves and begging friars were the worst visitors we had to fear.

Our rank and file consisted of the Boss, his clerk, two American teamsters, the cook, an old mestizo of all work, and five Mexican carreteros, or brevet teamsters, as one of the Americans, an ex-sergeant of the United States cavalry, called them.   I was the only passenger, but Don José Barreto, a coffee-planter of the neighboring Vega, had accompanied us from Guaymas, and accepted an invitation to supper.

Before he left he shook my hand with all the unreserved cordiality of a North Carolina country squire.   "To requite your kindness, I will give you a bit of advice, señor," said he in a rapid *patois* which he knew to be Greek to the Boss.   "Do you know what makes your American teamsters so inferior to our old Mexicans on the march?   It isn't want of practice, for some of them have been at it all their lives, and their physique is all that could be desired. The matter is this,—they eat too much: I mean they eat

SONORA INDIANS.

too many meals. A Mexican teamster takes a big meal in
the evening after going into camp, but he hardly eats any
breakfast at all. The habit could be formed during a single
trip, and the advantages would be lifelong; for such meals
as I saw your countrymen swallow at the posada this morning are sure to make the stoutest man torpid for the next
five or six hours, no matter how many drams he puts down
to stimulate digestion. A carretero hardly drinks a drop
of water all day long: a Yankee teamster pumps himself
full whenever he gets a chance. It's not the heat of the
sun that makes him thirsty, but the inward heat, the stack
of beefsteaks under his belly-band."

Paso del Cabo (" the Chieftain's Ford") the natives call
the place where we crossed the river, and the origin of the
name is explained by an old tradition of the Sonora Indians. When the Spanish conquistador Valdez established
himself at Guaymas, his freebooters used to go adventuring,
singly or in troops, into the interior of the country, but they
could rarely extend their forays beyond the Rio Yaqui, a
deep and rapid river that runs parallel to the coast for a
good many leagues, while on account of the shoals near the

boca none of their heavy boats could ascend from below. They had reason to suspect that there was a good ford somewhere near Guaymas, but the Indians of the neighborhood refused to specify the locality, and finally confessed that El Cabo, a powerful chieftain on the other side of the river, had threatened and sworn that if any man should dare to divulge the secret he would cut his throat and throw his body into the Yaqui River. The Spaniards did not like to meet the cabo on his own ground, but during a dark night of the rainy season they surprised a village on the north side of the river which the chieftain honored with his occasional visits, and were lucky enough to capture his son, a youth of eighteen or twenty years. The prisoner was arraigned and questioned in regard to that ford, but he pleaded ignorance, and was sent back to jail with the hint that they would permit him to cross the river at any time if he would just be kind enough to find that shallow place.

About that time, or a week after, a Spanish hunter bivouacked on the bank of the Rio Yaqui at a place where certain indications let him hope that deer would come to drink after dark. He fell asleep, but after midnight he was waked by a loud splash in the river a little farther up, and, hurrying to the spot, just caught a glimpse of a human figure disappearing in the bush. The bright moonlight enabled him to see that there were wet footprints in the sand, as if the nocturnal traveller had emerged from the river. He could hardly trust his eyes, for the current was strong and swift at that place, but when he met a troop of horsemen the next morning, and was informed that Cabo junior had effected his escape during the night, he told his tale and conducted them to a spot which he could identify by those footprints, and where, with the aid of a sounding-pole, they found the long-sought-for Paso del Cabo, the only ford of the lower Yaqui River. The rapidity of the current at the ford makes the water turbid, and thus conceals its want of depth. But the story of the Cabo has a disagreeable sequel: the truculent old chief ascertained the circumstances of the discovery, and a few days after the Spaniards found the jugulated body of their ex-prisoner in a pile of driftwood near the mouth of the river.

When we crossed the foot-hills of the Encinal on the following morning I stopped repeatedly to take a look at the northern horizon, where the Gila Desert spread its sand-waves over an apparently boundless expanse of fallow plains. El Pays de la Muerte (" the Land of Death") the Spaniards called this region; and the name is certainly appropriate. If Northern Africa can boast of any worse desert, the fiercer heat may justify the claim, but the most desolate portions of the Central Sahara can certainly not surpass the barrenness of the Death-Land. The morning air of that October day was so clear that I could distinguish the rocks and ravines of a group of hills in the distant northeast, and even the bluish-green shimmer of the cactus-hedges on the table-land beyond, but, turning my eyes to the north, I could not discover the faintest trace of vegetation, though the view was only bounded by the outline of an airy mountain-range at the edge of the horizon.

The Gila Desert extends, in fact, from the Rio Yaqui to the foot-hills of the Sierra de Pinos in Southern Arizona, and its eastern spurs form an almost continuous chain of sand-hills to the valley of the Concho River, where the American Timbuktoo, the city of Chihuahua,* with her gardens and orange-groves, lies like an oasis between two dreary table-lands.

---

* Pronounced in three syllables, almost like Chee-wà′wa

Professor Buckland asserts that there is no such thing as
an *original* desert on earth : the destruction of forests, he
says, has converted the garden-spots of the northern hemisphere into sand-wastes ; and his view is certainly supported
by the remarkable circumstance that the most treeless regions of four continents are found on the sides *turned toward
Asia,*—Southeastern Europe, Northern Africa, Western
America, and Northwestern Australia,—where the early
advent of man may be inferred from the proximity of the
common cradle of the human race. That deserts do not
spread—i e., blight the vegetation of adjacent districts—
seems proved by the fertility of regions which are not only
bordered, but almost surrounded, by the most hopeless sand-
wastes. In Eastern Persia forests alternate with alkali-
steppes ; in Fez and Algiers gardens bloom on the very
edge of the Sahara ; and the Encinal, at the border of the
Death-Land, teems with vegetable and animal life, though
it is a wilderness indeed if only tillage can redeem a country
from that stigma. Its human population is exclusively pas-
toral, and I do not think that the vast plateau that stretches
from Guaymas to Southern Sinaloa has ever been touched
by a plough ; but its spontaneous flora comprises nearly all
the species of the subtropical zone, and, seeing the multitude
and variety of game which our dogs started during the next
forty-eight hours, I could credit Xenophon's account of a
Thessalian chase. Pheasants, prairie-chickens, and rock-
partridges whirred up whenever we approached a mimosa-
thicket, and the crack of a whip or the vociferous profanity
of a Mexican teamster started the rabbits across the hill-
country in every direction. Black-tail deer, chaparral-
bucks, and turkeys were seen at longer intervals, and at
night the yelping of the hill-foxes and the occasional scream
of a wild-cat proved that the rocks and ravines were not

altogether tenantless. What zoological gardens such regions must have been in the good old time of animal liberty and equality, before the power of the scientific biped became too irresistible!

RUINS OF AZATLAN.

Sunset found us still on the road, and the *oriyas*, a species of whippoorwill, were repeating their watch-song in the mezquite-thickets when we reached the ruins of Azatlan, near an old rock-well that has never been known to fail in the dryest seasons. The night was calm and warm, and after a glance at the cloudless sky the Boss pitched his tent under a leafy walnut-tree near the well, while the teamsters took camp in one of the deserted buildings, whose stately dimensions and well-preserved roof have earned it the name of the *Casa del Cura*, "the parsonage." The Spaniards, who destroyed many cities and nearly all the temples of the old Aztecs, are not responsible for the ruins of Azatlan; the four *casas*, with their sculptured walls and broken colonnades, are relics of that problematic nation which inhabited, and perhaps desolated, the western table-lands of our continent, and disappeared before the earliest dawn of aboriginal tradition. The origin of the Casas Grandes on the Gila River and the ruins of Northwestern Mexico is as obscure as the significance of the Sphinx and the purpose of the Pyramids.

Soon after midnight the dogs in the casa began to bark, and, peeping from under the folds of my blanket, I noticed that the little clerk was getting uneasy about the noise. He raised his head and was looking wistfully, first at the Boss and then at me, and finally stretched out his hand in a diffident way, but drew it back, as if unwilling to incur further responsibilities. I lay motionless, waiting for the second act of the dumb show, but the barking became furious, and when our big greyhound joined in the chorus, I jumped up and walked over to the casa.

One of the American teamsters met me at the gateway. " I can't keep them quiet, sir," said he. " I was just going to take a look at the courtyard, or what d'ye call it, back there. I think there must be cats or thieves somewhere round here."

We went to the north side of the casas and walked over a heap of débris and through a dilapidated building, but

when we stepped out on the moonlit terrace at the opposite
end, two light-footed animals leaped over the broken stones,
whisked noiselessly across an open field, and disappeared
like shadows in the night-mist.

"Coyotes: I thought so," said the teamster. "I hope
they won't come back. We had a late supper last night,
and those long-legged thieves had smelled the bacon, I
guess. I had a good mind to let the dogs loose, but it
won't do; we have to keep them tied up, or they would
hang around the mules and get kicked to death."

"What was it? robbers?" whispered my little bed-
fellow, who had picked up a pistol and followed us from
a distance.

"Yes, sir—six of 'em," said the teamster; "but they
galloped away like race-horses when they saw you cock
that six-shooter."

Ten miles south of Azatlan we crossed the Rio Mayo,
ascended a steep ridge on the opposite shore, and found
ourselves on the table-land of Sinaloa, the southern and
grander portion of the Encinal. The rolling hill-country
swells here into mountains and valleys, and the chaparral
alternates with stately and extensive forests,—cork-oak
forests, some of them, and open chestnut woods that form
an agreeable contrast to the impenetrable tanglewood of the
Vega. Our cook had been still-hunting in the chaparral
while the train crept up the ridge, and said that he had
seen buffaloes from the summit of a grassy knob,—a statement which jeopardized his reputation for veracity; but
our doubts were removed by an *argumentum ad hominem*
before noon. On approaching a grove of hackberry-trees
on the bank of a little mountain-creek whose windings the
road had followed for some time, our greyhound gave
tongue, and was answered by a quartet of strange dog-voices

so much deeper and louder than his own that the foremost team came to a full stop, when a broad-shouldered *ranchero*

THE RANCHERO.

stepped from the grove with a merry halloo, and bade us "Advance and draw our meat-rations, and bring all our friends along."

There was, indeed, meat enough to ration a cavalry regi-

ment with numerous veterinary surgeons and attached
officers with their respective families. On the shady side
of the hackberry-trees a party of hunters had hitched their
horses and relieved them of their burden,—five full horse-
loads of fresh buffalo-meat, including a bagful of livers and
kidneys and a ponderous string of tongues. They told us
that, without firing a shot, they had bagged six bulls and
four calves with the aid of their Aragon shepherd dogs,
gaunt, shaggy, and long-legged brutes, that stood around
the beef in a semicircle, and leered at us as if calculating
the amount of meat our rump-steaks and livers would add
to the pile.

The Aragon hound exceeds the mastiff in size, and the
greyhound in strength though not in swiftness, and resembles nothing so much as an overgrown, long-headed, and
hirsute wolf. On account of his ferocity he is seldom employed as a watch-dog, but his strength and his reckless
courage make him a useful domestic beast of prey. He will
rend a mountain-goat as a terrier would kill a rat, and two
or three of them will keep a buffalo at bay till the hunter can
despatch him with a lance or even with a long knife, for a
trained Aragon flies at the throat of the strongest bull and
disables him in spite of his heavy dewlap and matted mane.

The Boss declined the offer with thanks, but the ranchero
would not be fobbed off, and every one of our teamsters
had to stuff his mess-chest with gratuitous beef.

"How did you like the looks of those 'shepherd-dogs'?"
asked the Boss when we had resumed our march.

"Sheep-stealing must be a risky trade in these parts," I
replied; "but, now you remind me of it, I am sorry I did
not ask them for a pup of that breed. In some of our
buffalo territories such a hunting-wolf would be worth his
weight in silver."

3

"Yes, in a country where beef is cheaper than powder, but where you have to pay a butcher's bill they would be expensive pets; one of them eats as much as three hard-working blacksmiths. They earn their rations, no doubt; but, to say the truth, I would not give my greyhound for a dozen of them. A good venison steak is worth all the bull-beef in creation; and I should like to see one of those lubbers try to catch a chaparral-buck or a cotton-tail deer. You will see Nepo (the greyhound) do it before night, if I am not much mistaken."

Another steep up-grade, and we kept along the level ridge of a long-stretched mountain that afforded a fine view of the park-like valleys below.

"Say, Boss, here's a chance for your *galgo*" (hound), said the cook, who had overheard our last conversation "You see that mezquite-coppice on the slope down there? Those black things a little to the left of it are *cabras* (antelopes), or I'm a blind-worm."

The Boss stopped his team. "Say, sergeant!" he hailed one of his American teamsters; "come here a minute, will you? I know you have eyes like a chicken-hawk· can you make out if those are antelopes, those black things near the mezquites down there? I should like to give Nepo a chance, but it's too far to go there on a wild-goose chase."

"Yes, I see them," said the sergeant; "they are cabras, —genuine pronghorn antelopes,—but it would be a wild-goose chase for all that There's too much cover here: a greyhound can't follow them through the bush, you know. There's timber all around, and Nepo couldn't begin to overtake them before they got across that open prairie."

"He couldn't, eh?" said the cook. "That's all you know about it I tell you they are lost if you get him half-way down before they start."

"What do you bet on that?"

"I bet you my *cuchillo* (dirk-knife) against a plug of tobacco that he will catch a cabra within ten minutes from the word *go!*"

"Much obliged," laughed the sergeant; "my old bull-sticker is getting played out. Who's going to steer the pup?"

"I leave that to his boss," said the cook, "but I'm going to saddle one of the spare mules and get my meat-bag ready."

"You may as well get your cuchillo ready too. Shall we stop the train for a few moments, Mr. Davis?"

"Well," said the Boss, "you may pull slowly ahead, but don't make any more noise than you can help; it wouldn't be fair play, you know. Come on, doctor: let us take our guns along, anyhow."

We kept the galgo in leash till we reached the lower end of a bushy ravine, at a point from where the antelopes were in plain view. There were eight of them,—five does and three bucks, one of them a fat old fellow with the grayish upper neck that distinguishes the full-grown specimens of the *Antilope americana*,—all browsing quietly and evidently unconscious of any danger, though two of the old does faced the ravine and seemed to look directly into our eyes whenever they stretched their necks for digestive purposes.

"Confound the dog! he hasn't seen them yet," said Mr Davis; "but it's a lost game if we go any nearer. Just hold his head a moment."

Nepo had understood the meaning of our manœuvres for the last five minutes, and, fully conscious of being the cause of the perhaps fatal delay, had wrought himself into a state of nervous excitement; but after straining his neck and eyes in all possible directions, he still turned his head and looked at us in a helpless and deprecatory way.

"That's it! hold him steady," whispered the Boss. "That will do now, he has seen them—by Dios he *has* seen them! Now take care! keep hold of him till I get that leash off. That's it! What do you say? shall we try to get a little nearer?" It can't do any harm *now*. Let me go ahead." He grabbed the hound by the collar and walked, or rather crept, toward a juniper-bush some twenty yards farther down; and still the cabras browsed in profound peace. He reached the bush, and after a little pause crept around it, more slowly and surreptitiously than before; but he had not advanced the length of his own body when two, three, four sibilant snorts from the coppice gave the signal for the beginning of the race. One of the does led off with a dashing caper, and the troop wheeled around the coppice and went down the slope at a rattling gallop.

I have seen English race-horses on the home-stretch and a wolf in full pursuit of a roe, but the career of the galgo reminded me more of the rush of some long-necked water-fowl sweeping down a river with that impetus that sends it flying through the surface-water for ten or twelve yards if it tries to alight. With his head, neck, and breast stretched forward, he shot ahead in a direction that was well calculated to intercept the fugitives if they should try to take to the timber on this side of the lower valley, and headed them off before they had passed the bottom of the ravine. They turned to the left then, now fully aware that they had to run for their lives, and went over the undulating hillocks of the opposite slope at a rate that would have defied the pursuit of the best rider in North America. Hedges, gullies, and rocks they cleared with flying leaps which only a kangaroo could emulate, while the greyhound had to break through such obstacles or get around them the best way he could.

There was an extensive forest on the ridge of the opposite slope, and, though still at a distance of half a league, the chances seemed even that the cabras would get there in time. But before they reached it they had to cross a level plateau where neither rocks nor bushes gave them any advantage over the pursuer; and here the race for life began in earnest. The antelopes strained every nerve, and their flying leaps became wilder and more frequent, but the galgo's chance had come. No intermittent flying could save them from that steady rush, and just when the foremost cabra dashed into the wood the troop flew asunder like a pile of pebbles under a sudden blow: the greyhound was in their midst, and a loud hurrah from the ridge above told us what we could not see from our lower stand-point: the cook had won his bet, and Nepo was throttling an antelope in the outskirts of the forest, which she had reached a second too late. The race had lasted a little more than ten minutes, but the plug of tobacco was duly paid.

When we returned to the road the Boss took a détour through the coppice-wood, and soon after I heard the report of his shot-gun.

"Look at this fellow!" said he, when he rejoined me at the train, pulling a long-tailed gallinaceous bird from his hunting-pouch: "do you know any English name for this kind of chicken?"

"It is a pheasant, isn't it?" said I, after a glance at the long neck and feathered tarsi of the nondescript.

"Looks like it," said the Boss, "but a pheasant can fly, and these creatures can't: at least, I never saw them do it. Chaparral-cocks, we call them in Texas: I don't know the Latin for it, but if there is any word for a shy bird, that would be his right name. Holy smokes! can't they run! They go off like a flash if they spy a human being in the next county. I tell you, where you can get one of these long-tails within shot-gun range, you may be sure that you are a long way from the next Methodist Episcopal church."

The chaparral-cock (*Phasianus alector*) inhabits the wooded highlands of North America from Arkansas to Yucatan, and is probably the shyest bird of our continent. He *can* fly, but is so sensible of his deficiency in that accomplishment that he takes to his heels at the most distant intimation of danger, except where lifelong peace has made him careless. The sportsman who bags his first chaparral-cock may sacrifice it to Æsculapius: he can be sure of having escaped from the malady of civilization into the healthiest wilderness of our old planet.

PLATEAU OF ENCINAL.

But the Encinal is a semi-tropical wilderness. Wild plums (Chickasaw cherries, they call them in Texas) and mulberry-trees abound along the water-courses, and the hill-forests are full of edible nuts. On southern slopes, even on the higher mountains, we found wild citron-trees, now in their second bloom, and diffusing an aromatic at-

mosphere that swarmed with butterflies and humming-birds.
The southern Encinal is crossed by the twenty-seventh degree North,—the parallel of Cashmeer and of the Bay of
San Lucas in Florida, where De Leon landed in his search
for the Fountain of Eternal Youth. He could not foresee
the extent of the swamps and the other obstacles that barred
his way to the west, but his instinct certainly guided him
to the right latitude, if freedom from such cares as hunger
and frost can prolong the term of our existence. The wind
Euroclydon can never pass the northern bulwark of the
Encinal,—the main chain of the Sierra Madre, that stretches
its cloud-capt ramparts from the head-waters of the Rio
Yaqui to Eastern Durango and shelters the American Italy
against the ice-winds that sweep from Labrador across the
territory of the United States.

"That means rain," said the Boss, when I called his attention to the electric twitches in a big bank of clouds on
the eastern horizon. "But we needn't mind if it does not
come this way before sunset," he added. "Now I think of
it, there is a jolly old greaser living on the Cañas River, six
miles ahead, and if you have any preference that way we
might as well sleep under a good roof to-night."

"Some kind of a country inn, is it?"

"Not exactly: it is a stock-farm, but with our antelope
and the bull-beef, and a plug or two of tobacco, we are sure
to be welcome."

Hospitality is the virtue of sparsely-settled countries,
and Don Pancho Garcia, the proprietor of the Cañas stock-
farm, received us with that hearty affability which mercen-
ary politeness imitates in vain. "I knew there were strangers coming this way," said he: "this afternoon I heard a
shot on the Rio Mountains that did not sound to me like a
Mexican shooting-iron. Well, I'm glad you found the old

place, capitano: my squaws are gone to a wedding at Mr.
Ichar's place, and I felt kind of lonely this afternoon.   It's
a good job for that boy of yours" (meaning the clerk) " that
you did not meet them on the road : they would have lugged
him along and danced him to death.   But just wait: we
are going to have a war-dance of our own if one of your
men will help me to get the cider-barrel out."

On the pavement of the corral a fire was lighted : the
galgo and we Americans, as strangers *par excellence,* got
reserved seats on the veranda, while the rest of the biped
and quadruped guests formed the pit in the background of
the corral.   After supper a guitar and a keg of cider (the
Boss had vetoed the barrel) completed the happiness of the
gypsy camp, and Señor Garcia invited us to make ourselves
comfortable on the piazza, and set us a good example by
throwing himself at full length upon a pile of white wool
which his wife had probably deposited there for different
purposes.

"Mas que bien, señor," he said in reply to a compli-
mentary remark of mine, " but I am afraid you would
have had a very poor supper if it hadn't been for your
own cook."

"The cook himself," I replied, " prefers truth to glory,
and says that your corn-meal is superior to the finest Northern quality.   Do you raise much corn on your hacienda ?"

" No, thank you," laughed the ranchero · " I get it from
Trinidad, with the rest of my grub.   I don't believe in
farming."

" It is a stock-farm," explained the Boss: " stock-raising
pays better hereabouts than any kind of agriculture."

" Yes, and it's less trouble," said the Mexican.   " How
many days' work do you think it would take a man to raise
a full crop of corn?   Sixty or seventy at the very least,

wouldn't it? Now, I can drive my cattle to market and be back with a stack of provisions in less than sixty *hours*. Besides, I can get my work in on horseback; and that is more than a poor planter can say." The sophistry of the unsophisticated is sometimes hard to answer.

VAL DE CAÑAS.

The Cañas Valley, we learned, is pretty well settled. There used to be a colony of Confederate refugees twenty miles farther southeast—New Texas they called it—who lived there in a free-and-easy way, and quite comfortably, for five or six years; but when times got sunnier in Dixie they left like birds of passage, and their pretty cottages are now tenanted by Durango Indians. A year before they left a pious old Scotchman came from Los Angeles to buy land in the Cañas Valley, and established a mule-farm,—*i.e.* a stud for breeding and breaking mules,—which he tried to work with a lot of imported hands, North Californians

most of them. When he first came to the Cañas he was a
most dignified-looking old gentleman, long-haired like a
missionary, and remarkably choice in his language, but
when Don Pancho saw him again, some nine months after,
he had only a handful of hair left, and the profanity of his
remarks appalled even the Mexican experts. As soon as
his Texas neighbors left he returned to California, a heavy
loser by his rash experiment, though his commonplace-
book had been enriched with two aphorisms: First, that
Mexican mules can only be managed by Mexican muleteers;
and, second, that under certain circumstances emphatic language becomes an imperative necessity.

"Do you employ any travelling horse-breakers in this
part of the State?" asked the Boss.

"In certain cases we do," said the ranchero. "There are
some brutes that defy all fair means of bringing them to
terms; but, as a rule, I try everything else first. There
are plenty of *monteros* in this country who can break *any*
horse, but the question is how long the horse will survive
the operation   There is no word too ugly for the sort of
tricks which some of them use in that business."

"They make a trade-secret of their methods, I suppose?"

"Yes. nearly every one of them has a system of his own,
and they often manage to keep it secret for a lifetime. I
knew a fellow down in Sonora who had a recipe for curing
runaway horses, and he had a monopoly of such cures for
more than fifteen years. He would take a wild *broncho*
out in the prairie, and bring him back as steady as a professor,—nobody knew how till his own son betrayed the
secret. And what do you think it was? He had contrived
a headgear with a sort of copper eye-flap that shut down
like a spring and blinded the creatures completely. He
frightened them on purpose, and as soon as they started he

pulled a strap, when down came the copper like a clapboard, and the wildest mustang came to a full stop. Then he opened the lid, reset the trap, and went through the same manœuvre till the brutes got satisfied that daylight depended on their behavior."

"That man was a Yankee, wasn't he?"

"No, señor,—a native, homebred Mexican; but you are right in supposing that the Americanos of the North are hard to beat at such tricks. You know that our young bucks once in a while manage to lariat a buffalo,—just for fun, of course, for St. Samson himself could not tame an old buffalo bull,—but a Yankee rancher near Mazatlan showed us that you can make them behave for a day, anyhow. His *vaqueros* captured a monster of an old bull and dragged him to the hacienda, where they chained him to a tree, but the length of the chain just showed exactly how near a man could come to that tree without losing his life. But Don Yankee was too much for him. He got four lariats around him, and made his men hold him steady for a while, and then went to work and hitched one end of a rawhide strap to his tail, and the other to his horns, and then tightened the strap. Now, you know a bull cannot gore you without lowering his head first, and in the fix he was this one couldn't nod without pulling his own tail out."

Our little clerk, whose knowledge of Spanish was confined to the written language, had fallen asleep on the hard boards of the veranda; but before the ranchero retired he put an armful of wool under his head and covered him up with a knee-high stratum of the same material.

Toward morning the long-expected rain began with a chilly gust, but without any of the electric phenomena which usually accompany a transient shower in the tropics, and after a short council of war we anticipated the ranchero's

permission to take refuge in the interior of his house. He
met us in the hall with excuses and a lighted candle, a
cera santa, remarkable for its odoriferous rather than illumi-
native qualities. These candles, composed of a mixture of
beeswax and frankincense, are prepared by the Mexican
ladies for the exclusive use of the church; and after a con-
fession to that effect Don Pancho ushered us into the next
room, shut the windows, and left the ecclesiastic candle on
the table.

The residence of the average ranchero is one story, and
contains four apartments,—the bedroom (reserved for the
members of the family); the kitchen, used also as a dining-
and sitting-room; the *almacén*, or larder; and the *silleria*,
or harness-room, where the ranchero keeps his saddle, his
tools, and often his dogs. Strangers sleep in their own
blankets,—in fair weather on the portico, in stormy nights
in the sitting-room. Besides the long dining-table and
kitchen furniture, the apartment contained a clothes-press,
and upon it a cage full of turtle-doves, the favorite pet of
the Mexican farmer; two looms, a spinning-wheel, and a
contrivance that would have created a general sensation in
a Northern industrial fair,—a combination of concentric
cudgels, not unlike a forty-legged saw-horse, which the
Mexican women use in the manufacture of polychromatic
ponchos and bandannas. They entwine the arms of the
wooden Briareus with as many different patterns of woollen
yarn, and need only to twirl the implement to get any desired shade uppermost and handy for immediate use. The
cera santa began to fill the room with a resinous odor of
sanctity, but every now and then it sputtered like a blazing
sausage; so we put it out.

Before we left the stock-farm the kind ranchero presented
us with a bagful of wild pineapples which his daughters

had gathered in the sierra, and had already commenced the
valedictory handshaking when he remembered that one of
his sheepwalks up on the river needed looking after, so
that he might as well accompany us for a couple of miles.
We followed the windings of the Cañas Valley for some
distance, and then turned to the right into a deep mountain gorge at a point where a wayside tavern displayed its
red-and-white flag as a sign that the *posadero* had *pulque*
(aloe-sap) for sale. But good wine needs no bush, and the
gayest pulque-flag cannot redeem the reputation of the
vender of an inferior article; so we took the ranchero's
hint and pursued our road, which led us gradually up hill
and back to the main plateau of the Encinal.

"You never feed those hogs, do you?" asked the Boss,
apropos of a sow that hastened across the road with her
litter of pigs.

"I don't, for one good reason: I have nothing to give
them," laughed the Mexican; "but they find all they want
in the woods and creeks the year round. Creatures that
can digest snakes need not starve in this country."

"If I may ask, señor, have you ever ascertained if it is
true that only *black* hogs can eat poisonous snakes with
impunity?"

"It's strange now, isn't it?" said the Mexican. "I suppose you heard that in your own country, and the same
belief is very common in many parts of Mexico. The
truth is, that *all* full-grown hogs are snake-proof; the
thickness of their hide and bacon protects them, for snakes
do not bite very deep,—anyhow, not deep enough to penetrate the callous upper skin of a pig. But it is true that
black hogs are more active as a general thing: the white
ones, you may have noticed, have reddish eyes: they are a
sort of *pallotes* (albinoes), I think, and not very quick-

witted; but catch a live rattlesnake and throw it right in front of a white hog, and you will see if he doesn't make short work of it. A dog or horse in such a case would jump aside as if it had seen the devil."

"Are there any wild hogs in the sierra?"

"No hogs, but you find plenty of wild goats in any of the mountains around here."

"Cabras (antelopes), you mean?"

"No, señor,—*cabras reales*, genuine bearded white goats; I shot five of them last winter."

"They must have run wild,—descended from our common domestic goat, I mean."

"I think so, but it must have been long ago. I remember my father telling about his dogs killing them by dozens in the Altar Mountains. They are not very different from our domestic goats, but they run like deer if they get sight of a human being."

"Would it not pay to hunt them for their hides?" asked the Boss.

"Hardly, unless you have a tannery of your own, but I tell you what does pay first-rate,—wolf-hunting. The government pays five *pesos* for every wolf-scalp and two for every coyote, and before they abolished the State bounty a man could 'kill *vermin* for his livelihood'"

"You don't use strychnine, do you?"

"No: that can only be done in a free country like yours: our people cannot buy or sell any kind of poison without a special permit. *It would make matters too easy for our dear squaws.* That's my sheepwalk, gentlemen," said the ranchero, pointing to a black-and-white dotted slope on a neighboring mountain-side. "I must leave you where that road turns off to the right."

"I wonder," said I, "if English prize-sheep could ever

get up that mountain? Just look at these fat monsters, caballero," handing him a copy of the *Illustrated London News:* "have you ever seen the like in this part of the world?"

While he inspected the paper I nudged my companion and whispered in his ear, "Try to make him accept some compensation."

"He wouldn't do it."

"Try, anyhow."

"The English would take our wethers for antelopes, if that's what they call sheep," laughed the ranchero. "Here is your paper, sir."

"Caballero," said the wagonmaster, "would you do me a favor?"

"If I can."

"You know I am a tradesman, and I should like to establish a market for our smoking-tobacco in this part of the country: would you oblige me by accepting this sample?" offering him a four-pound package. "Please keep it, and let your neighbors try it, and let me know how they like it if I come this way again."

"What is it worth?" asked the ranchero.

"I don't remember just now, but I shall let you know before Christmas. Prices are changing continually, you know. Please keep it in the meanwhile."

"No, that would not do, señor. Be kind enough to tell me the average price. This is nearly five pounds, I should say?"

"Oh, that package you mean? Why, that's a sample: they are always free to reliable parties."

Don Pancho's eyes twinkled under his broad-brimmed *sombrero*. "You are very kind, sir," said he. "Well," with a good-humored smile, "you may always *rely* on one

thing,—that my old house-door will be open whenever you
or your companions return to the Val de Cañas. Let me
have another one of those apples in your lunch-basket.
Thank you; and now good-by, *amigos*."

He shook hands all round, and made us a respectful
parting bow, as if we had put him under some great obli-
gation, instead of having been feasted and lodged at his
expense, for when he was gone we found the four-pound
package in the lunch-basket.

The horizon cleared up before night, and when we
reached a mulberry-grove on the bank of the Rio Fuerte
the sun set behind a streak of that fleecy white mist which
is a surer presage of fair weather than a perfectly cloudless sky. I do not know if the cicadas of ancient Greece
were identical with the West Mexican species, but the enthusiasm of the classic poets would appear less inexplicable
if the locust orchestras of their woods were not quite so
monotonous as the katydid concerts of our Northern summer nights. I think I distinguished a dozen different
notes in the insect-music that came from the tree-tops of
our mulberry-grove,—the well-known chirp of the locust
proper, a long-drawn whir, a twang, a low whistle, a singular bell-like ring, a combination of a click and a squeak,
and a variety of insect-diphthongs for which the English
alphabet yields no equivalent. Singly repeated, they would
have been tiresome, but their combined effect was quite
entertaining. The smallest of the Mexican tree-locusts
(*Cicada dryas*), a thing about as large as a castor-bean, chirps
louder than a sparrow; and if it is true that it produces
those sounds by rubbing its hind legs against the edge of its
wings, the energy of the tiny fiddler is truly astonishing.

I could not help admiring the wisdom of a merciful
Creator, who has not increased the vocal power of animals

in proportion to their size, when the overture of a coyote serenade sounded over the hills about an hour after sunset. It commenced with a slow crescendo, so irresistibly lugubrious that two of our dogs at once raised their heads and swelled their voices into a responsive tremolo, which may have been heard and appreciated by their distant relatives. A kick brought their antiphones to an abrupt finale, but every now and then their irrepressible feelings found vent in a low whine.

It cannot be hunger that makes the Mexican coyotes howl, for the forests of the Encinal are inexhaustible storehouses of animal food, and the occasional disappointments which may attend their predatory enterprises would hardly furnish an excuse for such loud and protracted laments. It is rather an elegiac tendency, which manifests itself in all the varieties of the genus *Canis*, for even the dingo, the voiceless dog of the Australian wilderness, breaks forth into sympathetic grunts if he hears a puppy whine. It is the one touch of Nature which makes all canines kin, and has probably been inherited from their common ancestor, the wolf, once "a mighty hunter before the Lord," but who may have learned to howl when his business declined under the competition of Nimrod & Co, till the hunter became the hunted, unless he preferred to enter the service of his rival at dog-wages.

CHAPTER II.

COLIMA.

Know ye the secrets of the nether sea,
Or what the pathless virgin woods conceal?
CHAMISSO   The God of Earth

ABSOLUTE monarchs must be absolutely abolished, but it can do no harm to confess that they were generally good roadmakers. The great highways of Hadrian were military march-routes, and those of Peter the Great all converged upon his pet capital; but, whatever may have been King Philip's private motive, it is certain that he and his successors expended a large portion of their bonanza revenues on the construction of broad and imperishable wagon-roads throughout their Transatlantic dominions. The Mexican republic has found no time to extend or repair the "royal roads" (*caminos reales*) of their territory, but the public works of the vireys can stand neglect, and, like those of Appius Claudius, will not be much the worse for the wear and tear of a series of centuries.

Sixty miles north of San Luis Potosi we struck one of these ante-republican roads, and thenceforth were sure to find a solid bridge at every creek and a massive safety-wall along every precipice. The bird's-eye views from a slippery bridle-path often suggest possibilities which only a bird can contemplate with equanimity, but the bulwarks of our *camino* enabled us to admire the abysmal valleys at our feet with more than the safety of travellers over a Pacific Rail-

54

ON THE ROAD TO SAN LUIS.

way viaduct. While my eyes wandered through the cloudland of blue heights that border the eastern horizon of the
Val de Potosi I noticed repeatedly a curious column of
white smoke that seemed to ascend from a lateral valley
in the southeast, and stood in sharp relief against the background of dark-blue pine-hills when our road brought us
opposite a gap in the intermediate mountains. Right over
the valley hung a streak of grayish clouds from which
the white pillar seemed to depend like an icicle, but its
upward rotatory motion and the immobility of its lower
end proved its terrestrial origin. What could it be? My
pocket-telescope failed to solve the puzzle, so I put it back
and looked at my companion, who had watched me with a
cunning smile.

"Can't you guess?" said he, anticipating my question.

"No; but it looks like a large steam-factory,—unless it's
a volcano."

"You came nearer the truth the first time," said the
Boss: "it isn't smoke, but pure steam. That's the geyser

of Aguas Calientes, near Los Baños. We are only forty
miles from San Luis now."

"A geyser? Why, that column must be at least four
thousand feet high!"

"If you mean the steam, *that* goes up on cold days
higher than the highest clouds; but the water itself spouts
up from a pond at the head of a little creek not more than
ten or twelve feet over the level of the banks. If it didn't
come up through the pond you would not see any water
at all, they say; it is superheated steam, hotter than the
hottest springs, and the noise it makes reminds you of a
copper-furnace in full blast. A sheer waste of fuel wherever it comes from: I saw the place four years ago, and I
do not think there is as much as a bath-house there."

"Is there anything like a watering-place at the *baños*
over yonder?" I asked an intelligent-looking caballero who
overtook us a few minutes after and appeared to be in a
communicative mood.

"There ought to be," said he, "but the place has somehow failed to become fashionable. We have a hotel at
the springs, besides a dozen taverns in the village, but it
doesn't pay. the valley is too far out of the way, and the
poor people of the neighborhood can bathe anywhere below
the hotel: three miles this side of the pond the creek is
still warm enough to be pleasant in winter-time."

"Excuse my curiosity," said the stranger, after half an
hour of topographical small-talk; "are you not from
France or of French descent?"

"Almost, señor: I was born in the French Nether-
lands."

"Didn't I guess it?" laughed the caballero. "I was a
good while on the Rio Grande, and I can recognize the
pronunciation of a Yankee or an Italian before he has

spoken a dozen words. There's a countryman of yours owning a pretty farm a few miles above my place, on the other side of the river. I could never remember his name, or I should advise you to stop there to-night; he would be the happiest man in Mexico to have a *paysano* under his

AGUAS CALIENTES.

roof. We have a horse-fair at Montellano to-day, and if I should meet him there I would bet my spurs that he'll overtake you somewhere between here and San Luis."

The Belgians and French abuse each other as rancorously as the English and Scotch, but, like the English and Scotch, they fraternize if they meet in Spanish America, as they

would fraternize with a Spanish American if they made
his acquaintance in Samarcand. "Pour aimer votre voisin," says Montaigne, "il faut le rencontrer dans un pays
étranger;" and I fully believe that Muktar Pasha would
embrace a Russian general if he should meet him in the
Mountains of the Moon. More than once after the caballero had left us I looked back, as if I expected a message
from my unknown half-countryman; and toward evening,
when a Mexican boy came tearing after us on a naked
horse, I somehow knew his errand beforehand.

"Mr. Laurent is coming this way with a tent-wagon,"
he gasped when he reached the wagonmaster's team, "and
if you will please to slow up a little, he will overtake you
on this side of the ford."

"Who's Mr. Laurent?"

"I suppose it's some acquaintance of that gentleman we
met on the ridge this morning," said I: "he told me something about a farm on the other side of the river, where he
advised us to stop to-night."

"Yes, sir,—that's Mr. Aimé Laurent's place," cried the
boy.

"Well, then, tell Mr. Emmy Laurent to hurry up," said
the Boss: "we're going into camp before the sun goes
down."

The banks of the Rio Fuerte are lined with stately bignonia-trees; and here I saw for the first time the singular
reptile which the Spaniards call *iguana* and the Portuguese
cayman do matto,—i.e., "tree-alligator." The latter name
may have been suggested by the formidable appearance of
an animal which attains a length of seven feet and a weight
of sixty-five pounds, and jumps from tree to tree with the
impetus of a tiger-cat; but there is no doubt that the iguana is the most harmless creature of that size which ever

jumped or flew or swam on this planet of ours,—the most harmless creature of any size, we might say, for the little goldfish and the robin redbreast are beasts of prey compared with the tree-alligator; they *will* hurt a fly, but the iguana is a strict vegetarian, and like an orthodox Hindoo

"TREE-ALLIGATOR" (IGUANA).

endeavors to prolong his life without shortening that of a fellow-creature. Still, with its saurian beak, its preposterous claws, and the row of bristles along its backbone, this giant lizard is a scandalous phenomenon; and a big green one, with a head like the seventh beast of the Apocalypse, plumping down from a bignonia-tree and scampering into the underbrush, had provoked me to snatch up a tent-

pole and start in hot pursuit, when the monotonous rumble
of our freight-wagons was interrupted by the rattling of a
lighter team that seemed to approach at a lively trot.   As
I emerged from the thicket a pair-horse country-wagon
passed our rear teams and the wagonmaster tightened his
reins.

"Oh, here he is now," said the Boss when he caught
sight of me.   "Please come over here, sir; here's a caballero from the other side of the river wants your casting vote
on a point we can't agree upon.   He wants us to camp in
this bottom or else on his farm on the other side, but I'm
afraid we must forego that pleasure; it's only a mile and a
half to Mr. Carmen's place, and I have to stop there either
to-day or to-morrow."

The "caballero from the other side" was leaning against
the front wheel of our team,—a black-haired farmer with a
semi-Mexican hat and shawl, but in the unmistakable black-
trimmed leather jacket of the Pays de Vaud.   Our eyes
met, and monsieur saluted me with a gesture that established his nationality before we had exchanged a single
word.

"I am sorry that you passed the ford," said he, in tolerable Spanish, "but my rancho is right across there, and if
I can supply you with anything you expected to get at Mr.
Carmen's place——"

The Boss made no reply, but looked meditatively at the
western horizon.

"If you permit me a vote on the subject, Mr. Davis,"
said I, "it seems to me that we could do worse than camp
under such trees as these   There's any amount of firewood
in that thicket,—good water, too; and what else do we
need?"

"Well," replied the Boss, "the truth is, we are short

of corn; but if this gentleman can sell us four or five bushels I guess we could camp here as well as anywhere else."

"If you stop anywhere in this bottom," said the farmer, "the corn shall be here before you have unharnessed your horses."

His boy galloped toward the river and our caravan wended its way to the bignonia grove.

These preliminaries settled, Mr. Laurent took me aside and the floodgates of his vernacular then opened. He had purchased his farm fourteen years ago, and lived here ever since, twenty-eight miles from the next sympathizing fellow-Frenchman, a linguistic exile which only hope and a volume of Béranger's *Chansons* had enabled him to support. Mexican conversation, Mexican gossip, Mexican sermons, and untranslatable Mexican blasphemies from morning till night,—his very children vexed his ears with their Spanish volubility. He had launched them in the right direction, hoping that the inherent force of the *langue de France* would make head against wind and tide, but the surrounding elements had prevailed. "I give them up," said he: "it takes a headstrong man to hold his own against the current, but if it comes to pulling a whole family the other way, you might as well try to paddle a raft against the stream."

"Who is your next countryman?" I asked, after answering a number of direct and indirect questions.

"The next one is Monsieur Vallier, the nurseryman, two miles this side of San Luis, but there are four more in the city."

"I suppose you know Dr. Rambert, the superintendent of the city hospital? How is he getting along now?"

"Old Jacques Rambert? Oh, he's all right. I see him

almost every month: he's got a large practice outside of the hospital among the rich burghers."

"It's a wonder how he can manage that in such a holy-saints place as San Luis"

"Now, isn't it, sir? It seems you know him, then, the godless old heretic! It's an everlasting puzzle to me that they haven't cut his head off yet, nor even his nose: they hate him like a were-wolf, and he tells me that they suspect him of witchcraft, but that's his salvation, maybe: they let him alone because their superstition gets the better of their spite. Still, he ought to be more careful: his best friend, the alcalde, died last summer, and I have an idea that the black rats are getting ready for him. I should not like to be in his boots next Christmas when the town is full of mounted Indians: somebody ought to warn him."

"Never mind. Those Indians must come well mounted if they expect to catch him next Christmas: I am going to relieve him to-morrow."

"You are? Well, sir, that accounts for it that he was in such good-humor last week. Where is he going to?—back to Europe?"

"No, he is going north, to Upper California. I was on his brother's farm near Los Angeles a month ago, and I see they have everything ready for him: they are going to cure him with California honey and country milk. His brother will meet him in Guaymas next week."

"Ah! that's the reason he was so anxious about that rumor from Sonora. By the way, what's the news from the rebel army?"

"They are still at El Paso, so far as I know; but the Eastern mail was over-due when we left, so there's no saying what they may have been up to since. But who cares?"

"Not I," said my courteous landsman, "since you got through all right. But what's the matter with your American friend? Listen: there he goes again. Is that a sickness or an English song?"

"A supper-signal, I suppose."

"Good-night, then, mon voisin à venir," said Mr. Laurent: "I owe you a visit, and I shall pay it in San Luis next Sunday."

Our teamsters trimmed their horses and trappings the next morning, and I tried to indulge in the luxury of an hour's sleep after sunrise, but the neighborhood of the large city announced itself too audibly. Wagons and carts rumbled along the camino, mules trotted to market with a load of squealing pigs, a fulling-mill in the valley commenced its noisy work, and from three different mountain-sides I heard sounds which affect me more than other discords in the harmony of Nature,—axe-strokes, preluding a splintering crash and a fall, followed by the sympathetic shudder of the surrounding hills. In a thinly-wooded country those echoes always sound in my ear with a sad significance, like a dirge of the wood-nymphs or a lament of our Mother Earth for the loss of her first-born. The tree-felling axe is the sword that has expelled the children of the East from their Paradise, and which in the West too has struck deep into the root of Ygdrasil, the Life Tree of the Edda, whose downfall will involve the final ruin of gods and men.

Mr. Carmen's place proved to be a turnpike tavern with a large corral, where ten or twelve horses were haltered in a row. The veranda was crowded with muleteers and travellers, and one of them stepped down and met us at the turnpike. "I think I passed you last night at the Rio, caballeros," said he: "do you come from the frontier?"

"Yes, from Guaymas, sir," said the Boss.

"From Guaymas! Why, on what day did you leave there?"

"Let me see——"

"We left there on the nineteenth of this month," said the sergeant

"Is it possible?" cried the traveller. "Look here, caballeros!" he hailed his friends on the veranda: "this conducta has left Guaymas on the nineteenth of this month! Santissima! just at the nick of time!"

A crowd was around us in a moment and fairly bewildered us with a flood of questions and congratulations. Did we hear the news? Pedro Mendez had captured Guaymas on the twenty-first and avenged his late defeat by plundering every house in Western Sonora.

"Ye have more luck than sense!" yelled a little *arriero:* "you must have a good-sized guardian saint about you, or is there a friar in your crowd?"

"No, sir," said the sergeant, "we are heretics, every one of us: at midnight you can smell the brimstone for a mile and a half around; but, you see, we are Americans, and old Pedro knew better than to tackle the town before we were out of the way."

"There wouldn't have been much time for prayers if he had catched ye," laughed the landlord; "but never mind, you're all right now: we will attend to the old man if he comes this way."

We reached Potosi an hour before sundown. The city was agog with rumors and political demonstrations, and one of the teamsters had to help me get my baggage to my room, the landlady of the hotel informing us that all her male employés had run off to join the mass-meeting on the plaza. Even Dr. Rambert marched me up-stairs into his studio and handed me a newspaper as soon as he had answered my first questions. There seemed to be no doubt about the fate of Guaymas. The insurgents had defeated the government forces near El Paso, the garrison of San Miguel had capitulated, and the rebels held every important town in Western Sonora. Sixteen regiments of regulars under General Parras were advancing from Monterey, and a brigade of loyal volunteers from Chihuahua, so that the suppression of the rebellion seemed only a question of time; but the fortified towns on the coast might protract their resistance for a month or two, and in the meanwhile all traffic *via* Guaymas must be suspended.

"Well, I have got you the place," said the doctor, returning at last from politics to personal affairs, "but with a *sine qua non:* you have to pilot me through to San Blas. I was in conclave with the agent of your trading company yesterday, and the matter is settled so far that the caravan is going back by way of Jalisco and San Blas instead of Guaymas, and he has to provide us transportation from here to Santiago: from there I can take the stage to Mazatlan, or let your teams lug me to San Blas and wait there for the Panama steamer."

"But I thought Dr. Patterson was going along?"

"So he was, but he *has* to go by way of Guaymas: in other words, he has to wait for a month or two. I got him to relieve me till New Year, so you needn't report for duty before Christmas. No excuses, amigo: it's my last week in Spanish America, and it shall be a pleasant one."

"You are over-kind, but was it worth while—worth the expense, I mean—to——"

"Yes, it was. Your agent's terms are devilish high, and the roads are wretched, but all that goes for nothing: we shall see Lake Chapala, and be reconciled to an earthly pilgrimage that has led us through Paradise. It's 'the scenic masterpiece of the Creator:' that is the phrase of a man who never used a superlative in vain,—poor Colonel Holty of the Austrian volunteers,—though he only saw it on that unfortunate expedition to Pascarro, and after Rion's guerillas had riddled him with buckshot. 'If St. Peter turns me off I shall ask him for a pass to Jalisco,' he told me when he got his last marching-order."

"It wouldn't be much of a pleasure-trip for you if you are not used to prairie-schooner voyages; but, as you say, I suppose we are in for it. I am sorry, though, we cannot postpone it for a couple of weeks."

"So am I, but I am due in Los Angeles. And as for your prairie-schooners, I shall be thankful for any kind of locomotive contrivance that moves me from this town. My time is up: the place is getting too tight for me."

"Why? Are the saints getting the better of you, after all?"

"Yes, amigo, I'm going to the wall: they're too many for me. Do you know that I had to pay those ten dollars, anyhow?"

"What ten dollars?"

"For that saddle-horse I wrote you about: don't you remember?"

"I can't say that I do."

"Bon Dieu! Didn't you get my last letter? You recollect that I used to hire a horse once or twice a week: they have no regular livery-stables here, but I had made an arrangement with a baker down on the plaza, who generally lent me the same old mare every Saturday. About a month ago the brute had a sort of seizure; I think it was nothing but what our veterinary surgeons used to call 'blind staggers,' but my worthy neighbors put their heads together and seemed to have a good mind to mob me. It was a preter-

natural disease, they said: the mare must have been bewitched; and no wonder, if she had to carry a monster who
kept his pockets cramful of heretical books! They talked
about searching my room for necromantic implements, and
the owner of the beast left me an alternative between a
compromise and a lawsuit."

"Would a Mexican judge actually commit you on such
a charge?"

"He would not acquit me in his heart, whatever he might
do for fear of the European consuls; and the wretches threatened to cure my infidelity with a potato-masher; so, for the
sake of holy peace that surpasses all reason, I let the fool
have his ten dollars and kicked him down-stairs."

"Do they only pretend to believe such things, or is it
possible that they are in earnest about it?"

"Their faith recognizes no impossibilities at all. If you
think that their stupidity has any limits, that affair of the
Protestant miner in Belcarras should undeceive you. Did
you ever read the account of his trial?"

"I read the report of the English consul: they sentenced
him for 'witchcraft in the first degree'—ten years, wasn't
it?—and three months extra for contempt of court because
he attempted an *argumentum ex absurdo*."

"You would not mention such trifles if you had read the
'circumstantial evidence,'" laughed the doctor. "I will
show you a copy of the proceedings: it's valuable from
a medical standpoint if you have a taste for the study of
mental diseases."

The Rocky Mountains of the United States cross the
Mexican frontier in two main chains, which gradually converge toward the south till they unite near the head-waters
of the Rio Lerma, about fifty English miles northeast of

Acapulco. Near the Rio Grande their water-sheds are at
least two hundred miles apart, and the intermediate region
is comparatively arid ; but as the ridges converge the central
valley becomes more humid and fertile, till south of Potosi
the cornfields, the orchards, and finally even the chestnut-
groves are supplanted by the rankness of the spontaneous
vegetation. The forest-trees of the temperate zone gradually give way to luxuriant evergreens, and where the two
sierras coalesce they enclose a forest-delta of three thousand
English square miles, which white men have but rarely
entered, and which no human being has ever attempted to
cross. This delta is drained by the Rio Lerma, which farther down expands into a glorious lake, and carries more
water to the sea than the Rhine or the Rio Grande ; but no
human eye has ever seen the source of that river. Fishermen from San Blas and the Jalisco turtle-hunters have ascended it in their canoes to its junction with the Rio Balsas,
but there the virgin woods of the delta begin to interpose
their barrier of driftwood, bush-ropes, and aquatic trees,
and the upper course—perhaps the upper half—of a broad
American river is as unknown as the fountain of the Nile.

The eastern slope of the mountain-range which borders
the Rio Lerma below the lake is extremely steep and rugged,
and farther south, where its height sinks from fourteen
thousand to six thousand feet, its western foot-hills are
flanked by the thickets of the delta. The roads which unite
Mazatlan and San Blas with the cities of the table-land have
therefore to take a strangely circuitous route. The air-line
from Potosi to San Blas, for instance, would run due west,
but terrestrial travellers have first to go south to Cuerna-
vaca in the valley of Anahuac, thence west up to the backbone of the sierra, due north along the ridge toward the
lake, and again west to a pass in the coast-range, from where

ON THE LERMA RIVER.

points on the Pacific can be reached by a less tortuous route.

We followed the highway as far as Queretaro, where we engaged a professional guide, and then launched our prairie-schooners on the old military road to the west. Our caravan had passed through seven degrees of latitude since we left Guaymas, and near the tropic of Cancer that polar distance makes an appreciable difference. We had entered the summer zone. The river-sides were covered with rhexia-thickets, intermingled with wax-palms and wild fig-trees, and the southern slopes of the foot-hills flamed with yellow orchids and the long red pipe-flowers of the *Salvia splendens*, and even exhibited some good-sized varieties of arborescent

5

ferns. The valleys of Eastern Michoacan produce a thorny
shrub of the genus *Lycium* that is covered with a profusion
of apparently perennial white flowers of a nauseous sweet-
ish smell, which seem to exercise an irresistible attraction
on all honey-loving insects They swarm with beetles, blue-
bottles, and formidable black wasps, but they are veritable
butterfly-traps, and enriched my collection with a number of
tropical swallow-tails and a fine specimen of the dark-blue
Papilio castor. We saw iris-crows and different parrots, and
wherever cattle grazed they were attended by flights of the
black cow-rider (*Crotophagus ani*), which benefit themselves
and the cows by relieving them of numerous troublesome
parasites. The southern Mexicans are strangely prejudiced
against these birds, and a Jalisco farmer, after requiting
their labors with an effective discharge of his old *trabucco*,
informed me that they were a worse pest than weasels and
chicken-hawks. "They flay our stock alive," said he. "a
black rascal of that race seems to think that I keep my cattle
for no other purpose but to furnish him with cow-hairs."

On the evening of the second day after our departure
from Queretaro we crossed the Rio Balsas on a rope-ferry,
and encamped near an abandoned *maderal*, or lumber-yard,
in the opposite foot-hills. The darkness of the night, increased by the gloom of the cedar forest, made it at first
rather difficult to collect the material for a camp-fire, but a
blaze of dry grass and furze revealed abundant pineapples,
and when the flame rose high enough to illuminate the outskirts of the maderal we found that the ground was strewed
with chips and good-sized logs, and that we had all the
wherewithal of a first-rate barbecue.

The teamsters had exchanged some of their superfluous
bacon for a six-gallon keg of pulque, and while we watered
our horses at a prairie-creek the sergeant had shot a pig : a

sick *peccari* (wild-hog) he preferred to call it, though he trusted that its flesh might be eaten with impunity,—in the absence of the owner. Only Dr. Rambert was out of luck. in unloading the baggage-wagon the men had dropped his mess-box and converted its contents into a mass of smashed eggs and cohesive flour; and as he disapproved of pork and all stimulants, including tea and coffee, he had to borrow a handful of soda-crackers from the cook and soak them in water with a little brown sugar.

"Try some of these spare-ribs, doctor: be persuaded," said the Boss: "we have the sergeant's word for it that it isn't pork, but venison."

"No, thank you," laughed the doctor: "I should soon be a great deal sicker than the peccari. I used to puff the temperance movement as a sanitary gospel of salvation," he continued, "but I have made up my mind that its chief purpose is defeated unless it goes hand in hand with a dietetic reform."

"That's all well enough," said the Boss, "but you can make up your mind that you're not going to starve in my camp. Look here, boys: doesn't one of you know a ranche or something hereabouts where we could raise a few eggs or a potful of milk?"

"Yes, there's a *cabaña* (log shanty) over there on the creek," said the guide. "I sent one of your men down there a while ago: he will soon be back."

Ten minutes after one of the Mexican teamsters returned from the cabaña with a hatful of leaf tobacco and a string of onions. "Mean as Jews!" said he. "They wouldn't take any sugar: I had to give them money."

"Do you know if they sell any eggs?" asked the Boss.

"No, sir, but they have *chilé colorado* and milk, and some green chilé."

AN INDIAN RANCHO.

"Never mind the chilé. Here"—handing him half a dollar—"take this pot and get as much milk as they will give for three rials."

We had to wait more than twenty minutes before our delegate returned with half a quart of skim-milk and a bunch of yellowish-green leaves. "They couldn't make the change," said he, "so they send you some chilé blanco (pepper-cress), since you don't like the other kind."

While we ate our supper a ragged Mexican—probably the proprietor of the cabaña or one of his neighbors— emerged from the darkness, and, upon the invitation of his countrymen, took a seat at our fireside.

"I had a good mind to make him eat his pepper-grass," muttered the Boss. "Confound his impudence! he might as well have sent us a handful of bulrushes. It puzzles me what he wants here."

Our visitor, after a whispered conference with one of the mestizo wagoners, at last solved the puzzle by drawing a dirty little package from his bosom and handing it to his neighbor.

"Excuse me, gentlemen," said the teamster, "but this *paysano* wants to know if you would like to buy a cake of fine beeswax. Nearly two pounds, he says,—enough for a big church-candle, and good for ten years of *gracias* (purgatory-indulgences) at the very least. It's first-rate for harness-leather too, especially in rainy weather," he added after a pause and a *sotto-voce* suggestion from his prompter. "Would you like to look at the cake?"

"Never mind," said the Boss: "tell him we are fire-and water-proof here."

The paysano nudged his interpreter, and exchanged the package for a larger article.

"Maybe you would prefer a *panuelo*," said the teamster, displaying a large red cotton handkerchief. "Look here! as good as new, and he says he lets you have it at less than half price, Mr. Davis."

"Take that rag away, or I——"

"Never mind him," said the doctor. "Listen! what's going on in that tree up there? It can't be birds at this time of the night?"

In different intervals of the camp-hubbub we had heard a shrill twitter from the summit of a large *pinabete*, or mountain-larch tree, as if a multitude of swallows were chirping in unison. But the invisible vocalists had either disagreed on some private business, or the glare of the camp-fire began to excite them, for their twittering was now intermingled with a vehement flutter and piercing squeaks that sounded through the cackle of our Mexicans like a boatswain's whistle.

"Goatsuckers perhaps, or some other kind of night-bird."

"They must be squirrels," said the Boss: "birds couldn't squeak like that."

"But squirrels can't flutter: they must be bats or birds," insisted the doctor. "Let me get over there: now watch if you don't see them fly away." He picked up a billet, and, after flinging it repeatedly against the upper branches, inspected the trunk of the pinabete, and owned himself puzzled when he returned. "There is a twenty-inch stratum of animal excrements under that tree," said he. "You may be right, after all, or there must be something else up there besides my birds,—maybe cats or *monoschicos*" (tree-raccoons).

"They are *murciegalos*" (a large kind of bats), said the guide, guessing at the context of the English conversation by the last word· "that tree is chuckful of them."

"What makes them flutter so?"

"I don't know, sir: they keep coming and going, and some of them are as large as wood-pigeons."

But the fluttering in the larch-tree was as steady as the flopping of a fan-ventilator; and after propounding and rejecting a variety of other theories, we came to the conclusion that the upper branches of the pinabete must be the flying-school of the bat colony, where their youngsters were exercised in the rhythmic movement of their membranous wings.

Smaller bats and a swarm of moths and beetles hovered about the camp, and in the light of our fire we could see night-rats chasing each other through the grass and flying-squirrels flitting from tree to tree; and the near and far voices of the forest made it rather doubtful which part of the twenty-four hours could here be called, *par excellence*, the wide-awake time. The business of animated nature is carried on by relays in the tropics.

We had almost forgotten our Indian visitor, when his interpreter resumed his functions: "With your permission, caballeros, this paysano asks me to mention that the pañuelo can be used as a neck-cloth. It is a patriotic handkerchief, with a Mexican eagle on it: all it needs is a good washing, and a little starch——"

"Doctor, you had better attend to that man; he must be seriously sick," laughed the Boss.

"A little starch, caballeros, would make it as good as new," he says; "and you needn't pay him in money: he'll take it out *en alimento*,—in comestibles."

"Aha! we are coming to the point now. Say, Pancho," to the guide, "just ask him what he wants, or he'll auctioneer his breech-clout next."

"I needn't ask him," laughed the guide; "he wants a little ground coffee, sir."

"That's talking sense, now. Here! fill him this pint cup. Now ask him if he wants anything else."

"He says he is very sorry to trouble——"

"Never mind; what is it?"

"A little bacon, sir: that's all."

"You relieve me. Here! I guess this chunk will grease his way to heaven if he should lose his bee-wax. Give him his pepper-cress back, too."

Cresses, coffee, and bacon were wrapped up in the patriotic handkerchief, and our Indio hopped off rejoicing.

"Indians are very fond of coffee, sir," explained the guide. "It doesn't grow here, and they've got no money hardly. There was no necessity, though, for giving him as much as all that."

COLIMA PEASANTS.

"Oh, he's welcome. But what's the reason the lazy loafers can't raise their own bacon? Don't they keep any pigs?"

"It's very hard to raise any hogs here, sir. The Indians are too poor to keep them in pens, and out in the bush they get snapped up as fast as you turn them out. The woods are full of panthers and bears, and God knows how many alligators down in the bottoms. Besides, they are liable to get sick, and——"

" To be mistaken for peccaris," suggested the doctor.

" Yes, and they are so worried with vermin,—leeches and bush-lice, and ticks as large as your finger. The same with chickens. The wild-cats eat them in the bush and the *pulgas* (sand-fleas) in the stable; so the Indians have to live on vegetables and milk."

" Why don't they go hunting, if the woods are so full of game ?"

" They don't dare to, sir; they might run across the wrong kind of game, or lose their way, as has happened more than once. You have no idea what sort of tangle-wood they have along this river; the best hunter can't find his way without a trained dog."

" There are no hunters at all here, then ?"

" Only a *Guero** here and there, but very few of the colored people. They told me about a deaf-and-dumb Indian lad down on the Balsas River who used to wander about the woods in every direction for days together, and somehow always found his way back. But one day he came flying home in the wildest excitement, and gesticu-lated as if he was out of his senses altogether; and he would hardly trust himself out of the rancho after that. They think he must have met a *renegrón*."

The backwoodsmen of Southern Colima believe in the existence of an animal which, according to their accounts,

* *Guero*, in Spanish America a generic name for all non-Spanish Europeans The European Spaniards are called *Castellanos*, but more frequently *Gachupines* (Tories)

must be a large, black-haired feline, of extraordinary strength and ferocity and of strictly nocturnal habits. The *renegrón*—blackamoor (*carraguar*, or night-tiger, the Indians call him)—has broken into adobe cabins and torn their inmates into pieces before a puma could kill a cow; and neither a bear nor a jaguar would follow a fisherman and capsize his boat in the middle of the stream, which feat is ascribed to a renegrón of the lower Balsas. In warm nights the rancheros of the Colima backwoods have often heard a peculiar howl which they could not mistake for that of any known beast of prey, and seen footprints in the river-sand which prove that the jungles harbor a brute whose size far exceeds that of the puma. They have found the mangled carcass of the *hormiguero*, or large ant-bear, an animal which from its mastership in the use of its long claws is never molested even by the jaguar. The jaguar also visits the *tierras frias*, the summit regions of the Sierra Madre, while the voice of the night-tiger is only heard in the river-jungles.

I was told that only a year ago the appearance of a carraguar in the Indian wigwams on the Rio Piñas created a perfect were-wolf panic; and the description of the brute, which was then seen and heard by a number of persons at the same time, though differing in details, agrees in the above-named essentials with the accounts of other forest tribes. But the renegrón sensations are by no means confined to the Indian settlements, and all the farmers of the Balsas Valley remember the tragedy of the Cazador Guëro (the "white hunter"), a sturdy ranchero of Portuguese descent, who had different rencontres with the murderous night-walker, and at last sealed the truth of his accounts with his life.

Juan Rivéra was a cattle-herder and trapper of the

Val de Mascalo, near San Nicolas, and proprietor of a clumsy but very efficient old *trabucco*, or Portuguese army-musket, which had freed the valley from so many wolves and panthers that he was generally known as *El Cazador*, the champion hunter of the Rio Mascalo. Among his trophies was a large shred of black fur torn by his hounds from the hide of a renegrón, which their master had crippled by a shot through the haunches, but which nevertheless effected its escape after disabling two of its would-be captors; and more than once had he seen the sable form of a "night-tiger" when he visited his beaver-traps in the morning twilight. But since the inundation of the Balsas bottoms, in 1869, his ranche had been more frequently harried by other enemies, and when he missed a fine white milch-cow he ascribed the loss to a puma that had carried off one of his goats a month before. The carcass of the cow, minus the entrails and one of the hind-quarters, was found near a salt-lick in the river-jungles, and the Cazador resolved to watch the next night and pay the butcher in heavy currency. He loaded his trabucco with two handsful of chopped lead, and started at sundown for the salt-lick, accompanied by his son Miguel, a fearless lad of fifteen or sixteen, who had lately been presented with a shot-gun by the Cazador's father-in-law, and wanted to prove himself worthy of the gift.

They watched behind an ambuscade of brushwood till the moon rose above the ridge of the Sierra de Mascalo, when Miguel heard a low rustling in the neighboring thicket and the click of the trabucco of his father, who motioned for him to cock his own piece and keep very quiet. After waiting in dead silence for ten or twelve minutes, during which the rustle was heard at intervals, but without coming any nearer, his father whispered to him to stay in the hiding-place and keep a sharp lookout, while he went to reconnoitre the jungle. He slipped away, trabucco in hand, and Miguel waited nearly a quarter of an hour, when he thought he saw a dark form creep upon the white carcass, which began to shake and roll in a way that satisfied him that the long-expected guest had commenced his supper. Bundles of brushwood had been deposited along the ground between the bait and the ambuscade, and Miguel could creep near enough to distinguish the whole outline of the cow-killer, and thought he recognized the broad head and long tail of a puma. His father had warned him not to fire at anything larger than a wolf, for his piece was only loaded with buckshot; but the brute presented a fair broad-side,—the left side, too,—not a pellet could miss, and no such opportunity might ever occur again. Miguel raised his shot-gun, and, resting it in the fork of a bush which completely hid him, covered the ribs of the supposed puma a little back of the left shoulder, and pulled the trigger.

He remembers that he dropped his piece and ran off, screaming for help, with the tiger at his heels, and that he was awakened from a stunning fall by the crunching of his shoulder-bones and a fierce tugging at his shawl, as if the murderer was trying to get at his throat. But in that moment he heard his father's trabucco go off like a thunder-clap close to his ears, and staggered to his feet. The brute had recoiled, and in the next instant received a blow *por tumbar un toro* (that would have felled a bull), for it splintered the butt of the heavy musket like a walking-stick. He saw his father swing up the gun-barrel for a second stroke, but before it descended the brute had made a spring at his legs, and in the next second had him prostrate on the ground.

" *Corre, muchacho! por tu vida! por tu vida!* " yelled

the hunter between his screams of agony,—" Run, my boy, for your life ! It's a renegrón !"

Miguel stood stupefied for a minute, and even the death-shriek of his father brought him only half to his senses, for he dashed into the woods at random, and arrived at midnight, not at his mother's ranche, but at an Indian wigwam on the river-shore, where a former *vaquero* of his father's bandaged his shoulder, and carried him home on a mule the next morning. The boy's excitement and his frightful wounds attested the truth of his statements, and before night the battle-ground was visited by a large party of armed rancheros. The corpse of the hunter had disappeared, but they found his hat and shreds of his clothes, and the two guns. On a spot where the sods were torn up by the rough-and-tumble fight, and on the butt of the broken musket, they discovered tufts of coarse black hair, which could not have belonged either to a jaguar or a *cuguar*, as the Indians call the yellowish-gray puma or Mexican lion.

The next morning we resumed our journey at sunrise, and passed through a majestic forest of pinabetes (*Larix montana*), which covers a considerable portion of the lower foot-hills. Even coniferous trees do not monopolize the soil of the virgin woods, and in the shade of dense and widespreading mountain-firs many bushes and arborescent shrubs—sassafras, *chrysosplenium*, or monkey-pot trees, and white-blooming oleanders—manage to dispense with sunshine and rain.

But the *selvas bravas*—the primeval forests proper—begin only beyond the foot-hills of the Sierra de Jalisco, where the erythrina thorns and wood-myrtles spread their thickets through the underbrush, while the upper foliage is interlaced with a network of wildering lianas. The road through the-e mountain jungles cost the vireys millions of dollars and untold human lives, and is kept in tolerable repair at the expense of the Mazatlan merchants; but the overhanging boughs of the giant trees and the swaying tendrils of the bush-ropes, that reach out like eager hands toward the bush-rope tangle on the other side, convey the impression that if the road was left to its fate the forest would swallow it and close above it in a single year. Here and there a creek issues from a dusky archway that leads into the penetralia of the tree-labyrinth like a tunnel into the bowels of a mountain. The arcades of the wild fig-trees, too, open vistas into leafy vaults where owls and goatsuckers commence their plaintive cry long before sun-set, and the gloom of the deeper recesses is unlike anything we see in our densest pine-groves in daytime.

The experience of a lifetime teaches the Jalisco hunter to distinguish the strange animal voices of these mountain forests,—the cries of yelping birds and whistling quad-rupeds, the shrill piping of the squirrel-monkey from the note of the crested curlew, and the hoarse bark of the toucan from the coughing scream of the tree-panther. But the remoter depths of the selvas now and then send forth sounds which puzzle even the natives, like voices from an unknown world, and awaken a suspicion which the theo-retical completeness of our natural histories cannot wholly remove,—namely, that the Forest has kept some of its secrets as well as the Ocean.

CHAPTER III.

THE LAKE-REGION OF JALISCO.

Yet would you scale those mountains if you knew
That they enclose the vale of Paradise?—CAMOENS

WHEN we reached the plateau of the first—*i.e.*, the eastern—range of the double mountain-chain that encloses the
lake-region of Jalisco, the valley at our feet was shrouded
by a misty veil, but the mountain-heads had doffed their
hood, and the ridge of our own sierra was sunlit for many
miles ahead. Our road meandered between boulders of calcareous tufa, but along the centre of the plateau the main
stratum had cropped out in a ledge of massive granite,
which approached the western brink at different points,
forming as many headlands of dark-gray cliffs.

"We could see the lake now if it wasn't for that wretched
fog," observed our guide, "but I guess we shall have the
south breeze before long if the sun gets a little higher."

We saw the breeze in the tree-tops of the lower mountain-regions before it reached our plateau; and when we
approached the western slope the next time the cloud-
masses had actually got under way, and a gap here and
there revealed the blue forests of the opposite sierra, and
even a dazzling though only momentary glimpse of the
great lake below. But when we reached the third headland our caravan stopped and the teamsters dismounted,
and one by one our men stepped up to the brink of the
projecting cliffs. The veil had been lifted.

The river at our feet was as wide and quite as blue as the Susquehanna at Harrisburg; but its banks were not gentle slopes, but savage cliffs rising abruptly into tower-like foot-hills and mountain-walls that approached the re-

LAKE CHAPALA.

gions of everlasting snow. But as the mountains diverge the river widens into a lake whose shores follow the zigzag line of the foot-hills, till, in the far west, where the two sierras part at right angles and forever, the lake expands into a boundless sea, glittering like a mirage and studded with hundreds of wood-covered islands that fade into light-blue hillocks at the edge of the horizon. Just below our feet the river was hidden by a grove of balsam-firs, the home of a colony of black herons, and the open lake was crossed and recrossed by swarms of waterfowl, which, at a greater distance, seemed to drift slowly along like a streak of silver-white clouds.

It has been said that the world in general knows nothing of its greatest men, but it is more certain that men in general are unacquainted with the fairest regions of their world. I am almost sure that there are towns of ten thousand inhabitants in the United States, and much larger cities in Western Europe, where it would be impossible to find one man who ever in his life heard even the name of Lake Chapala, while every other village schoolmaster in Europe and North America could write a treatise on Lake Leman or Loch Lomond. Thousands of North American school-boys have read about the Lago di Como, and many illiterate Western farmers know that the Boden-See is drained by the Upper Rhine, but not two men in a cityful of European professors would be able to say if the fairy lake of the Rio Lerma is in Mexico or in the Philippine Islands. Yet this fair *lacus incognitus* is ten times as large as all the lakes of Northern Italy taken together, and forty times larger than the entire canton of Geneva,—contains different islands whose surface area exceeds that of the Isle of Wight, and one island with *two secondary lakes* as big as Loch Lomond and Loch Katrine !

" Well, boys," observed one of the American teamsters, " it's no use to deny the truth if you can see it in broad daylight : this beats California."

" It does indeed," said the sergeant, who had stood at

my side as immovable as a fugleman on parade. "Well, sir, I have often wondered how that Maximilian of yours could be so foolish as to leave all those castles he had in the old country and come here and get himself shot like a highway robber; but I see now that his head was level enough, after all. He was right to risk his life for a country like this "

I walked over to the other side of the cliff, where Dr. Rambert stood, hat in hand, pensive and mute. "Que dit Monsieur le Docteur" You wouldn't find such a lake in California? Don't you feel like going back to San Luis, in spite of your heresy?"

"*Retourner?* Yes," said the heretic, turning suddenly and gimleting me with his keen eyes—"Yes, I do feel like going back a long way,—back to the fourth or fifth century B.C. There it is, my friend: that's the world we have lost for the privilege of exchanging a pantheon for a charnel-house, —a company of happy gods for an assembly of tearful saints, who ruined their bodies to save their souls and *ce monde-ci pour l'amour du ciel.* Have you ever wished to know what Southern Europe was like in the times of Homer and Xenophon? *Circumspice.* That's Greece with all its ancient forests and happy islands, and without its modern deserts and convents. Take a good look at it. I have an unfortunate talent for historical clairvoyance, a sort of inverted second-sight, and I can see it: I see a Mediterranean Paradise getting from year to year more desolate and Semetic, but——"

"Go on."

"No, I won't. The guide tells me we are going to have fried salmon-trout for dinner, and I don't like to spoil my appetite."

The forest thickened around us as we descended, and

before we reached the lake our road shrank to a narrow
senda, a mere trail through the wild tanglewood. The
jungles of the foot-hills, our guide told us, swarm with game
of various kinds which are but rarely seen in the *alturas*,
as the natives call the open forests of the summit-regions.
In the matted thickets of styrax and myrtle-wood they
find safe retreats from the arrow of the Indian hunter, and
even the panther visits their haunts only at midnight, for
fear of the *maraños*, or wild hogs, that charge him with
headlong fury if they spy his freckled hide in daytime.

The foliage was fairly drenched with dew, and the
morning wind diffused a medley of most astonishing odors;
but the weather was already too warm to be agreeable, and
when we emerged from the bottom-jungles opposite a pebbly beach our mules jostled and kicked each other in the
press for precedence. The shores of Lake Chapala had not
borrowed their enchantment from the distance of the view.
Sturdy hemlocks and bignonia-trees crowd the impertinent
underbrush out of the way, forming natural avenues along
the beach, which slopes so gradually that the water-line is
almost everywhere accessible. The water is steel-blue and
wonderfully transparent, in spite of the algæ and pond-
weeds that weave their tangled tendrils wherever the bottom is a little less obdurate. From the racks of an open
wagon we could see the mountain-forests of the opposite
shore glittering with a moist and tremulous light and a
thousand hues,—all possible shades, variations, and combinations of green and blue, darkened here and there by the
gloom of a mountain-gorge or the floating shadow of a
cloud. But on the eastern shore the sierra presents a
mural front to the lake, and discharges its drainage in the
form of dripping springs and cascades, tiny rivulets mostly,
except at the northeastern extremity of a triangular bay,

where the falls of the Rio Blanco come down with a thunder that can be heard and felt for leagues around. A mile below the falls a few jagged rocks rise from the water, forming the southern outposts of the motley archipelago of cliffs and islands that extends along the eastern shore for at least sixty English miles. A meadow of pond-reeds near one of the mid-lake islands seemed to be a rendezvous for all possible kinds of waterfowl. Moor-hens, surf-ducks, flamingoes, a long-legged bird that looked like a stork, but might be a species of white heron, coots, and black divers, arrived and departed from and in all directions; and a little apart from the rest a flock of *gansas*, or swamp-geese, disported themselves in the open water,—grayish-white, long-necked fellows with black heads, floating at times in a sleepy way till some old gander craned his neck, and then, as if suddenly stirred by the spirit of locomotion, shot ahead with flopping wings for a hundred yards or so, and excited the whole flock into a fit of aquatic gymnastics.

"How would this suit you for a camping-ground, capitan?" asked the guide when we passed a grassy slope at the foot of a styrax-coppice.

"There isn't much tent-room here," said the Boss. "I guess I shall steer for that mangrove-thicket over yonder: it looks like a nice level place. When are you going to that hacienda you were talking about?"

"If the gentlemen are ready we had better go now," said the guide, with a chronological squint at the sun: "it's very near noon, I should say. Can't you manage to join us?"

"Not now," said the Boss, "but I guess Billy here could."

The clerk assented, and we crept into the cabin of our prairie-schooner to supply some essential defects of our toilet

"Please don't go out too far that way," cried the clerk when he jumped down, "or else we sha'n't be able to find you to-night."

"Don't you fret," shouted the cook. "you'll know the place by the smell if you don't see the camp-fire: we are going to fry all those Dutch bananas of yours while you are gone," meaning the bologna sausages, of which the young gentleman kept a full stock on hand.

"How far is that hacienda from here, anyhow?" asked the doctor after we had followed the windings of a meadow-brook for some time.

"We are on the hacienda even now," replied the guide, "but the dwelling-house—the Casa Morena, as they call it —is about half a league from those mango-trees over there. That orchard has grown into a regular forest with all the new trees they have set out, and they are still at it."

"You have been here before, it seems?"

"Yes, sir, many a time; and the Señor Vidas is an old friend of mine: he used to live in Queretaro, and I knew him a long while before he ever came here."

"He has only purchased this place lately, has he?"

"He doesn't own it, sir, but I guess he will before long: the proprietor, old Mr. Martinez, is his father-in-law, and lets him boss the place as much as he likes. He might as well be dead: he has never a word to say."

"Bedridden, I suppose?"

"Lord bless you, no, sir! he could ride a wild buffalo. But he is hardly ever home: he's fishing from morning till night. That's all he cares for; and I really think he could beat a fish-otter at its own game."

The Casa Morena was a two-story, flat-roofed stone house, constructed of a kind of brown syenite of great durability, but of a color that gave the stones the appearance of overgrown bricks: the house, the corral, and half a dozen out-buildings were enclosed by a citron-hedge whose flowers shone like drifted snow against the background of dark-green mango-trees.

The señor was not at home, but the housekeeping mestiza informed us that she expected him for dinner, and promised us a superlative potful of *trucha con papas*—broiled trout with potato-chips—if we would tarry a little while. In the mean time one of the stable-boys volunteered to show us the sights of the hacienda,—the flower-plots, the chapel, a pyramid of alligator skulls, the Shanghai cock recently imported from Mazatlan, a little wind coffee-mill, and the skeleton of a big swamp-boa. But a greater curiosity, at least to our eyes, was the tame *porcasso*, or hog-tapir, the fattest, laziest, and, with the single exception of the tree-alligator, the ugliest habitant of the Tierra Caliente, and the first of his tribe I had ever seen in a state of captivity. He was confined in a pig-pen of solid construction, though in his present condition he seemed hardly able to use his legs for migratory purposes. When we approached the pen he surveyed us with a misanthropic—nay, pessimistic—expression of his jaundiced eye, and even when the stable-boy offered him an armful of water-cabbage he turned away with a weary look and grunted protest against the vanities of this world. But by and by the aroma of the succulent vegetable seemed to revive his secular propensities: the wrinkles of his proboscis began to work; he turned his head gradually, and with crescendo sniffs eyed the garbage with the mien of a connoisseur, and suddenly broke forth into an exultant snort that contrasted painfully with the moral tone of his previous utterances. I think there were about sixteen pounds of cabbage, which vanished in as many seconds, and after smacking his chops meditatively for two or three minutes he raised his head to apply for a second instalment. The functions of his mental apparatus

THE HOG-TAPIR.

seemed, indeed, quite as sluggish as his visible movements. The stable-boy handed him another bundle, larger and heavier than the first, but, after allowing him to devour a hatful or so, he jerked the rest away, leaving him nothing but a few scattered leaves. While the tapir gobbled these leaves he kept his eye on the main stake, but a full minute elapsed before he realized the magnitude of his bereavement. When the truth flashed upon him it seemed to strike his brain like an electric shock: he jumped around as if possessed with all the hog-goblins of Gadara, snapped at his own buttocks, and finally stood still, leaned his head back, and uttered screams that continued for a long while after his property had been restored.

A bell sounded from the kitchen-window, and we returned to the casa. "You must excuse my appearance, gentlemen," said the señor when he came in, wet and mud-bespattered. "I have a lot of Chechemeca Indians at work in the swamp getting the vanilla-crop in; and you know you cannot trust them round the corner: you might as well rely on a troop of monkeys to behave in your absence. Had the caballeros a pleasant trip?"

"Yes, sir, from the moment we sighted your mountains," said Dr. Rambert; "but the pleasure will end here too: it's hard on a man to have to crawl back to the humdrum Tierra Caliente after having been in heaven."

"How's the old man?" inquired the guide.

"Thanks: oh, he is all right,—still at it, of course," laughed the señor: "he wouldn't care for any other heaven either unless he could take his angle along.—Well, help yourselves, caballeros, and excuse me for a few minutes."

When Don Vidas returned in his black jaqueta we found him "a gentleman in dress and address." He had been an alcalde of the court of session in Queretaro, and could not only read, but had evidently put that accomplishment to some account.

"I understand my honored guests are versed in the medical sciences," said he, after dinner, "and I have often wished for an opportunity to hear a competent verdict upon the value of a hot spring in this neighborhood. Would you like to take a stroll down to the creek?"

We took our hats, and the clerk, who had only understood the last two or three words, followed our example.

The thermal springs of this region deserve a hotter name. The weather was so warm that we envied the broad-

brimmed sombrero of our companion, but in spite of the
heat and dryness of the atmosphere Mr. Vidas's little spa
smoked like a Canadian waterfall on a cold winter morning.
Where it joined the creek, and for some distance below,
the water emitted curling little wreaths of steam that soon
dissolved in the upper air, but to our surprise we noticed
the same vapor in the creek-water above the junction. The
mineral thermæ proper were farther up, explained the
señor, and he took us to a place where a number of tiny
fountains welled up from a smoking puddle at the edge of
the creek.

"Whew! that's a sulphur spring, it can't be denied,"
said Dr. Rambert, rubbing his nose. "Very popular with
the natives, I dare say,—miraculous cures effected, lepers
restored to health, etc., eh?"

"Well, I don't know," laughed the señor. "It's a popular maxim, though, that whatever tastes bad must be healthy;
and if that's true the sanative efficacy of this puddle must
be preternatural indeed: it tastes like a mixture of rotten
eggs and turpentine. The Indians call it the *pestazole*"
(stink-hole)—"your nose testifies to the fitness of the term,
I suppose—but they worship it, nevertheless, though it all
but suffocates them. I have often seen them take a mouth-
ful and wait to let it cool off, and then swallow it with a
sort of resignation; but the moment they get it down they
explode like fermenting beer-bottles, and never stop sneezing
and hacking for hours together. A clerical friend of mine
calls it the 'Fountain of Eternal Coughs.' It's no eternal
fountain, though, I'm afraid: the creek keeps encroaching
on its left bank, and will swamp the spring—maybe both
of them—before long, unless I can stop the mischief with
a dike or something."

"Save the lower spring, then, the one without brimstone.

A warm spring, sir, is a great blessing in winter-time,—as a bath I mean, not as a beverage."

"That's what I often suspected," said the señor. "If I understand you right, you mean to say that it doesn't matter much whether this puddle gets swamped or not?"

"Not one straw. If that stuff were healthier than pure water, the Creator would have covered the face of the earth with pestazotes. The truth, señor, is what you hinted at a while ago: that people in general have an unhappy reverence for out-of-the-way things,—hartshorn, miracles, cod-liver oil, mandragora, and such like. If some wretch should discover a spring of sulphuric acid, he would be hailed as a benefactor of mankind. Thousands of cures ascribed to our mineral springs are in reality effected by open-air exercise, climatic influences, music, and other incidental advantages of a watering-place, but especially by the dietetic restrictions which are commonly involved with a sentence of sulphur-water. And the power of faith can even dispense with such adjuncts."

"Our Indians are saved by faith then," said Don Vidas, "for they certainly dispense with dietetic restrictions. I have seen them put down potsful of sulphur-water and broiled eels, turn about, or a greasy mess of cabbage with lard oil and red pepper. Their digestive apparatus is different from ours, though. There's a chap on this farm who can devour an arroba of sweet potatoes with pansful of bacon-fat and onions at a single session; and my Cheche-mecas have regular eating-matches that last four or five hours, and do not prevent them from walking as many leagues the same night, puny monkeys as they are. My only explanation is this: they are strict teetotalers; fermented and distilled drinks are almost unknown in their settlements; and I have often thought that a stout white man or an African could digest almost anything if he would just leave alcohol alone."

As we sauntered back to the casa the señor informed us that he had to meet a cattle-dealer in the village of Barrios that night, but that he would return in the course of the next morning, at all events before noon. "In the mean time," said he, "the house and the hacienda are at your disposition, and I think you will find the proprietor a man of excellent good-humor, though the same cannot be said of his manners."

"What in the name of witchcraft can this be?" whispered the doctor when we were alone with our guide,—"this unearthly smell, I mean: it gets worse every minute."

The guide chuckled: "It's the vanilla, señor; they have just brought a load of fresh-cut in, and they are spreading it on the veranda. It can't be done in the hot sun—it would spoil all the aroma, you know—so they have to wait for a dry night; and about an hour before sunset is the right time to spread it."

"It's the right time for us to be off, then," laughed the doctor: "let's go. Yes, come on: here they bring the second load."

"Me too?" asked the guide.

"If you like. On second thought, no· you had better stay here, my friend, till the old gent comes home, and make up an excuse for us, like a good fellow."

Flocks of white herons were returning to their roosts in the mountain-forests, and the reed-frogs struck up the prelude of their evening concert when we reached the lake-shore. On an old pasture at the foot of the hacienda the children of the farmers and day-laborers were at play with that vociferous mirth which only the evening hour awakens in boys and rooks. The little Indians looked at us with shy curiosity, but their less naked, semi-Caucasian playmates gathered around us when they saw us stop near a group of guava-trees; and they had no sooner understood that we wished to get some of the *madreselvas* (yellow honeysuckles) in one of the top branches than six or seven of them swarmed up the tree like squirrel-monkeys and pelted us with a golden shower of blossoms and flowery tendrils. When we left we treated them to a penny scramble, while their comrades were chasing a tame antelope around the pasture or rolling in the dry grass in a very ecstasy of frolic and exuberant health.

"Wasn't poor Holty right?" said the doctor; and then muttered, as to himself, "A man might live here like a wood-god and forget that there are such things on earth as tobacco-smoke and an anti-natural religion."

Before we sighted the mangrove timber the guide overtook us and informed me that Don Martinez—"the governor," as he called him—would join us at the camp to-night.

"So he was not offended at our leaving the casa?"

"Not in the least. I told him you belonged to a sect of Protestants that have to be baptized every Saturday night, and he was determined to see the fun."

"Why, what made you tell such——"

"Don't get mad, now: let's hurry up, and I'll tell him you have just got through when he comes."

After sunset the clerk had repeatedly called my attention to the gigantic bats that steered their fitful flight through the trees at the lake-shore, and, finding our cook still at work, I took my shot-gun and sauntered along the beach in the vain hope of bagging one of the prodigies before pitch-dark. On my return I found my friends squatting around the camp-fire, and in their midst an old gentleman whom I should have taken for a Hollander if I had met

him in a seaport-town.   He shook my hand without stirring
from his seat, and even without interrupting his conversation with Dr. Rambert, who, knowing his hobby, had
already got him astraddle and was listening to an account
of his recent piscatorial exploits.

"Gar-pike," said he, "do not spawn in this lake,—they
come from below,—but I caught an old slick-tailed one this
morning whom I've seen for weeks and weeks, and who
knew me too well to try any of his tricks on me when I
pulled him home.   It made me laugh to see the way the
dog winked at me."

"I hear this lake is full of alligators?" said the Boss

"No, no: we can't complain.   My father used to hunt
them unmercifully, but I have been living here nigh on
sixty years, and I do not think they ever did me sixty
shillings' worth of damage.   They stick to the south side,
where there are plenty of swamps, and few people living:
we shouldn't know there were any about if we didn't hear
them splash in the night-time."

"Do they ever come ashore?"

"Only in the rutting season: in March and April I have
seen the males chase each other across the beaver-meadows
near Cape Ramas.   There's one exception, though," he
continued: "whenever one of those big *lagartos*" (caymans)
"comes up from the coast-swamps our alligators combine
against him and run him down, *coûte que coûte*, though they
should have to follow him through the jungles and up
stream for miles.   I went down to San Marica about five
years ago, and near the ford I met some countrymen flying
up the road almost out of their senses; and they told me
there was a snake in the creek as long as my picket-fence,
—*i.e.*, about sixty-five yards.   I told them they must be
crazy, but when I got down to the creek I thought there

must be something in it,—not in the creek only, but in the snake-story. For a considerable distance up and down the opposite shore the water was in motion as if an everlastingly long snake kept turning over and over, and when it came a little nearer it struck me all at once that it was quite natural for those Indians to run away. But before I turned my horse I happened to notice that the critter seemed to have three or four tails, and when I watched closer I thought it must have at least a dozen. And what do you think it was? A string of alligators after a lagarto that must have led them a six-mile chase from the lake till they got him up to the rapids; and there they had him foul,— a current like a mill-race ahead, steep banks on both sides, and no place to hide. I can't say if they killed him or not, but I know that somebody got hurt in that corner, for after they left the water was as red as a puddle behind a butcher-shop. A lagarto can go against the stream like a surf-duck, but the fool should not have run into a little creek with a *cul-de-sac:* if he'd gone up the Lerma, he might have laughed at all the alligators in North America."

"What is your theory about the Rio Lerma, señor? Where do you think it comes from?"

"From a greater distance than any of our sierra-creeks, —that's all I am sure about,—for it isn't possible that it could collect all that water on this side of the *juntura*" (the junction of the two mountain-ranges); "so I think the Indians were right, after all. The Indian chiefs of this valley told the Spaniards that the Rio Lerma is fed by subterranean affluents, by creeks that take their rise in the Orgas Mountains beyond the sierras, and that the limestone-caves near Toluca are the upper end of these tunnels. I suppose you have heard of the great mica-cave near Temascaltepec, where you can walk for half a league alongside of a deep

river that goes to nobody knows where? Well, the Indians
have a tradition that a Toluca chieftain once entered that
cave with sixty warriors, and asked which one of them had
pluck enough to jump into a canoe and commit himself to
the current of the cave-river? Fifteen or twenty volunteered, so he made them draw lots, and it fell to a naked
spearman of his body-guard. The chief gave him his red
mantle and a cargo of provisions, and the man pushed off.
They say the current carried him to the farther end of the
cave and into the interior of the mountain, and that was
the last they saw of him. But two months after his canoe
and the red mantle were found near Benjamo on the Rio
Lerma."

"I have heard of that cave," said Dr. Rambert; "and
I'm sorry we did not take a look at it when we passed
through Toluca. Have you ever visited that neighborhood,
señor?"

"No, sir: I've passed my life in this State," said the ha-
ciendero,—"never was farther east than Celaya I haven't
even seen the ocean yet, though it is only forty leagues to
San Blas, and I guess there are greater wonders in the sea
than a little underground water-course. Tell me, caballeros,
—though you may laugh at me for repeating such stuff,—
is it true what I've been told once and again, that there are
luciernas" (lightning-bugs) "in the sea that live under water
the year round and don't get extinguished? It's a sailor's
yarn, isn't it?"

"Not quite," answered the doctor. "you can see them
in warm nights, but only where there are millions of them
together, and even then it's only a green shimmer. The
sea doesn't extinguish them, but nobody would miss them
if it did; and who could say that of your *luciernas*? Just
look at them, all of you!"

The Mexican lightning-bugs seemed, indeed, to have turned out with all their colleagues and relatives that night. Fire-flies, fire-midges, and fire-bluebottles drifted and dodged through the branches of the mangrove-thicket, the skirts of the forest behind us scintillated like a reflection of the Galaxy, and even the scattered trees in the valley could be distinguished by a blaze of circling sparks. The lake-shore too glittered with intermittent stars, mere luminous points at a greater distance, but in the canebrake on the south shore a larger light flared up every now and then—like a sudden flash, rather than like the continued flicker of a will-o'-the-wisp. What could it be? Not the tropical lantern-fly, which I had seen in Yucatan and Panama, and again near Tampico, and which nowhere exceeded the brilliancy of the common luciernas more than two or three times, while the flashes in the canebrake fairly illuminated the reeds for yards around. Was it an electric phenomenon, or what in Florida they call " bush-fire" ?

" I couldn't tell you," said the planter. " I have often seen it on the beaver-meadows near the *boca,* and sometimes in the vanilla-swamps, but never near enough to find out if it's a living thing or something else,—something the heretics don't believe in. Say, Coco," turning to his Indian attendant, "just look at those bulrushes: do you see that light? Wait a moment: there it goes again. Now, what would you call that?"

" That's a *luz huanal,*" said Coco, combining a Spanish noun with a Chechemeca attributive

" A—what?"

" A *fuego huanal,*" sticking to the doubtful adjective.

" Describe it : is it an animal or something else?"

" Si, señor "

" How do you mean? Is it alive?"

"Yes, sir, but—" after some reflection—"it hides in the daytime."

"What is it like? A bird, a bug, or a fish?"

"Oh no, sir."

"What, then? Can it fly?"

"Yes, but not like a bird."

"Describe it, then, can't you? What is it, anyhow?"

"A *luz huanal*, señor."

We gave it up. The art of definition does not belong to the primitive faculties of the human mind.

"Whatever it may be," said Don Martinez, "I have never seen it after December, but often in August, and generally towards midnight or early in the morning. But that reminds me it's getting late, at least for people who have crossed the sierra this morning. I shouldn't have bothered you anyhow, I suppose, but you have no idea how much I should like to have you stay here for a couple of weeks. My neighbors are mostly Indians and hog-tapirs, and it's so rarely we see any strangers in this valley! Well, it's my own fault too. Fifteen years ago a French company wanted to build a railroad from here to San Diego, and I was against it, like every other fool in the country, because I thought we might as well do the job ourselves and pocket the profits. Now we can wait a long while for another chance like that. Mexico is ruined, and the French seem to have got rid of their loose change during that last war."

"We'll attend to that, señor," said I: "my friend here will be in California this day week, and he will take orders for any desired number of railroads. There's plenty of time: we sha'n't start before nine A.M. to-morrow."

"To-morrow!" cried the Mexican. "Santissima! you are not going to travel on Sunday, are you?"

7

" Yes, they are," said the guide. " I told you they were
heretics: they always travel on Sunday, especially on
Easter-Sunday and Whit-Sunday: it's their merriest day in
the week."

"Don't believe it, señor," said Dr. Rambert: " it will
be a sad day for us if we have to bid farewell to Lake
Chapala. But, as my friend says, there's a remedy for it:
we'll build you a railroad down here at our earliest con-
venience and invade you with an army of commercial travellers. It isn't fair that you should have a Paradise all to
yourself."

" All right!" laughed the planter. "I'll let you go on
those terms, even on Sunday. But before you leave the
lake you ought to baptize that guide of yours: he's in need
of it, I'm afraid."

We went to our tent. A night-chill had stolen upon the
air, and the candle in the doctor's field-lantern was flickering rather low in the socket, but before we put it out we returned to a little hillock behind the tent to have one more
look at the great mountain-lake. The camp all around was
fast asleep, and so still that we could hear the low creaking
of the tent-poles and the half bark of a dreaming dog whose
soul was perhaps roaming through the thickets of the alturas. The camp-fires and stick-torches had burned down
to the last chip, but the deepest night was already past.
Above the heights of the Sierra de Inua the moon was
rising, and all along the eastern shore the dark forests of
the foot-hills began to gleam with a magic light that seemed
to spread with the night-mist till it glittered through the
tree-tops of the coast-islands and painted the lake with
silver streaks and spangles. From the dark north coast
the scream of a waterfowl came now and then like a distant trumpet-note, but the chorus of the lake-frogs had

CHECHEMECA PLATANERO.

subsided into a minor key, and even the booming of the
Rio Blanco had a muffled sound, as if the water-spirits
were yielding to the slumberous spells of the night-wind.

We stood silent till my companion tapped me on the
shoulder: "This evening you said something about inveig-
ling a railroad company into the valley. You will have to
do it yourself, amigo: I don't want the weight of such a
sin on my soul."

The Rio Lerma enters the lake as a rock-bound moun-
tain-river, and leaves it a broad stream with low shores and
sedgy shallows; but before it reaches the coast it contracts
once more to force its way through the tortuous defiles of
the Sierra de Santiago, while the road takes a short cut

through the Porta Marina, a deep gap which intersects the mountain-range about fourteen miles north of the river-cañon and hardly eight hundred feet above the water-level. From the apex of the pass we could see the south shore of the lake in all its grandeur ; also a lateral valley with different smaller lakes, one of which, the Ojo del Cayman, became " bottomless" a few years ago, when an earthquake overthrew a steep rock on its western shore and swallowed a little island which, as our guide told us, had been cultivated by one of Don Martinez's neighbors for many years. The western slope of the sierra stretched away to the very edge of the Pacific, whose coast is indeed an almost continuous mountain-slope from Oregon to Patagonia, while the west shore of the Atlantic is flanked with equally persistent swamps. On a headland of the coast that looked like the northwestern extremity of the continent we could see the church-steeples of Mazatlan, but the direct distance could not be less than sixty leagues ; so we decided to follow the road to San Blas, a little seaport at the mouth of the Rio Lerma and hardly twenty English miles from the ridge of our mountain-range.

About three miles beyond the pass we overtook a gang of Indian *plataneros*, or banana-hucksters, who trudged along manfully under loads that would have staggered a mule, and attested their gratitude with unintelligible but not less expressive exclamations when we permitted them to deposit their burdens in one of our empty wagons. One of them, an ex-mail-carrier, could talk a little Spanish, but his five comrades were unqualified Chechemecas, and wore the turban-like head-dress which distinguishes the bush Indian from his half-civilized city cousin. They carried long bows of bignonia-wood, and gave us a sample of their skill when we passed a swampy lagoon at the foot of the mountain. We heard a rustle in the canebrake and a splash or two in the open water behind it, but the pool was

CHECHEMECA BOWMAN.

screened by a hedge of hackberry-trees, and we were about to pass by, thinking of the common swamp-turtles that frequent such lagoons, when one of the Chechemecas peeped through the hedge and beckoned to us to stop. The front teams had already turned a corner, but our wagon was one of the last, and four of us jumped down.

"*Maraños!*" (wild hogs) cried the Indian: "hurry up! you can see them yet."

A herd of peccaris had been rooting in a reed-thicket in the middle of the lagoon, and were now swimming for the opposite bank with an energy that stirred the little pond from shore to shore

"Why don't you shoot, compañero?" I asked the mail-carrier: "they are not out of range yet, are they?"

"No use, sir," said he, "not water enough to swim, and too much mud to wade it; but we can try it for fun. Be quick, boys," reaching for his bow with an exclamation in the vernacular: "Here goes!"

The first volley scattered among the swimming heads, but a big sow that landed on a peninsular mud-bank received two arrows at the same moment and almost in the same place; and one of her pigs was crippled in a way that would have ensured its capture if we could have reached the other shore. The rest were cautious enough to swim around the peninsula, and landed on the safe side of a mangrove-coppice.

The peccary (*Sus torquatus*) is one of the few migratory quadrupeds of our continent, and roams from the Rio Grande to the Orinoco in search of swamps and inundated forests, and in wet seasons often appears *en masse* in upland regions where it has not been seen for a half-century. It is smaller and uglier, but much more active, than our domestic hog,—the sow we saw in the lagoon cleared a broad sand-bank at a single leap, and rushed into the mangrove-thicket with heroic disregard of the prickly under-brush. Some of her pigs seemed to have been littered in the preceding summer,—*i.e.*, three or four months before, —but they swam like ducks, as, indeed, all young animals do, at least as soon as they can run, the children of man alone excepted. Have we incurred such disabilities by our abnormal habits? Now and then I cannot help suspecting that Jean Jacques Rousseau was right: *non est quod fuit Natura.*

One of our Indians seemed to be sick or weak-minded: he tramped along without ever raising his head, and repeatedly stumbled over obstacles which even a short-sighted man might have avoided. "What's the matter with that comrade of yours?" I asked the mail-carrier: "can I help him in any way?"

"No, sir; it can't be helped, I guess: he is blear-eyed and nearly blind. Eel-hunting did it."

"Hunting—*what?*"

"Barcas eels or eel-snakes," explained the guide: "they come ashore in moonlight nights, you know, and the Indians often collar them by the sackful."

"What has that to do with his eyes?"

"I do not know, sir, but they ascribe it to the moon, like a good many other diseases. If their children are playing out-doors in the evening, the old ones are sure to drive them in as soon as the moon rises. Moonlight makes them *anochido*" (night-eyed), "they say, and unfit to work in daytime."

The last four miles of our journey brought us in sight of, and finally back to, the banks of the Rio Lerma, a happy river that passes from the hills to the sea without muddling its waters in an intermediate swamp-estuary, after the fashion of our Atlantic streams. We entered the town through a double gate that forms the main sallyport of a fort and gives the place something of a mediæval appearance; and San Blas is really one of the oldest Spanish towns of the New World,—nearly a century older than New York and *New* Vera Cruz, for the seaport where Hernan Cortez landed in 1518 was abandoned some ninety years after Ruiz Lacerdo fortified the mouth of the Rio Lerma

While the custom-house officers inspected the doctor's baggage, I accompanied the wagonmaster to the Morgan agency, and our first question was after our old mail-boat, the Gila City, whose schedule we knew to have been changed since the capture of Guaymas.

"She went up this morning," said the clerk, "but you can take the Panama steamer. Yes, to-morrow is Wednesday. she will be here in the evening at four or five o'clock, if she is on time."

Going back to the custom-house, we met the agent himself, a very intelligent young Scotchman of the Mackenzie clan, who gave us all the particulars of information we could desire, and offered us the hospitality of his own quarters in the agency building But Dr. Rambert was suffering from his old complaint, chronic rheumatism, and preferred the dreary solitude of a *posada;* and I joined him in order to spare him the delays and chicaneries of a Mexican hostelry.

On the following morning Mr. Mackenzie called upon us at the Posada de la Cruz, and, finding the doctor dozing after a sleepless night, asked me to come down town and take a look at the harbor. "It's *down* in the geometrical sense of the word," he added: "this old hole is carved out of a mountain-side like a slate-quarry."

We inspected the wharves, the American warehouses, and the old Spanish fort, where we witnessed the guard-mount of a ragged regiment with an excellent regimental band, and then sauntered along the beach to the mouth of the Rio Lerma, where the coast assumes a rugged and cavernous character and harbors countless gulls and a colony of *nutras*, or sea-otters, that sport in the surf like porpoises, and seem to have their nests in the penetralia of the honeycombed cliff. From there we returned to the harbor by a circuitous route,

A NEGRO POLYGLOT.

and took a look at a licensed gambling-house and at the
"Suburb of the Chinamen," who, finding no shirts to wash,
have devoted themselves to the manufacture of fish-pies
and iced lemonade. Among the living curiosities of the
town is a tame alligator, the property of an English agent
and a great pet of the 'longshoremen, and a negro polyglot
who speaks two American and four European languages,
and has even mastered the principal monosyllables of Hop-

Wang-Lee. His industrial talents are still more versatile. He acts as runner for two hotels and one stage-coach company; peddles relics to the native Christians, Chicago jewelry to the heathen Chinee, and sea-shells to foreign rationalists, with impartial eloquence and effrontery; keeps magic oils and yellow-fever pills for the benefit of mankind in general, and a deck of Spanish monte cards as a side-show. "He has numerous native rivals," observed Mr. Mackenzie, "but they do not find it very easy to compete with a man who can lie in seven languages and cheat at fourteen different trades."

The agency clerk in the meanwhile had found room for our caravan in a suburban corral, and Mr. Mackenzie quartered our teamsters in a private posada

"Travellers in Spanish America," said the practical Scotchman, "should never put up at a public hotel unless they are saddled with invalids or ladies, but should take rooms at a posada" (lodging-house), "stipulate beforehand for such extras as drinking-water and errand-boys, and take their meals wherever they find a sensible dish ready made. By doing so they will avoid the inflated bills and inflamed pepper-pots, as well as the noise and the kitchen fumes, of the public meson."

I spent the afternoon with Dr. Rambert, and had just persuaded him to send for a little lunch when a messenger from the agency brought us word that the San Salvador had been signalled in the offing and would reach her landing at about four o'clock. The doctor grabbed his hat, but I prevailed on him to stay and break his fast while I escorted his luggage to the wharf.

Since the completion of the Pacific Railroad the vid-Panama steamboat line has to fight the struggle for existence against desperate odds, but it has spared no efforts to maintain its old popularity by novel devices. The San Salvador steamed up the harbor like a floating opera-house, her deck on fire with music, flags, and gorgeous uniforms, and the suavity of the employés could not have been surpassed by the ushers of a new metropolitan meeting-house. They got all the baggage aboard in a trice, and then waited with respectful deference till the last of their passengers had shaken hands for the last time with the last of his bereaved friends. Dr. Rambert looked a little glum when he trod the last furlong of Mexican soil, but once on the plank he stuck his hands into his pockets and marched aboard with all the nonchalance of a Gallic philosopher.

"You are now going to find what you need most, home comforts and perfect rest," said I, "but your Protestant friends in Potosi will be selfish enough to miss you sadly, for all that."

"Oh, they'll get over it," said the doctor, gayly, "but it's rough on the orthodox party: they're quite disconsolate. I really cannot think of them without feeling like a runaway debtor."

"What do you owe them? You paid for that bewitched horse, didn't you?"

"Yes," laughed the doctor, "but I cheated them out of a first-class solemnity: they'll have to burn me in effigy now."

The San Salvador had landed some Mexican passengers, who had hardly left the wharf-boat before the proprietor of a neighboring restaurant began to hammer his supper-gong. The day was indeed far spent, but the merry sports of the sea-gulls promised a fine evening, and Mr. Mackenzie invited me to take a stroll to the promontory.

San Blas is a humble *pueblo*, and cannot boast of any

city parks with flowery promenades and monumental hotels; but a lonely sea-shore can dispense with such embellishments: at least, I am sure that we did not regret their absence when we reached the cliffs that overlook the otter-cave and the murmuring surf at the headland, where the Rio Lerma confides the secret of his birth to the Pacific.

CHAPTER IV.

THE WESTERN SIERRAS.

Their ways are not like ours, but wild and rugged,
And, unlike ours, they lead to happiness
DE MORA   *El Nuevo Mundo*

THE stormy September equinox of the American tropics is followed in Southern Mexico by a halcyon season of three or four months, during which even the Tierra Caliente, the sultry lowland of the coast-regions, enjoys successive weeks of that genial and absolutely cloudless weather which sometimes precedes the midsummer heat of our Northern clime, while the skies and breezes of the sierras are only equalled by the happiest October days of the North Carolina Alleghanies.

There is a boat-house at San Blas where sailing-yawls can be hired at six reals (seventy cents) a day, and my rambles in the Coast Range were so much more pleasant than the dust and racket of the caravan-journey that I was almost sorry to learn that the Gila City had landed her cargo, and that the teams would start in a couple of days. I had half a mind to stay and take my chance of reaching Potosi in time by the next trip, but Mr. Mackenzie informed me that the same boat had brought such favorable news from Guaymas that the Morgan teamsters might possibly resume their old route with the next month.

"Are you in earnest about that?" he asked, when I told him that I should even prefer to cross the mountains afoot

SAN BLAS.

if I could find a re-
liable guide, though
my arrival in San Luis
might thus be delayed
two or three weeks.

"Why not? They
do not want me before the end of next month, and certainly
not before Christmas."

"No, I mean in regard to that pedestrian project," said
he; "because if you have a mind to rough it for a couple
of weeks I could recommend you a guide who would put

you on your mettle,—a chap that took us overland to Vera Paz last spring,—my brother Aleck and me. When my brother was sixteen years old he could beat our Lanark- shire guides at their own trade, and I would have backed him against any living American mountaineer; but I modified my opinion when we tried conclusions with this Mexican in the Sierra de Colima last March. He is honest, too,—at least for a Greaser,—and a personified gazetteer of Western Mexico: he and his father used to belong to a company of *operadores*, who travel around prospecting for silver ore, and they took him all over the country from California to Honduras. He is a native of Orizaba, near Vera Cruz."

"So he is acquainted with the eastern slope, too?"

"At least with the State of Puebla. Yes, I should advise you to take in the eastern Coast Range: the Sierra Madre between Puebla and Perote is, after all, the Switzer- land of this continent. You could take a détour through the Val de San Juan and back to Potosi by way of Que- rétaro."

"What does he charge for a three weeks' trip?"

"Oh, anything you will give: he is very poor. His prospecting company broke up some years ago, and he's now peddling pastry for a second-class confectioner. I suppose you will need a *portador* (a carrier) for your blankets and comestibles: we had two of them, and paid them and the guide ten reals per diem. If you find the tortillas, he will guide you all over Mexico and furnish an Indian portador at a dollar a day."

"What! portador and all?"

"Certainly. There are Indian adobe-carriers in our suburbs that work like mules from morning till night for three reals, without a crumb of board: they enjoy such a

trip as much as the travellers do, and make money besides.
But before you start you ought to stipulate for the amount
of baggage they are to carry, and promise them a few dollars extra at the end of the business if they behave well."

"Where can I find that guide?"

"I'll find him for you: just let me know how much time
you can afford to spend on the trip."

I completed my mountaineering-gear with a couple of
rubber blankets, two hatchets, a coil of *pellejos*, or rawhide
ropes, and a Mexican army-tent with a set of joint poles.
The wagonmaster promised to deliver my trunk and a
couple of letters in Potosi.

"I have got one of your men here now," said Mr. Mackenzie when I passed his office in the afternoon: "I was
just going to send my clerk to your posada. You can start
as soon as you are ready. Step in, if you like to take a
look at your man. This is José Milano, the guide I told
you about."

A barefoot mestizo rose from his seat on the balustrade.
"*No mira mi mugre, caballero,*—please overlook my
squalor," said he, with a deprecating glance at his feet: "I
have been out in the dust all day, and was just going home
when the señor called me in."

The original color of his trousers seemed rather doubtful,
and a well-worn and somewhat greasy *scrape* constituted
his only upper garment, but he was clean-built, lithe, and
black-eyed as an Hungarian gypsy, and prepossessed me by
a certain graceful frankness of speech and manner that contrasted agreeably with the usual cringing submissiveness of
his countrymen.

"I am in business here," said he, pointing to his cake-
basket, "and I ought to stick to it, but I couldn't resist
when Don Ricardo told me that you are going to visit *mis*

montes naturales,—my native mountains: it's perhaps the last time I shall see them. My time is nearly up,—got just five months of free life left: I'm going to be married next March."

He engaged to find an expert *portador* before night, and to report the next morning at eight o'clock in full marching order.

In order to avoid the dust and the tedium of the Vega, Mr. Mackenzie advised me to take the Mazatlan stage as far as San Pedro, where a spur of the Balsas Mountains connects the Coast Range with the main chain of the Sierra de Inua. From there José knew a ridge-way—or, as a California teamster would say, a high-level road—to the plateau of Eastern Jalisco.

The harbor was veiled by a sea-fog the next morning, but the upper town was light, and a look at the mountains satisfied me that the sky would clear up again before noon. On my way to the *officio de correos,* or stage-coach dépôt, I was joined by Mr. Mackenzie and one of his clerks, and a few minutes before eight the guide made his appearance with a stout Indian carrier, ready packed and strapped for an immediate anabasis. José was equipped in correct *montero* costume,—pressed-leather sombrero, leather breeches, sandals, and a short jacket covered with a brand-new scrape. He carried a kit with sundry camping and cooking utensils and a portion of the comestibles, which Mr. Mackenzie had been kind enough to furnish us from the agency store, and had brought a little terrier along, which he assured me would prove a very useful watch-dog in our sierra-camps. The carrier was a stolid but good-natured-looking old Tuxpano or mountain-Indian, barefoot and almost bare-legged, with an arm-hole serape that displayed a bull neck and a pair of powerful arms At the dépôt we met his

8

wife, an emotional old Tuxpana, who insisted on carrying my gun and shawl to the coach ; and when **Mr. Macken-zie's** clerk happened to splash his boots in the muddy corral, the poor old body knelt down and cleaned them with all the spitting and rubbing eagerness of a Castle Garden bootblack. Before we could get rid of her she showed me a piece of paper folded and tied up with bits of red yarn, handed it to the guide and patted his shoulder to coax him into a faithful interpretation of her comments.

"That's his testimonial," explained José: "she says her husband's last boss wrote this for you to read."

"All right! just keep it: I'll read it by and by. How far is it to San Pedro from here?"

"You'll get there before noon," said Mr. Mackenzie. "San Pedro lies at the foot of the black hill just below that double-peaked mountain," pointing to a range of sun-gilt hills in the northeast.

"Are they not beautiful?" said the clerk. "They just remind me of the Stirlingshire Grampians, and that cluster of mountains in the middle has nearly the shape of Ben Roonis, near Levendale."

"Hush up, you rascal!" laughed the agent, "or I join the party and leave you in the lurch. Indeed, sir," said he to me, "I can stand it only by sticking to the lower part of the town, where the sierra is out of sight. It makes me homesick, though it's a libel on an alpine range like that to compare it to our Caledonian molehills. You will see wonderful scenery, and the Jalisco highlands are full of curious ruins, temples, *teocallis* and cairns, and a still more interesting ethnological relic,—two tribes of pagan Indians, the Jaliscos and Tuxpans, who have pre-served their religious and political freedom in spite of monks and muskets. You must pass through Mayapan,

and get Josey to show you the great rock-temple in the
Tuxpan village. Oh! and I almost forgot," taking a
paper from his breast-pocket: " If you stop at the Hacienda
del Monte, as they call it, you will do me, and perhaps
yourself, a favor if you will forward this letter to Jimmy
Cardenas, the ex-governor of Jalisco. Give him my best
respects. He is quite an exceptional Mexican: you will
understand what I mean if you make his acquaintance."

The coach started, and, after rumbling through the
débris of the old Spanish city-wall, took the Mazatlan
camino real, a sand-road, through the open Vega. There
were only two inside passengers besides José and me, but
the Tuxpan had deposited his pack and himself on the
pescante, the roof-seat behind the coachman's box, from
modesty rather than in accordance with any established
rule, for the conductor of a *diligencia* tolerates not only
Indians, but dogs, and, as José assured me, even *goats*, on
the reserved seats.

The Pacific glittered through the tree-tops of the mango-
plantations when we reached San Pedro, but the same wind
that had dissipated the sea-fog swept blinding sand-clouds
across the Vega that became almost suffocating where they
mixed with the dust of the unpaved pueblo.

"We shall soon be out of this," said José. "Look
there! Half a mile above that little gap we shall strike
the Saltillo trail and a mountain-meadow, to where no dust
ever reached."

The first ascent was rather steep, and made more difficult
by the multitude of jagged stumps, half hidden in weeds
and brambles, for opposite, and for some distance northeast
of the village, the slopes had been cleared; but after
reaching the next terrace the trail improved, and, as we
kept along the ridge, I saw that farther north the foot-hills

were covered with dark-green *Bombax* forests, and that
the main chain of the Coast Range was densely wooded
almost up to the steep cliffs of the summit regions.

South of the twenty-eighth degree of latitude the Cordilleras of Western America are generally *boscados*, or
forest-mountains, in strange contrast with the western
coast of the old continent, where the same climatic, if not
geometrical, parallel marks the boundary of the *northern*
forest-lands South America has an African sun, but no
African deserts; Colorado, the climate of the Alps, but
no Alpine forests: in other words, our continent has a
fertile Morocco and a virgin-wood Sahara, but a desolate
France and a barren Switzerland.   According to the traditions of the Aztecs and Toltecs, as well as of the Western
Peruvians, their ancestors came from the North,—very
likely across Behring's Strait, where Western America
approaches the fatherland of all tailless monkeys,—but
before they reached the tropics they tarried north of the
Rio Gila for a millennium or two, and probably committed
the same outrages against the vegetable kingdom by which
the Numidian sylvania was changed into a sand-waste.

We halted at a dry arroyo to pick a cupful of small
yellow raspberries, and, finding them well-flavored, I followed the creek as far as it ran parallel with our trail.
Half a mile farther up it connected with a broader valley,
where we found a running stream and larger raspberries,
but also an appalling number of venomous snakes.   The
grass wriggled with dwarf rattlesnakes and *vivoras pardas*
(gray vipers), and whenever we came near the creek a score
of water-moccasins dropped in with a simultaneous splash
that reminded me of the broadsides of bullfrogs plumping
from the reed-islands of the lower Potomac at the approach
of a canoe.

" Why, that's nothing," laughed José. " Do you see that swampy bottom back there where the creek comes from ?—the *Val de Culebras*, the Serpent Valley, they call it: that's the place where a Semasquito (snake-eating Indian) could put up a year's provisions in two or three hours. There's a viper-nest in every bush and every bunch of Spanish moss up there."

" What do the snakes all live on ?"

" Tadpoles, I believe," said José. " In the rainy season that bottom is full of water, and the marsh it leaves breeds vermin of all sorts. In the dry season they have to starve, I guess, except the tree-snakes and vivoras pardas: they are smart enough to find a square meal every day in the year."

I killed and dissected a large blacksnake, but found nothing to indicate that it had broken its fast for the last week or two, but the autopsy of a fat vivora revealed two half-digested birds and tufts of hair that looked like the fur of a young red squirrel. A sluggish reptile that can raise such tidbits where the swift blacksnake has to starve must indeed be " more subtile than any beast of the field which the Lord God has made," but the specimens I saw were as slimy as leeches, and so disgustingly fat that they could only have tempted an Eve of the most depraved taste.

By persistent climbing and short halts we managed to reach the upper ridge before sunset, and on the eastern declivity of a narrow plateau, capped with wild currants and cedar-bushes (*Juniperus spicatus*), the granite alps of Jalisco and the jagged peaks of the Sierra de San Juan rose suddenly to view. The mountain-walls of the eastern highlands, which glittered like snow where their cliffs reflected the horizontal sun-rays, I found, on examination with the telescope, to consist of white limestone or granular quartz; but those of the Coast Range, as well as the intermediate sierra, are of volcanic origin, and present the most fantastic outlines, as if the gaps between their summits had been escarped with a splintering instrument, rather than by the hollowing and rounding influence of the mountain waters. Some of their pinnacles resembled the minarets of a fanciful mosque, and it needed the circumstantial evidence of perspectives from different points of view and the gradual extension of the evening shadows to convince me that a group of turreted peaks in the main chain of the San Juan range were not a mirage or a cloud counterfeit.

I have often found that in clear nights the air of an elevated plateau is perceptibly warmer than that of the valley regions The evening seemed very mild when the wind subsided together with the sun, and as our canned provisions would last us for a day or two, I thought we might as well dispense with a camp-fire; but when we approached a grove of cork-oaks in a hollow of the eastern slope, we all agreed that a little fuel-forage would promote our comfort as well as our appetites.

While we collected brambles and dry twigs, the old Tuxpan dragged up a good-sized fallen tree, chopped it into handy billets, helped me to pitch my tent, and then retired with a strip of dried beef and a chunk of wheat bread—*por en-mascarse*—to chew himself to sleep, as the guide expressed it. To judge by his deep breathing, the old chap was comfortably asleep half an hour after, though his serape was not much heavier than a good-sized bedsheet. He was a native of the Jalisco highlands, and had preserved his hardy habits through twenty years of town-life. His younger comrade was rather a *mozuelo*—a city lad—in manners and tendencies, an expert in opening

preserve-cans and wide awake as to the merits of oiled
sardines and the superiority of catchup over the finest *chile
colorado.* After helping himself to the best our mess-bag

THE TUXPANO.

afforded, he spread his couch with his feet to the fire, and
collected a large blanketful of Spanish moss for a pillow.

"According to what you told me about vipers and tree-
snakes," I observed, "you must have about a two-bushel
bagful of them in that pile."

"*Ya no hay cuidado*" (No danger of that now), said he:
"we are twelve miles above their head-quarter valley. Up
here you wouldn't find anything bigger than a *cecilia*

(blindworm); they can't make half a living in these rocks."

"How big will they grow in their head-quarters?"

"In the Val de Culebras? Oh, there's no limit to their fatness and length, sir. I saw a blacksnake there as long as a lariat, and a vivora parda with a head like a good-sized pug-dog's."

"What's the biggest snake you ever saw, Josey?"

"I could hardly tell you, sir. When we crossed the Sumasinta River, in Yucatan, they offered us the carcass of a boa with a belly on him like an English shipmaster; but down in Honduras they have water-snakes that could swallow such boas alive. They told me about a party of turtle-hunters that came across a monster of that sort on the Belize Bayou,—a river as broad as the Rio Lerma,—but the snake crossed it as a blacksnake would a little creek, and when its head reached the opposite bank the tail end was still trailing through the canebrake on the shore on which they stood."

I thought of Don Martinez's alligator phenomenon, and it occurred to me afterward that the great historical serpent which (as Pliny assures us) disputed the passage of the army led by Regulus along the banks of the Bagrada belonged probably to the same composite order.

The night was almost cloudless, and after the moon went down the stars glittered with a brilliancy which is rarely seen in our Northern lowlands. When I awoke, at about four o'clock the next morning, I saw for the first time a distinct zodiacal light in the north*east*, its axis passing through Cancer and Gemini, with the apex of the pyramid nearly touching Alpha Leonis. The planet Mercury rose soon after, and I could comprehend the morning-star worship of the ancient Peruvians, but also the meaning of the

Regio septentrionalis. The seven chief *triones* of Arcturus loomed through the mist of the northern horizon with a ruddier and more remarkable light than the largest fixed stars of a higher latitude, and were thus probably seen and named by the shepherds of Southern Italy. In the higher North, where they never reach the horizon, their arctic position is much less obvious.

We took our breakfast at the next spring, and followed our trail nearly due east into an ascending valley of the Inua ridge. Our little terrier ranged the gullies and coppices with indefatigable energy, and flushed at least twenty different coveys of prairie-chickens in the first two hours, and started a flock of bighorn sheep, which bounded into a ravine with an impetus that made the stones fly in all directions. A little farther on the same ravine widened into a broad valley, and we passed different cedar-groves with an undergrowth of wild plum-trees alternating with fine mountain-meadows.

"This would make a good place for a settlement," said I, as we crossed a meadow of stone-clover and buttercups at the bank of a pebbly stream.

"It might," said José; "there are Indian villages in much poorer valleys; but a settlement of white rancheros would hardly have farming-land enough up here, and a single man might find it rather lonesome. He wouldn't hear any chickens crow but his own: the farmers around the pueblo we left yesterday morning would be about his next neighbors."

Men and dogs seemed, indeed, to be rare guests on these heights, for while we ascended a little bluff at the head of the valley a troop of *berendos*, or mountain-antelopes, approached us from the left, crossed and recrossed the trail hardly forty yards in front of us, and escorted us across the bluff, trotting at our side and eying us with evident surprise. When the terrier charged them the next buck leaped aside with a loud bleat, and the troop seemed on the point of stampeding; but as soon as we recalled the dog they returned and followed us at a trot, mincing their steps when they had reduced the distance to thirty or forty yards, as if fearful of incurring our displeasure by any nearer approach. During the next half-hour I could have killed any two of them before the rest could get out of range, but we preferred their merry company to their meat, which, as José—perhaps in the interest of his heavy-loaded countryman—assured me, was tough and rank, and "*peor por el changatál*"—worse now on account of the rutting season. In the course of the same afternoon we saw different bands of bighorn sheep, which gave us a wider berth; but their notions of danger were evidently founded upon bow-and-arrow data, for they permitted us to approach within easy rifle-shot range. I also noticed that they let a gray wolf (*Canis nubilus*) get within ten yards of their outpost before they scampered away. I suspect that the shyness of our European and North American game is something quite abnormal and unnatural. The aspect of an armed Hoosier must inspire an Indiana deer with a terror of which no emotion of the human breast would give us any adequate idea, unless we should stumble upon a country whose tigers could leap upon us from a distance of five or six hundred yards.

Our road led along the base of a steep ridge of argillaceous limestone, which obstructed the view to the north and northwest, but the scenery became more interesting when we at last reached the valley of the Rio Raton and ascended it into the defile of Santander, the gate of Eastern Jalisco, and the main pass of the Sierra de Inua. The mountain-walls on both sides become steeper and higher as the defile narrows, and at the eastern gate, where they rise to a height of four thousand feet above the trail, the tiny stream almost fills the bed of the cañon, and a full-grown man might touch its rocky banks on both sides at the same time. Where they recede, they open abruptly upon a broad and level lawn, and a resolute defender of such a Thermopylæ could only be crushed by unimaginable odds, and would be safe against all flank attacks, for the eastern front of the sierra for many miles to the left and right is an almost perpendicular precipice.

Our trail now turned to the left, winding along the declivity of a mountain-spur, but with a deep valley at our right, which would have attracted my attention by its chaotic cliffs and exuberant vegetation if a sudden turn of the road had not opened a vista to the north and revealed the grandest scenery of Western Mexico,—the Coast Range of Sinaloa, with the giant-peak of Culiacan.*

It is an old French saying that every high mountain is a sermon which directs the human soul to heaven; and Lamartine remarks that a peak adds *point* to the sermon. He is right: at least I think that a *nil-admirari* philosopher who could view this mountain without surprise might consider himself emotion-proof. The extinct volcano of Culiacan rises thirteen thousand feet above the level of the Pacific and about seventy-five hundred above the ridge of the Coast Range from a wild mass of pine and cedar crags, while the upper peak is covered with snow, streaked farther down with jet-black basaltic ribs. But it is not so much

---

* Pronounced *Cool-ya-can'*, an Indian word signifying flint-head or arrow-peak. The volcano of Culiacan is fifty miles north of Mazatlan, nearly opposite the southern extremity of the Californian peninsula

the height or color of the volcano which distinguishes it from all neighboring summits as its form, which makes it, indeed, incomparably grander than almost any other moun-

PEAK OF CULIACAN.

tain of that altitude. As viewed from the Sierra de Inua, the cone rises in a jagged slope, whose steepness for the first three thousand feet does not exceed that of the Great Pyramid, but the peak tapers towards the top, so that the sharp outlines of the upper four thousand feet form an angle of hardly thirty-five degrees, and, being flanked by no other summits of more than half its height, the great mountain towers up against the sky like the spire of a stupendous Gothic cathedral.

The Peak of Teneriffe is a blunt knob by comparison, though its perfect isolation makes it almost equally conspicuous, and the sharp pinnacle of the Matterhorn is hidden in a cluster of rival heights. So far as I know, the shape of the Pic de Culiacan can only be compared to one other mountain on earth, a much smaller peak,—the Col du Midi in the Southern Cevennes, which, as seen from the head-waters of the Aveyron, looks, indeed, more like a pointed turret than a natural mountain.

Towards the northwest the Coast Range subsides rapidly, and presents an even or slightly undulating outline, but its eastern continuation, the Sierra de San Juan, abounds in inaccessible peaks and alpine ranges, capped with precipitous white cliffs. Yet these heights are inhabited, and, on the whole, better cultivated than any portion of the fertile terrace-lands.

The guide called my attention to a column of milk-white smoke that seemed to rise from the edge of a lofty ridge bordering the valley of the Rio Raton in the northeast. " That's a limekiln in the wigwam of Villapaterna," said he : " the Jaliscanos will soon have a regular village up there."

" Have they permanent wigwams on top of a sierra of that height?"

" Yes, it's their reservation, where they have pastures and orchards of their own, and do not permit any white man to settle among them unless he promises not to tax them for roads and *diezmos*" (church-tithes).

" They do not want any roads, then ?"

" They don't need them, sir. Look at Benito here" (the carrier) : " he could tote that load of his up the steepest slope in the sierra, and he's nothing but an old granny compared with some of his countrymen. There are only three or four thousand of them, and they keep all Christendom at bay."

The savage Jaliscanos have accomplished what the gentle Waldenses attempted in vain,—made the rocks of their mountain-home the bulwarks of personal and religious freedom; for the Mexican government—which permits the Comanches and Apaches to defy its authority on the plains of Sonora—has never even tried to meet the warlike mountaineers in their own fastnesses, and, in spite of their reckless bigotry, the Mexican priests have been daunted by a stronger fanaticism than their own. The Jalisco Indians, like the Pintos in Yucatan and the Cocharcos in Peru, adhere to the religion of their fathers, are privileged from civil and military duties and pay no direct taxes, and, so far, have contrived to preserve an armed peace with their neighbors without permitting them any interference in their municipal affairs. Their homes, in the literal sense, are their castles, for the tribe, which once was scattered over a territory of fourteen thousand square miles, has been isolated by its chiefs on the most inaccessible plateaux of the highest mountain-range, though there are valleys at their feet where they could raise abundant crops with onefourth of the labor which now only wins them a bare living. They are hated and envied by their priest-ridden neighbors, but men deserve their liberty who are ready to purchase it at such a price.

We met two of their bag-carriers that evening,—stout, broad-shouldered men, with fists and knee-bones that might have excited the jealousy of a Gaelic moss-trooper. Their only piece of apparel was a short jacket or waistcoat, with a pair of shoulder-pads to support the cross-straps of their burdens, two capacious leather bags full of a whitish substance which I supposed to be flour or salt. They came up with swift, steady strides, answered my greeting with a grunt and their countryman's jest with a laconic repartee, and pursued their road at a pace that would have braved the field at an international walking-match.

"These fellows earn their bread, and no mistake," said I, "but I should starve for a good while before I would shoulder a flour-bag of that size."

"You wouldn't carry it very far then," laughed José: "it's saltpetre from the Mayapan rock-caves,—about twelve dollars' worth in each bag."

"They sell it, I suppose?"

"Yes, or exchange it for shot and trinkets or a new rifle once in a while: that's about all they need,—everything else they make or raise themselves."

"Gunpowder too?"

"Certainly: they have all the ingredients for it. They keep cows and bees too, and raise big crops of yams and brown beans. They have no corn, but they make bread from *polenta* (chestnut-flour). They need no shoes and hardly any clothing."

"What do they drink?"

"Nothing at all: I mean, nothing that could do them any good. They are terribly down on wine and aguard-iente, because they believe the Spaniards invented them to poison them and get the better of them in that way. If they catch one of their young bucks drunk, they tie him to a tree and let him stand in the hot sun for a day or two to give him a relish for fresh water."

"They keep no horses, it seems?"

"No, they do their own horse-work. Those two fellows that passed us a while ago are going down to Cárcamos, forty miles from here, and must have crossed the Inua range since morning. It will be the roughest piece of our trip, about fifteen miles steadily up hill."

We were now approaching a part of our journey much dreaded by the Indians of the Tierra Caliente, on account of the icy winds that sweep over the backbone of the sierra the year round. Wishing to have our carrier fresh for the passage of the *mal pays*, we made a short day's march, encamping at the mouth of a deep cañon that winds up through the mountains to the plateau of Las Charcas. We kept up a good fire, and started before daybreak the next morning, but found the ascent more arduous than I had anticipated. We had to climb over boulders and fallen trees, and the cañon is a veritable wind-trap, a gate of the north wind, that drives and whirls through the winding gorge with the force of a furnace-blast; but the worst was over when we reached the plateau about eleven A.M. The Inua range forms the dividing ridge between the Rio Raton and the happy mountain-valleys of Eastern Jalisco watered by the streams of the Sierra Madre and the northern tributaries of Lake Chapala.

We were now more than four thousand feet above our last camp, and at least ten thousand above the sea, which was hidden by the Coast Range, and farther north by a yellowish haze, probably the dust-clouds of the Vega. The vegetation of these heights is almost arctic,—broom-furze, lichens, and rock-berries (*Vaccinium boreale*). In sheltered places I saw hedges of dwarf rose-bay, and here and there a few larger birch-trees. The birch, rather than the pine, is the polar tree *par excellence*, for the plurality of our Northern Coniferæ grow in the tropics as well, or better, while north of the last dwarf-fir regions the hills of Siberia are still covered with birch forests.

" There used to be a tavern up here when the Spaniards had a garrison at Cárcamos," said my guide. "Do you see that trail up there? That leads to the *Altar*, as they call it, a promontory where you can see the *hornitos* (mud-volcanoes) of Acubaya."

" Is it much out of our way, that promontory ?"

" Not more than half a league."

" All right: tell the Tuxpan to take it easy if he is tired, and let's have a look at the hornitos."

The " Altar" is a projecting cliff on the northern declivity of the sierra, and affords a bird's-eye view of a little tarn in the valley below. Close to the foot of the precipice, and apparently at the head of the lake, are the hornitos, five or six intermittent geysers whose outlets were hardly visible from our standpoint. But every now and then one of them emitted a puff of white steam which I should have mistaken for I don't know what if I had seen it unexpectedly. The declivity being almost perpendicular, we could not perceive the vertical expansion of the cloudlets, which dissolved almost as soon as they appeared, but for a moment looked like little white balls which suddenly flattened out to the size of a big round table, and vanished abruptly before the end of the next second.

We made up for lost time when our trail turned into a grassy valley with an easy down-grade, and reached a good wagon-road before dark at the bank of the Rio Parral, and, as José believed, about fifteen miles from the Hacienda del Monte.

Florida derives its name from *Pascua Florida* (Palm Sunday), but the true flower-land of our continent is the terrace-region between the Val de Jalisco and the highlands of Western Zacatecas. The morning air was saturated with the perfume of wild jessamine, and the creeks below our camp were almost hidden by a rank growth of *Veronica pungens*, with flowers like those of a light-blue variety of forget-me-not, while the slopes on both sides of our road were covered with larkspur, foxgloves, white euphorbia, rhododendrons, and orange-colored asclepias. The blue elder (*Sambucus pubescens*) was still in bloom, and, with an undergrowth of currants and wild licorice, formed dense hedges along the creek. Game seemed to abound in these thickets: we heard the whistle of plovers and different varieties of partridges, and met a man at the creek who had just gutted and cleaned a large bundle of *gazapos*, or mule-ear rabbits.

"*Que provecho?*" (What luck?), said he. "Oh"— seeing the carrier—"you are travelling, it seems, *de por abajo*" (from down below),—"from the coast, I suppose?"

"Yes, we left San Blas last Thursday," I replied. "You are in luck this morning, to judge by that string of gazapos."

"*Sin mejora*" (Hobson's choice), said he. "My dog started a fox this morning, and that's the last I saw of him. These brakes are full of turkeys and peccaris, and our Indians reported bear-tracks last week. Let's cross this creek: there is a better road on the other side."

"That's Padre Felipe, the governor's major-domo," whispered José: "you have a good chance to deliver that letter now."

"This valley of yours is the prettiest in the State," I observed,—"just the place for a country-seat. Do you know Governor Cardenas, who owns a hacienda somewhere in this neighborhood?"

"I saw him half an hour ago: he's my boss, sir. Why?"

"Would you please to hand him this letter? It would save me the necessity of troubling him at the hacienda."

"He will blow me up for not bringing you along. Are you going east?"

"Yes, to the Sierra Madre by way of the Indian villages."

"To Cañadas?"

"That's where we shall stop to-night."

"Well, come this way, then: I'll put you on the direct road, sir. Let's take a short cut through this bottom."

We followed a trail running nearly parallel with the creek through a rank jungle of brambles and wild licorice, interspersed with copses of alder and white mulberry trees. I was making some inquiries about the security of the sierra roads, when suddenly my Indian caught me by the arm and pointed in the direction of a *rambla* or dry ravine at our right-hand side. In the gravel-bed of the rambla, at a distance of some two hundred yards, I saw an animal about the size of a large hog engaged in rooting the ground below a little copse of alder-bushes. The hunter, too, following the direction of my gaze, had stopped and cocked his gun.

"That's a maranon boar," he whispered, "but too confounded far for my shot-gun. One of your barrels is rifled, I see: do you think it would reach there?"

"I can try. Stand still, Josey," said I; and, resting the rifle on his shoulder, I covered the broadside of the maranon and pulled the trigger. At the report the boar jumped convulsively into the rambla, snapped at his haunches, and glared around in a bewildered way.

Before I could give him the second barrel he made a dash at the alder-bushes and plunged into the jungle to the left, as if trying to reach the creek-bed a little ahead of us. We heard his rush through the brambles, but almost at the same moment a piercing scream and quickly-repeated cries for help. As if seized with the same idea, we all ran toward the creek at the top of our speed, and had hardly emerged from the thicket when an Indian boy leaped into the creek, followed two seconds after by the wounded boar, who, happily, stumbled at the edge of the bank, and fell, rather than jumped, into the gravel below. Before he recovered his legs our guns went off like a single shot, and the maranon sank back and rolled into the creek. The boy, who had thrown himself headlong into the canebrake, now recrossed the water and met us at the foot of the gravel-bank, still sobbing and trembling with excitement. He had been picking fox-grapes in the jungle when he heard the first shot, and, looking up, saw the boar charging through the bushes directly toward him, and, throwing his basket down, turned and ran for his life. He stumbled twice, and came within an ace of sharing the fate of Adonis before he reached the creek, and by a lucky instinct leaped, rather than climbed, down the steep bank.

"Do you think you could remember this place?" asked the major-domo, reloading his gun with great complacency.

"Yes, sir," still snivelling.

"Well, get your basket, then, and go home and tell your father to hitch up one of the black mules and drag the maranon home You show him the way and I'll make it all right with you to-night."

We resumed our path, and after an hour of devious marching and chatting came upon a well-beaten country road that led in the direction of the northern mountains.

"Well, sir, take care of yourself," said the major-domo. "If I could get a day's furlough, I should like to pilot you through to the sierra; but you can't miss the way now as far as Cañadas, and it seems you have a good guide of your own *Buen viaje!* Be sure now and send me a bottle of wedding-whiskey, Don José"

"All right, padrecito," laughed the guide, "but don't forget that I want you to baptize my first child."

JOSÉ.

"It seems you know that man, Josey?" I asked when we continued our way.

"Yes, he is the governor's overseer,—the funniest rake you could find on this side the Rio Grande."

"What makes you call him *padre?* Is he a priest?"

"He's a runaway monk, sir, and that's the reason the governor engaged him: it tickles him all over to have a fighting and drinking padre on his place."

" Doesn't that set the rest of the clergy against the governor ?"

" Yes, but what does he care?   He owns six square leagues of farming-land in this valley, and the priests would break each other's necks to please him."

We had just deposited our traps under an old hackberry-tree to take a little rest and a bit of dinner, when two horses trotted around the corner of the hill, and we thought we recognized our friend the major-domo on a pony, leading a saddle-horse.

" Yes, that's he," said José: " maybe he is going to accompany us to the sierra."

" Never mind those cakes now," said he, reining up his pony at our tree.   " I knew the governor would read me the lesson of the day for leaving you behind.   He sees by that letter that you are going to visit the Indian temples near Mayapan.   You are on the wrong road, then: the ruins are only twelve miles from here, but more than twenty from Cañadas, so you might as well make the hacienda your head-quarters.   You had better take this horse if you think that your men can find the way alone: the governor is waiting for you at the bridge, not far from where I left you."

A lank and lazy-looking old gent was reclining on a stone bench near the bridge, but rose at our approach and greeted me with an off-hand military salute.

" I am very sorry, sir," I began, " that I was so unlucky as to cause you all this trouble."

" No, you are lucky enough," said he,—" doubly lucky, sir, that we have a priest here to absolve you, and that he caught you so quick, for you may be very sure that I would have fetched you back from the other side of the sierra. No, sir, that would never do,—a travelling foreigner recommended by my best friend in America, and going to pass my place to sleep in a thundering hole of a Greaser wig-wam! Besides, 'tis Sunday to-morrow, when a gentleman mustn't endanger his Christian soul by any kind of labor, such works of charity and necessity as cock-fighting and gambling excepted."

The señor seemed, indeed, to be as independent in his habits as in his opinions. He smoked common tobacco in what looked very much like a Kentucky corn-cob pipe, and was the first Mexican I met who had sense enough to dis-card the cumbrous sombrero in the cool air of the high-land districts. He wore a sort of forage-cap.

I have often found that the scepticism of Northern Prot-estants has a deistic bias, while that of the Roman Catholics tends toward pyrrhonism and cynicism, and I suspect that the present century has been rather prolific of French and Spanish apostates from the Thaumaturgic Church, who would feel perfectly at home in the haunts of Diagoras and Petronius Arbiter. Ex-Governor Cardenas, too, was a couple of ages either behind or ahead of the speculative standpoint of his countrymen, and astounded me by the free-dom of his remarks, though I had reasons to surmise that Mr. Mackenzie's letter had indicated my dogmatic status.

The Hacienda del Monte had been built for a Spanish fort, and the orthodox inhabitants of the scattered village at the foot of the mountain might have subjective reasons for postponing a crusade against a heretic who could answer their arguments with a cross-fire from two howitzers at either corner of his parapet; but the ordnance, though apparently in good working order, was kept as a relic rather than as an *ultima ratio*. The Jalisco pagans, who should have valued the sceptic as a natural ally, avoided him for political reasons, but his tenants worshipped him

HACIENDA DEL MONTE.

as a liberal and indulgent master, and had attested their confidence by electing him their *corregidor,* or justice of the peace, and matters in general seemed to be conducted on the live-and-let-live principle. From my window, which overlooked the old parade-ground, I could see the preparations for a *gran funcion de toros* (a solemn bull-fight) which was to come off on the festival of Santa Maria de Guadeloupe in a week or two ; and the señor's retainers all looked healthier and more cheerful than the half-starved serfs of the average hacienda, for he refused to take advantage of the peonage law,* and paid his domestics and day-laborers

* The old Spanish and modern Mexican law, which authorizes a creditor to enslave an insolvent debtor.

at the uniform rate of two reals a day. The major-domo being a disciple of St. Dominic, and very apt to win at cards, received no direct compensation, but was instructed to apply for funds whenever his patron saint should fail to anticipate his wants.

The hall was crowded with country-people, it being the señor's justicing day; but he promised to join us before supper, and in the mean time recommended me to the spiritual guardianship of Father Felipe. After mounting the watch-tower and admiring the panorama and the governor's armory, we descended into the casemates, and by an exterior stairway into the court-yard. Behind the bastion there was a large water-tank, fed by a primitive aqueduct, and supplying in its turn a fountain at the opposite end of the parade-ground. The basin of the fountain had been constructed from the foundation-walls of the old guard-house, and a rock-built cell between the guard-house and the parapet was now occupied by a prisoner for life, a fat grizzly bear, who seemed to expect his dinner when we approached his den, for he turned round and round, licking his jaws in an evident state of self-gratulation. He had been caught very young, and during his minority had been taught to posture on his hind legs, to play 'possum, and various other tricks. He used to volunteer performances, the major-domo said, but lately required an external stimulus. Whenever he omitted any essential part of the prescribed evolutions, or gave other signs of being in the sulks, they softened his heart by turning the squirt of the fountain upon him. He looked thoughtful, but by no means very ferocious.

"No," said the padre, "chaining seems to spoil their pluck. Do you see that little fellow there?" pointing to an Indian lad who was filling a pail at the fountain. "The grizzly broke out a year ago, and got through the sally-port before we knew it, but that boy overtook him and kept him at bay with a common cudgel till our *montador*" (horse-breaker) " lassoed him and dragged him home like a calf."

" That little chap looks as if he would make a good montador himself some day."

" He's the most impudent puppy I ever saw; but we can't get rid of him, he's the governor's pet."

" An orphan, I suppose?"

" Worse than that. He was whelped in one of the Jaliscano wigwams, and came down here every other week or so with a gang of hucksters or wood-choppers; but one Easter Sunday they happened to come in with a load of huckleberries, when we had a dance and music in the house, and his comrades stayed all day to retail their berries, and made something like five dollars before night. But in the evening this boy got beastly drunk, and the rest of them went away and left him asleep in the straw-shed, and our foolish cook kept him full of brandy for three or four days. We wanted to send him back that week, but—what do you think?—before we could start him off his mother came in howling and crying, and asked the governor, for all the gods' sakes, to keep her boy and not send him home, because his father had loaded a musketoon and sworn to shoot him at sight, and the chiefs confirmed him in his purpose. That was three years ago."

" And you have had to keep him ever since?"

" No ' had to' about it," grunted the padre; " but the governor would not let him go. He's very sensible in some ways, our boss is, but he has a queer penchant for saddling himself with useless retainers. Of which penchant I myself am perhaps the most striking illustration," he added, seeing me smile. " Well, it takes all kinds of

pets to complete a menagerie. I could mention another
instance of his mania. We have a bull in that grass-garden
back there who has been smashing fences and frightening
our neighbors out of their wits for the last ten months, but
our boss refuses to shoot him. The brute was ruled out of
the arena for killing three bull-fighters in succession,—two
at Mazatlan and one at Cárcamos,—so they sold him to a
butcher, but the governor redeemed him, and keeps him
for a scarecrow to frighten the ladies."

"He is a bachelor, it seems?"

"No, but he is a widower, and he wants to die as a *freed-
man*, he says."

"You ought to convert him from that purpose."

"Well, you may try it, but at your own peril: it is the
one thing that never fails to bring him on his hind legs."

"I should like to take a look at those ruins to-morrow,"
said I: "do you think he will seriously object to a Sunday
trip?"

"No, no, not if your time is limited; but I'm afraid
that he couldn't accompany you. You may have noticed
that he is almost lame: he got a shot through the knee-
joint during the French war, and his leg has got worse
again. But I could go if you want to take me along."

"Well, please to get me permission, then."

When we were seated at supper two visitors were announced,—a horse-dealer and the Padre Timoteo, the village
priest.

"Show them in here," said the hospitable señor. The
trader excused himself after settling a little bill, but the
padre was persuaded to stay, and took a seat at the table
at the side of the ex-Dominican. Of the two padres, the
major-domo was decidedly the more respectable. He was
evidently trying to restrict the conversation to secular topics,

but his neighbor encouraged the governor's sallies by bursting every now and then into a fit of uncontrollable laughter, or modified his repartees in a way that seemed to invite a bolder attack.

"Never mind, you will change your opinions before you cross the big ferry," said he, with his mouth full of pork-pie: "you would have sent for a priest mighty quick if the French had captured you that time, just as your father did when the Spaniards boxed him up in Vera Cruz."

"You needn't keep throwing my father in my teeth," said the governor. "My father admitted that he believed in a future existence, because he could not get a fair show in this world, but you may be very sure that he did not join any church. He did not part with his senses altogether."

"*Valgame Dios!*" cried the padre, "*que hombre tan arastrado!*" (God help me! what an eccentric fellow this is!) "*Santa Maria Purissima!*" and he laughed till the shaking of his paunch threatened him with suffocation.

"Protestantism is the established religion in the States, isn't it?" asked the señor.

"We have no established dogmas, sir, except universal toleration and a Sunday law or two."

"Oh yes, I forgot: pantheonic and pandemonic liberty and equality, and that's the soundest plan. Let men and gods stand and fall by their own merits."

"So you would prefer our system?"

"Yes, as a man I would; but, being a superhuman governor, I prefer an idolatrous country like our own. But your institutions have always interested me more than those of any other nation, because they alone afford an opportunity of testing many curious theories by a practical experiment. Give every one a fair start: that's the way to find out if Africans can compete with Caucasians and women with men."

"Do you approve the woman's-rights movement?" I asked, with a glance at Father Felipe.

"I can at least explain it," said the heretic. "Since the world has got so full of effeminate men, he-coquettes, man-milliners, and perfumed dandies, it is no wonder that the girls think themselves able to beat us at our own game, and want to profit by that ability. In a manlier age, like the fourteenth century, when our forefathers hammered the Saracens in the battle of Velez Malaga, and made the sparks fly from their iron helmets *como los giró el viento*" (as if the wind whirled them), "I suspect that their ladies were not so very anxious to try their hands at masculine trades."

The major-domo waked me at five o'clock the next morning, and a little after sunrise we mounted a pair of glossy mules at the lower sally-port.

"You must take the consequences of your impiety," laughed the señor when he limped to the gate to wish me a good-morning. "I told Father Felipe that I wash my hands of this business, but he assures me that I can rely on his judgment in matters of casuistry. Well, I wish you a happy trip," said he, "and I think you will be pleased with the scenery. There is a famous view from the ruins of Mayapan, and the Val de San Juan is said to be the most magnificent in the State, though I do not doubt that you have seen finer valleys in France and Italy."

"France has no sierras," I replied, "and Italy no forests. No, sir: Mexico is the most beautiful country of the present world, and it would be the happiest, too, if you would just content yourselves with a reasonable number of revolutions, —say one in four years or so."

TEMPLE RUINS OF MAYAPAN.

"Yes," said the señor, "they are a grievous nuisance, but"—with a sort of shudder—"I must confess that they are still the lesser evil, though I am myself of Spanish descent. Even absolute anarchy would be more endurable than the yoke of a so-called man* who embroidered a petticoat for the Virgin Mary."

Before the Jaliscanos retired to their present strongholds in the upper sierra they had a large village near the hamlet of Mayapan, where their sachems resided and where their priests assembled the nation after a successful war and on other solemn occasions. Here also are the ruins of the

---

* Charles IV. of Spain, who employed his leisure in embroidering gowns and chemises for an image of the Holy Virgin in the chapel of San Ildefonso.

great temple of Catascotl, the fire-god, the Pluto of the Toltec pantheon, whose palaces are the volcanoes, and who has his headquarters in the subterranean halls of the Sierra Madre, where he dwells with the spirits of the Toltec warrior-kings, and where his voice can be heard during an earthquake.

We reached the site of this temple after a leisurely ride of five or six hours; and I think that in extent, as well as in the elaboration of the bas-reliefs and sculptured terraces, its ruins surpass those of any single edifice in Yucatan or Central America. It stands on the western brink of a plateau that commands a magnificent view of the Tierra Caliente, a portion of the Bay of Mazatlan, and the Coast Range, with the two peaks of Culiacan and Penasco; and the broad platform of the upper terrace must have been an exquisite place for a national assembly of mountaineers. There seems to have been a vault under the terrace, for the platform is full of crevices and holes that form regular man-traps, so that the interior of the temple is generally approached from the north, through a breach which the guides or stone-robbers have opened through a rubbish-mound of sand and broken columns. So far as I could judge by the vestiges of partition-walls, the enclosure was divided into three halls,—two smaller ones at the western entrance and a larger one at the east end, where a recess is blocked up with the fragments of a massive rostrum or altar-platform. The friezes of a cluster of pilasters on either side are ornamented with bas-reliefs and stuccoes which I might describe as sculptured mosaic, the figures being composed of close-fitting stones fastened with a vitreous cement, which the crumbling of the main wall has dislodged here and there. This platform, as well as the niches in the south wall, were formerly full of statues, but they have all been removed, and only torsos and broken pedestals can still be found in the rubbish-heaps.

The smaller idols were carried off by clerical and antiquarian vandals, and some of the larger ones may yet be seen in the next lowland villages, stuck up in the flower-gardens like *termini* or doing duty as easy-chairs and hitching-posts. The masonry of the side-walls is a heap of débris, and the façade is sadly demolished, but the south wall is better preserved, the outside cornice being sculptured in its entire extent, while the lower part is covered with lapidary inscriptions whose hieroglyphics, reduced to the size of common print, would fill about two of these pages.

My cicerone described a rather problematic eidolon which was taken from this temple and is now in the possession of the alcalde or mayor of Cárcamos,—a well-chiselled figure four feet long and about a foot in diameter, cut apparently out of a single block of magnesian limestone or coarse marble, of which the one half is yellow and the other almost jet black, the dividing-line running vertically and along the profile of the face. Tradition says that in a still more ancient temple six miles farther northwest the Jaliscanos had a sort of national palladium, known as the "Marvel of Atocha," a large statue or column which looked grayish-white and semi-transparent in daytime, but became luminous after dark, and was supposed to be a miraculous symbol of the moon.

The dwelling-houses I saw were generally stone-built, but low, and with mere loopholes for windows, yet they have one larger building in the hamlet of Villapaterna, where they store the saltpetre produce of the neighboring limestone caves and manufacture their own gunpowder, while the Christian proprietors of private powder-factories are hounded by revenue officers like the nocturnal whiskey distillers of our Southern Alleghanies. They pay no tithes and raise a good deal of tobacco, which also is a government monopoly in the lowlands.

These and other privileges make them rather obnoxious to their Christian neighbors, whom they scandalize besides by their passionate adherence to the religious rites and mysteries of their forefathers. When the south wind melts the snow of Tierra Fria and the chestnut forests are in bloom, they celebrate a May festival (*fiesta de Mayo*), a kind of thanksgiving demonstration inspired by the re-awakening of Nature from her winter trance, like the Feast of Tabernacles and the Roman Lupercalia. Later in the year, either in September or the beginning of October, they assemble for a grand carousal of three or four days, followed by athletic games, wrestling, running, and spear-throwing.

Every village has its wrestling-ring, where the contests of the young men divert the chiefs and wigwam belles in the cool of the evening; and this passion for manly exercises, as well as their resolute abstinence from the seductive beverages of their enemies, distinguishes them favorably from other tribes of the American race, and is probably the secret of their success in maintaining their religious and political independence. Though they still occupy the larger part of the great Sierra de San Juan, they have lost at least nine-tenths of their ancient territory, but they have preserved their health and their freedom, and, in spite of their present poverty, are probably the happiest inhabitants of the Spanish American highlands.

Two miles north of Villapaterna, on a level plateau of about a hundred square yards, is the tomb of a famous chieftain who checked the advance of the Conquistadores for more than a quarter of a century, and, from his many miraculous escapes, was long supposed to be bullet-proof. He is said to have made a charge into a fortified Spanish camp in broad daylight in order to recover a golden image of Catascotl; and when the enemy captured his son he abducted the wife of the governor of Sinaloa, to hold her as a counter-hostage

Near the tomb was a wrestling-ring, and an obelisk-shaped monument which the fire-worshippers of Jalisco erected in honor of their god when the large pyramid of Cárcamos was destroyed by the Spanish fanatics, about the end of the sixteenth century. The monument is in ruins now, and the best sculptured stones of the pedestal have been employed in the construction of the Franciscan convent of Las Animas near San Cristoval. The temple on the promontory, too, was thus repeatedly despoiled by the inhabitants of San Renaldo; but it may console the worshippers of Catascotl to remember that the sacrilege has been avenged by many a church-destroying earthquake, and that the god will not lack a monument while the volcano of Culiacan lifts his snow-capped pyramid above the clouds and superstitions of the lower world.

CHAPTER V.

The gods that left the lower world
Still haunt the mountain solitudes.—CHAMISSO.

DURING my absence Señor Cardenas had ascertained
that the mountains of Querétaro were infested with the
fugitive guerillas of Pedro Mendez, who had retreated to
his native State after his defeat in the north. For greater
security, therefore, as well as to make up for lost time, I
adopted the señor's advice to take the stage-coach to Cuer-
navaca and Tehuacan, and reach the Sierra Madre by way
of Orizaba.

We passed through the historic valley of Anahuac, where
the fate of Mexico was four times decided,—by the troops
of Cortés, Iturbide, Scott, and Bazaine,—and on the fifth
day reached the little mountain-village of Acolcingo, in
the Sierra Madre, where we readjusted our packs and
resumed our work before daybreak the next morning.

From the head-waters of the Rio Blanco to the Peak of
Santander the slopes of the sierra are diversified with grassy
terraces, holm-oaks, groves of larch-trees, cliffs of fantastic
shapes, and incipient valleys dotted with patches of straw-
berries and flowering rhododendrons; and in August, when
the berries ripen, and the days are warm enough to make
the shade of the larch-groves agreeable, these heights would
afford play-grounds for all the school-children and tourists

151

between St. Petersburg and San Francisco. In the park-like middle region between the continuous forests of the foot-hills and the upper limits of all arboreal vegetation, the fauna resembles that of our Southern Alleghanies; black-tail deer and rabbits prefer the fine grass and the aromatic mountain-herbs to the rank vegetation of the lower valleys; the ravines are frequented by a long-legged variety of mountain-grouse (*Tetrao tetrix*) that rely on their pedalistic agility and decline to take wing at your approach; black and gray squirrels divide the larch-nuts with a little bird of the cross-bill kind, and the rhododendron thickets swarm with a white-and-red spangled butterfly, similar to the *Papilio phœbus* of the Southern Alps. To judge by their confidence, the peace of these free *monteros* is rarely disturbed by visitors from the land of gunpowder and hunting-dogs. A bright-colored woodpecker, flitting about the rocks in pursuit of his entomological researches, repeatedly prolonged his sessions till I could have taken him with my outstretched hand, and when we passed through a small holm-oak grove a gray squirrel jumped upon a fallen log and sat right in front of us, chattering and switching its tail as if it had a good mind to refuse us the right of passage. A few hundred yards farther up, from the top of an overhanging cliff where we rested a few minutes, José started a big boulder and sent it bounding toward the foot-hills, but a projecting rock deflected it to the right and into the little holm-oak grove we had passed ten minutes ago. Not the boulder, but a band of black-tail deer, emerged from the trees and went through the juniper-bushes and round the corner like a whirlwind. As the grove did not contain more than thirty or forty trees, we must have passed within a few steps of the troop, and if they did not see us, they certainly must have heard us talk; yet they did not

MOUNT ORIZABA.

think it worth while to interrupt their matinée on our
account.

But the chief charm of such mountain-solitudes is their primitive character,—their entirely unimproved condition, as a Kansas farmer would say. No destruction of forests and construction of fences proclaim here that the sceptre of Nature has passed into other hands; no deserts and ruins remind you that the *Juventus Mundi* has departed with the youth of the human race. Thanks to his blessed laziness, God's vice-regent on earth has generally confined the abuse of his power to the level lowlands; and the immortals, who wanted to keep their private paradise unprofaned, did therefore very well to locate it in the summit-regions of Mount Olympus. For those who can climb earth is as young as ever.

We had to make a considerable détour to the left to reach the ridge that connects the volcano with the Sierra Madre, for the western slope of the peak is dreadfully steep, and we were unprovided with mountaineering-gear, as the members of the Alpine Club call it,—ropes, claw-shoes, and ice-axes. As we approached the ridge the rock-chaos became intricate and obstructive, but the grade was not very steep here, and at about nine A.M. we reached the divide and beheld now, for the first time, the eastern slope of the North American continent. The average height of the Sierra Madre surpasses that of the Western Alps by more than six thousand feet, and the greater elevation of the snow-line makes the highlands far more accessible, but the view from the summits of the Mexican Cordilleras owes its peculiar grandeur to the wonderful transparency of the air. Nowhere else on earth is the atmosphere at the same time so humid and so free from consolidated clouds; the radiation of heat from the elevated table-lands seems to transfigure all gaseous moisture into an aerial vapor that reinforces the light it transmits and endows the eye with a strange telescopic power. That haze of the horizon which limits the vistas from an Alpine height veiled the swamp-coast of Yucatan, but in the north, the east, and the north-west the view was only bounded by the incurvation of the globe, and the outlines of the peak of Culiacan, on the coast of Sinaloa, appeared as sharp and distinct as those of a jagged cliff at our feet. The gulf-coast, from Northern Yucatan to the islands in the Bay of Tampico, is visible, with all its harbors and white beaches; the flag on the citadel of San Juan d'Ulloa appears and disappears as the sea-breeze moves it; the ruins of Fort Antigua, where Cortés effected his first landing, can be plainly distinguished from the surrounding tower-like cliffs; and where water and sky meet, in the northeast, the light-house on the island of Bermejo glitters like a rising star. Farther to the right the peak of Las Milpas stands on the horizon, like an outpost of the sierra that crowns the plateau of Eastern Yucatan, and which can be traced through a suc-cession of snowy crests to the highlands of Guatemala, in the distant southwest. At your feet you see the terrace-land of Vera Cruz, a vast chaos of gray rocks and sombre pines, rising above the undulating foot-hills with their tarns and pleasant groves; farther down, the table-land, intersected by deep ravines and dotted with settlements here and there; and below that, the *tierra caliente*, with its evergreen forests that stretch away to the north and south-west as far as the eye can reach, and border the land with a frame of eternal summer. The numerous little mounds that rise like light-green billows above an ocean of darker foliage are groves of *Adansonia*, or monkey-fig trees, that attain a height of two hundred feet and monopolize their favorite soil by the vigor of their growth.

I looked around for a suitable camping-ground. The

ridge was dismally barren, but right below us, at the bottom of an accessible ravine, I saw a cluster of small fir-trees, some of them withered and apparently dry enough for firewood. I showed them to my guide: "Look here, Josey! wouldn't that make a good camping-place for the Indian, where he could cook our dinner while we try the volcano?"

"Just the place," said José; "and if you like we could sleep here to-night: it seems to be sheltered all around."

"Tell him to go down, then, and make himself comfortable. It would wear him out to drag his load to the top, and it wouldn't do to take him along and leave the blankets and things down here. Tell him we shall be back by three or four o'clock."

After a short dialogue in the Tuxpan vernacular, the Indian waved his hat, as if to emphasize his approval of the programme, and we resumed our road toward the peak.

"I knew the old man would be glad to get a rest," said José; "but as for the blankets, it would have been perfectly safe to leave them anywhere on the ridge. One visitor in two years is the average, I reckon, and they take very different routes."

"Are there no hunters coming up here? It would pay, I should think."

"Well, yes; but they find enough farther down. The foot-hills are full of all kinds of game, except the *cimarones*" (big-horn sheep): "they only come down in winter nights, I am told, but it is too much trouble to follow them up to the *tierra fria*."

"A man might live up here for years, then, and nobody know anything about it."

"Certainly he might. I'll tell you, señor, what happened here four years ago. A company of *operadores*" (exploring miners) "came up from San Patricio, and were grubbing around on the Lookout Cliffs, as they call that steep ridge over there, and when they crossed a ravine they

SLOPES OF THE SIERRA MADRE.

found the body of a man, lean and dried up like a piece of leather, as if he had been lying there for a long time. They reported the thing down in Val de Lucas, and the alcalde got the 'stiff' down in the course of the week, but it took them more than a month before they could identify him. And who do you think it was? An outlaw that had broken jail in Tehuacan when the French garrison left, and had not been heard of for full six years. It was a little before Christmas when he broke out, and they think he tried to cross the sierra in the snow, and froze when he slept in that ravine "

The backbone of the ridge got narrower as we approached the peak, but toward ten A.M. we reached the volcano proper, and then began the real ascent. we had to clamber up on our hands and feet when we failed to find an oblique ravine or a snow-field with a plastic crust.   Where the snow commences the last traces of vegetation disappear, and only on the southeast side the rocks are clothed with a sort of reddish moss, that helps to mitigate the dreary aspect of these supra-mundane regions.   I followed my guide in silence, and took the lead now and then, for I noticed that José trudged straight ahead with an apathetic disregard of coming obstacles, keeping his eyes on the ground as if he feared an attack of the "mountain fever"—the *mal de monte*— that overcomes travellers at the brink of a steep precipice.

The last thousand steps of the ascent were up-hill work in the steepest sense of the word, but a sharp north wind and the *spes finis* sustained us, and ten minutes before noon we reached the last barricade of jagged crags, helped each other up, and stood upon the apex of the North American continent.

"*O Santissima! mis rodillas*—my knees! my knees!" laughed José, throwing himself at haphazard upon the loose rocks   "I should doubt that there were such a thing as an all-merciful God if he had made this mountain any higher!   Santissima! I could not go up another slope like that if I knew it was leading *derecho al cielo*" (straight into heaven).

"Take care, amigo," said I, "or you might happen to land in the other place: you are sliding right toward the trap-door of it."

"*No hay cuidado*" (no danger), "sir," he laughed, lying

down at full length in one of the ruts that diverge from the crater: "the hole is stopped up. *El diablo* himself could not get in if he tried to go home by that route."

After a closer inspection of the supposed crater, I arrived at a similar conclusion. The rim of the summit still incloses a circular cavity, about twenty yards across and five or six feet deeper in the centre than at the circumference, but the volcano of Orizaba had been extinct for immemorial ages when the Conquistadores arrived, and has never since shown any disposition to resume business. The walls of the crater may have collapsed and obstructed the hole, or

CRATER OF ORIZABA.

the chief vent was somewhere in the deep gorges of the northwestern slope, but the cavity at the summit shows certainly neither a trace of volcanic ashes nor any aperture that could be supposed to have been the chimney of a subterranean furnace. The hollow is filled with basaltic rocks, decorated with icicles on the north side and grayish-white streaks of snow in their horizontal crevices, and here and

there between the crags former explorers had left memen-
toes of their visits,—broken bottles, a rusty pickaxe, shreds
of an old blanket, and a pile of charred sticks,—as if an
adventurous tourist had attempted to pass a night on the
summit, and had brought up the material of a camp-fire
from the sierra below.

The peak of Orizaba is perhaps the only mountain on
earth where, at an elevation of more than three miles above
the sea-level, the air can be breathed with impunity. The
lofty table-lands that surround its western and southern
base seem to send up a breathable atmosphere to a height
that would paralyze your lungs in Switzerland and South
America, while the tropical latitude has lifted the snow-line
to an elevation of more than fifteen thousand feet. Besides
a queer feeling about my knee-joints, nothing but the fact
that the noontide beams of a tropical sun were so utterly
devoid of warmth could remind me that I was standing
three thousand feet above the summit of Mont Blanc, and
at least twelve thousand above the "Tip-Top House" on
Mount Washington. My lungs were perfectly at ease, and
the dry cough that was provoked by every attempt at a
deep respiration might be ascribed to the north wind that
was sweeping over the summit in fitful blasts.

I clambered over to the south side, where the wind could
not strike me below the shoulders, fastened my hat with a
handkerchief, and looked around. The view from the
peak is a perfect panorama: nothing but an horizon as
sharp-drawn as the sky-line in mid-ocean bounds the land
almost all around. Almost, I say; for in the west the only
North American rival of Orizaba, the volcano of Popoca-
tapetl, equally remarkable for the strangeness of its form
and of its name, rises like a huge white cloud above the
outline of the Sierra Madre, and slightly above that of the

horizon. The rest is a map, rather than a picture, of Central America. The sublime glaciers of the Sierra de San Juan appear like glittering dots on a background of dark-green fir-woods, and behind the coast-range of Jalisco the Pacific Ocean reveals its islands and the smoke-trail of a steamer, perhaps on her way to Australia. That little mirror with an oval frame which reflects the rays of the sun in the northwest is the Laguna del Cayman, in Northern Durango, and that group of islands in the opposite quarter of the sky belongs to Spain,—Las Islas Amarillas, on the western coast of Cuba. Letting my eyes roam over the valleys and table-lands of the continent, I could not help wondering how greatly the area of the American wilds still exceeds that of the cultivated districts. In comparison with the Southern United States, Mexico can boast of a pretty dense population,—nine million inhabitants to seven hundred thousand square miles,—but a bird's-eye view of the country shows that the yellow-green corn-fields and the naked environs of the larger towns are only small islands in a vast sea of virgin woods and savage mountains, and only the trans-Cordilleras railroad, that extends a narrow sparkling line from the coast to the centre of the continent, impresses one with a sense of the power of that two-legged insect whose aggregated dwellings—Vera Cruz, Puebla, and the capital—appear like small whitish specks from these heights.

But from all their wanderings my eyes sooner or later returned to the Gulf-coast. By an association of certain geographical and historical ideas, I find a strange charm in those rock-bound coasts and mountainous islands that give this branch of the Atlantic a peculiar individuality. Eastern Mexico, Guatemala, Honduras, Panama, and the entire West Indian island-world bristle with mountains, and their diversified coasts and those of the northern continent contrast with each other as strangely as Southern Europe and North Africa. In this happy alliance of land and ocean, of waters navigable and coasts inhabitable to the very land-and-water line, the West Indian archipelago is the only parallel of the *mare internum*, the inland ocean, of the classic nations, the Gulf of Mexico is our Mediterranean Sea, and, remembering that the Old World saw its golden age when the westward progress of pagan civilization had reached the shores of that wonderful midland gulf, I cannot help thinking that America will not celebrate her happiest centuries till the Anglo-Saxon spirit shall have reclaimed the countries that border this great mountain-lake of the West.

I looked down, and was puzzled to account for the origin of the long streaks of vapor that drifted along the cliffs at our feet and away into the empty air, till I became aware that they must be clouds,—clouds, too, perhaps, of that fleecy, aerial kind which, viewed from the lowland, seem hardly to belong to the sublunary world. They were the only guests of these lofty heights. A couple of harpy eagles circled around the rocks at the base of the peak, but they had their eyries far below: they had no need to seek refuge in the dreary rock-wastes that shelter the brood of their persecuted European relatives.

"Look down here, Josey," said I: "the mountain throws no shade, hardly, does it? The sun must be now exactly overhead."

"Yes, it must be full noon," he replied. "I wonder if old Benito has got our dinner ready?"

I took the hint, and sent a farewell look to the eastern sky and the Gulf, whose silver plains I could not hope to see again for many a year "Yes, let us go," I said at last.

"I begin to yearn for that long-haired blanket of mine: it's getting rather chilly up here."

"There must be something wrong with our Indian," I remarked, when we had got about half-way down: "that's his cave below that cliff there, but I don't see any smoke. I'm afraid the old sinner has swallowed our bacon raw and thrown the crackers away."

"I can guess what's the matter," said José. "The wind has been getting pretty stiff, and he had only five or six matches: I don't think he has been able to get a fire under way."

The Indian walked up to his countryman and opened his hands in a deprecatory way when we reached his camping-ground.

"Just as I thought," said the guide: "he has been trying to light that wood with all the dry grass and pine-needles he could find, but he used up his last match in vain. It's too windy and the wood is too damp: it wouldn't be any use to try again, he says"

"Hadn't we better go over to the south side of the mountain? Or say, Josey: do you know any house or shelter of some kind that we could reach before night?—a cave or a *casucha?*" (a herder's cottage).

The Indian, listening eagerly, had understood the last word, and the two natives looked at each other meditatively.

"Hold on," said José at last; "there *is* a house down here, now I come to think of it, but there is nobody living there,—the old *quartel*" (storehouse) "of the Rio Blanco silver-mine. But we can hardly reach there before night if we want to cook our dinner first."

"That building you speak of—is it on our road to San Rafael?"

"Certainly, sir. The teamsters from Jalapa used to stop there before the Perote pike-road was finished: it isn't anything out of our way."

"What do you say, men? Shall we let our dinner go and try to reach that quartel before night, and have a big supper there and a good night's rest?"

"If you ask *me*, I should be glad to start right away," said the guide.

"Shall we find any firewood there?"

"Any amount of it, señor: it's right in the centre of the *piñal*" (the coniferous belt).

"All right, then. Ask the Indian if he can rough it out, or if he wants to take a cold snack before we go."

The Indian grinned.

"It seems he has attended to that already," said José: "I'm afraid the old man has put himself outside of a terrific lunch."

"Hand me my gun, then. So here goes for the quartel and a good supper."

After a somewhat risky scramble through the cliffs we got back to the grassy slopes of the sierra, where we could go down hill at a trot, so that we managed to reach the forest-region of the eastern slope while the sun was yet high up in the sky. Two lines, drawn at an elevation respectively of nine thousand and thirteen thousand feet, would mark the vertical extent of the coniferous belt. In full view of the palm-groves and sugar-cane fields of the coast, one can breathe here the resinous odors of a Norway pine-forest, and meet such flowers and shrubs of Old and New England as hollyhocks, tiger-lilies, mayflowers, whortleberries, broom-corn, and hazel-nut thickets. The meadows, too, have a decidedly northern appearance: fine short grass spotted with white clover and bluebells, and bordered by rushes and forget-me-nots along the mountain-creeks. Following one of these creeks, we passed through sunny glades and dark, rock-bound glens, till we entered a deep

IN THE PIÑAL.

mountain-gorge and heard below us the booming of the falls of Val del Torre, where a large creek tumbles over a precipice of three hundred feet into the cañon of the Rio Blanco.

Leaving the cañon to the right, we followed the windings of a *rambla*, or dry ravine, for half an hour, and emerged upon a mountain-meadow that would have gladdened the hearts of a New England picnic party, tempting us sorely

11

to abandon our quartel plan and go into camp under one of the shady holm-oaks at the edge of the forest. What chances here for summer hotels and sanitaria when the State of Vera Cruz shall have added a star to a certain spangled piece of cloth !

When we entered the woods again, a *gallinasso* (coq-des-bois), a large bird of the grouse species, flew up into a pine above my head, and, espying us, took wing again immediately, but in flying through the open branches gave me a chance for a snap shot. He dashed into the next tree and came flopping to the ground, but at our approach fluttered away and contrived to reach a laurel-thicket, where further pursuit became hopeless. Our terrier had started a black-tail doe when we crossed the divide, and we had never seen him since. Another four hundred or five hundred feet down hill and we reached a broader valley, at a point where a mountain-creek had been bridged with a few rough-hewn logs.

" *Gracias a Dios!* the worst of our trip is over," exclaimed José. " Here's the old military road: only four miles to the quartel now."

" Who owns that quartel, as you call it, or why has it been abandoned ?"

" It used to be the storehouse of the Rio Blanco mine, señor; but it doesn't belong to anybody in particular now: it has been vacant for years."

" The company broke up, I suppose?"

" Why, no, sir. It wasn't a company: it used to be a government mine. You heard of Captain Salinez, I suppose? Well, he——"

" Never heard of him. Whom do you say it belonged to ? The Mexican government?"

" No, the Spanish government, sir. Let me tell you how

it happened that our people had to abandon it. A few years before the revolution the Spaniards put an old Catalan officer in charge of the mine: he used to be a sea-captain, they say, and a very smart man,—the only one out of sixteen captains who saved his ship when the English captured the *cargada*" (the Spanish silver-fleet). "He got away that time, and his ship was the only one that reached Spain out of the largest cargada that ever sailed. So they made him superintendent of this mine when he left the navy; and when the revolution broke out, this Captain Salinez was again the only one who didn't get fooled like all the rest of the mining-officers: he knew beforehand how it would end, and saved his last year's bonanza in time. And what do you think he did before he left? He bribed all the *plateros*" (ore-diggers) " who had ever entered the shaft to follow him over to Spain, and the day before he cleared out he sent a dozen of them up to the mine to play us a trick of the meanest sort: when they came back he said the rebels were now welcome to work the mine—if they could find it. He had not been gone a week before the Liberals captured Vera Cruz; and a few days after the new government sent officers of their own up here to take charge of the mine.

"They found the furnace and hammer-works in good condition, but all the workmen were gone; and when they wanted a guide to take them up to the mine they had to hire one of the rancheros that lived down in the Peñas valley. He took them up the mountain as far as he could track the ruts of the ore-cars, but then the trouble commenced: the sierra was so rocky and full of caverns that the entrance of the tunnel might have been anywhere and nowhere all over a mountain-slope two miles high and forty miles long. They had to go back, and tried to hunt up the engineer of the mine or one of the plateros, but not a man could they find; and when they asked the farmers, they didn't know anything about it, except that the mine was somewhere on the southeast side of the Sierra de San Lucas. The officers threatened and promised, but the old captain had been too much for them: they didn't find a soul who could tell them the one thing they wanted to know. Well, sir, ever since that time there have been commissioners and private parties up here nosing around and clambering all over the sierra, but the professional *operadores*" (prospectors) "say that it would be a great deal easier to find a new mine than this old one. That rascal of a Salinez wasn't satisfied with hiding the right place, but left no end of counterfeit *señas*" (indications), "as the miners call them, that set the green-horns hunting for mares' nests in the ravines and limestone caves."

"So the right place has really never been found?"

"That's what I was going to tell you, sir. About ten years ago—a year before the French tackled us—an oper-ador from Durango came up here and had a long conference with a relation of his,—the old ranchero Hernandez, that used to haul wood to the furnace in time of the Spanish government. They went up to the sierra together and crawled around in the rocks till the old man got tired, but his relation didn't give it up, and went back alone the next week with a good pile of *tortillas* and dried beef. He came down again and got another supply, and so on, for a quarter of a year, till his relation asked the neighbors not to sell him anything after this: he was afraid the fellow would ruin himself. But Mr. Operador bought his tortillas in another settlement, and kept the game up till one evening he came down after sunset, made his uncle get up and follow him out into the woods, and told him there he had found the old bonanza mine,—no doubt about it, he said,—told him how he had discovered the *true* indications, and the way he had followed them up; and at last asked his advice how they should work the thing: should they keep it secret, or should they borrow some money and get a government license? 'Make sure of the thing first,' said the uncle. 'Did you go *into* the mine?'—'It's a tunnel,' said the miner, 'and I went in for a quarter of a mile, saw the timbers, the wheelbarrows, and all. What shall we do about it?' They had a long talk, and on the following day the ranchero applied to the alcalde of Redondo, a well-to-do man, who lent him some money and wrote for a license. As soon as they could get the necessary tools the uncle and nephew and four of the uncle's neighbors went up into the sierra to clear the obstructions away, so as to have everything ready by the time the license should come.

"But up near a place they call the Paso de Salsas" (Sassafras Gap) "the young Hernandez got uneasy, made them stop and went ahead alone, to make sure that they were on the right road. The men waited and waited till near sundown: some of them then went up into the rocks and hallooed and looked for that Hernandez in all directions, but they couldn't find him; so they all went back home, wondering if the man had gone crazy or what had become of him. They didn't hear anything of him for a good while, but four weeks after they found out that he had stopped at a tavern in Cuernavacas, where he told the landlord about his troubles,—that he had found the bonanza mine, and lost it again after sending for a license and going to great expense about it. He said he meant to come back and pay the alcalde and his uncle what he owed them. He did so, six months after, but with the money he had left he started for the sierra once more, and swore that he had found the mine once and would find it again. They say he sold all his property in Durango and lived in the Sierra de San Lucas like a hermit for the rest of his life; and it is sure that he has often been seen by the teamsters who crossed the gap between Perote and Santander."

I began to fear that my guide too had lost his bearings, but just before sunset we traversed a rocky *cerro*, or rib, of the sierra, and sighted our destination in a forest of hemlock-trees. From afar it resembled a ruined castle, but the stone wall on the south side proved to belong to a separate structure—the *rebosso*, or smelting-furnace—while the quartel itself was built in the orthodox backwoods style, rough-hewn logs laid crosswise and filled out with a mixture of grass and adobe-mortar. The building was two-storied, and after a glance at the ground-floor I ascended the staircase—a massive ladder with a railing—and found myself in the *bel étage*, where a plank floor and a rustic chimney offered decided advantages over the stable-like basement.

"Here we are, compañero!" said José, slapping his countryman on the back. "Put your freight in this corner and make yourself at home."

Man is a domestic animal, and the feeling of having "a roof overhead" has its charm even for the natives of a rainless clime. But the chilliness of the air reminded me that we were still ten thousand feet above the *tierra caliente*. "Hold on, amigos," said I. "let's have a fire before all other things now, and supper and a ten hours' rest after. You stay here, Josey, and attend to the cookery, and let me and the daddy fetch you wood enough to last us all night."

With a short axe that constituted an item of the Tuxpan's cargo, we sallied out into the *piñal*, chopped down a dozen of the withered little pine-trees in the underbrush, and broke a piece of timber out of the dilapidated furnace for a home-log, as they say in North Carolina. Half an hour

DESERTED MINING-WORKS ON THE RIO BLANCO.

after the smoke ascended from the chimney in a dense mass.

"*Ay, que canta mi fuego tan claro!*" (" How strong our fire is singing!") José exclaimed again and again as he crumbled his crackers into a panful of butter. " Now the old man can't make us believe that pine wood wouldn't burn."

The Tuxpan fetched a tin bucket full of water from the ravine, and we spread our blankets around the fire and sat, or rather lay, down—*more majorum*—to a supper of cracker-pudding, cooked apples, tortillas with a little butter and sugar, and water from the sierra creek. We had no stimu-lants, but ease is a far more essential element of comfort than luxury, and I felt that I would not willingly exchange my free-and-easy repast in the chimney-corner of the old quartel for a ceremonious supper at the table of Baron Lafitte.

"Halloo! there he is!" cried José, apropos of nothing, as I thought, and jumped up, and down-stairs into the basement. "Yes, it's him!" he shouted from below, the explanation being this time furnished by the joyful yelping of a dog. "I thought I heard him whine around the house," said he when he reappeared on the ladder, dog in arm. "Here he is: look at him, as wet as a muskrat and full of burs.— Come here, Sentinelita! Poor doggy! come to the fire."

There was no doubt of it: Sentinelita had come back, as short-legged and long-named as ever.

"Give him all he wants to eat," said I. "I wonder how the little fox tracked us across the Rio Blanco? He must have had a hard day's work of it."

"Mustn't he?" said José. "I bet you he followed that doe clear across into the Sierra de Pascarro: when I heard him give tongue the last time he was 'way on the other side of the San Lucas Mountains."

"You were afraid you had lost him for good, I suppose?"

"I wasn't sure about it," said José, with an admiring look at the gastronomic feats of his pet: "I know from experience that he commonly manages to be back in time for supper."

"What is this?" I asked, pointing to a little paper package which José had shaken out of his pocket, with different buttons and bits of chewing-tobacco, in his search for matches.

"That?" with a furtive look at the Tuxpan. "Why, that must be Benito's testimonial. It's very foolish: I thought I had given it to you long ago."

"What is it, anyhow?"

"Oh, he has been working for Mr. Calgar, a *ladrillero*" (brickyard-master), "and his boss wrote him a recommendation. Or I think Mrs. Calgar did the writing: she's quite a scholar, they say."

"Let me see it."

The joint literary efforts of the ladrillero and his spouse had achieved the following document:

"Una recomendacion por Benito Lucas trabaxo en mi ladrilleria hace dos anios 5 meses otros 3 meses jornalero por 4 Reales otros tres semanas y ahora 6 Meses dos semanas a precio a dos medios por carga otras 2 semanas tres reales Reales siempre diligente que le puedo encomendar Es esta seguro siempre diligente puedo encomendar el dia veintidos de noviembre 1875 manuel Calgar."

Literal translation: "A recommendation for Benedict Lucas worked in my yard two years ago 5 months other 3 months day labor at 4 Reales other three weeks and last 6 Months two weeks job work two medios per carga other 2 weeks three reals Reals always industrious that I can recommend Is he is reliable I can recommend twenty-second day of november 1875 m. C."

I walked across to the loophole in the opposite wall and took a look at the sky. The calmness and clearness of the air seemed to promise a cold night, so we put the home-log on, spread our couches in a semicircle and prepared for fire-worship. I had pulled out a volume of Calderon's *Canciones*, and my companions were gossiping with that talent for protracted confabulation which distinguishes the *Indio Manso* from his taciturn Northern cousin, when we were startled by a most uncanny sound—a long-drawn croak or a shuddering gurgle, I might call it—that seemed to come from the depths of the piñal, and made the terrier rise to his feet with a suppressed growl.

"What was that?" was the question implied by our puzzled looks at each other, till the Tuxpan offered a remark in the language of his tribe.

"He says it's an *onza de monte*" (a female mountain-panther), explained the guide: "that's the way they call for their mates, he says."

We listened in silence for a couple of minutes, but heard nothing but the low babbling of the mountain-brook.

"*Virgen purissima!*" whispered José, making the sign of the cross: "if that didn't put me in mind of the *Llorona!* We are lucky if it's nothing worse than what the Indian thinks it was!"

The *Llorona*—a noun feminine from *llorar*, "to weep, to mourn"—is an indigenous bugbear of the Mexican Cordilleras, a nocturnal lamia that haunts the rock-wastes of the Sierra Madre and chills the blood of the belated traveller with her boding voice. He who meets her face to face dies: to hear her presages an imminent calamity.

"Did you ever *see* the Llorona, Josey?"

"No, but my uncle in San Sebastian did: he saw her coming towards him across the road when he came home late one night. She had her mouth half open, and showed a set of snags like a tiger, señor; but he saved himself by galloping away like a buffalo. He's a powerful runner, my uncle is."

"Are there any other ghosts in the sierra?"

"Why, yes, sir. There's the *voz de luta*" (warning voice), "you know; but that's a propitious spirit, and warns people who are going astray."

"Helps travellers that have lost their way in the mountains, I suppose."

A full orchestra of singing-birds awoke us the next morning, and when we resumed our route along the banks of the Rio Blanco, I felt sure that neither sportsman nor landscape-painter could find a similar paradise north of the Rio Grande. Turkeys and *curacos* (pheasants) were scraping the dry leaves all along the mountain-side, and made the air musical with their calls. We found tracks of panthers and black wolves, and Sentinelita started three deer, but they hugged the river-bottom and would not break cover. From the sandstone cliffs that overhung the water we had a glorious view of the lower river-valley and the terrace-lands beyond. As far as the eye could reach, the country appeared like a boundless rolling ocean of wood-covered hills, fading away to the eastern horizon and rising to the northwest, where the Sierra Mesilla lifted her walls of sun-gilt cliffs and evergreen pines. I durst not analyze the feelings inspired by the morning wind that carried the fragrance and the greetings of this mountain-world, but I could not suppress a growing conviction that city-life is an unpardonable sin.

A little below its junction with the Yegua Creek we crossed the Rio Blanco once more, and followed the windings of a valley whose rock-walls became higher and steeper, affording us an agreeable shade as the sun rose higher. About ten English miles below the mouth of the Yegua the cañon expands to, or rather crosses, a circular valley of more than half a league in diameter, whose western wall is formed by an absolutely perpendicular cliff two miles long and about six hundred feet high. This citadel is garrisoned by an army of vultures, who have their nests among the summit-rocks, where their tribe may have roosted in peace since the end of the glacial period that escarped these mountain-ramparts.

"What are those chaps living on?" I asked, pointing to a long row of sentinels on the edge of the rock: "there can't be much carrion in this part of the sierra, I should think ?'"

"I couldn't tell you, señor," said the guide, "but they always find something, I guess. They take long flits down to the *tierra caliente*, and I have an idea that they *make* carrion if they don't find it ready-made. They are harmless, though," he added, "but on the south side of this rock there is a nest of mountain-eagles that often make the settlers wish the thing wasn't quite so steep."

"They steal a good many kids, I suppose?"

"Yes; and farmer Garcia, down on the Olmos Creek, suspects them of having kidnapped his boy."

"Carried him up into this rock, did they?"

"Nobody knows. The boy and his sister—babies, both of them—were at play in the garden behind Garcia's house, and their mother, passing near the garden-fence, saw the girl run toward the gate as fast as she could and just as if she was scared out of her wits, and when she went into the garden to look for the boy, he was gone. They didn't know what to think of it, for they had never seen a panther or puma in that part of the country, and a wolf couldn't get over the fence; but half a year after the girl got sick, and her mother took her down to Doctor Gonzales's place, near San Lucas, and when they came through the garden the girl all at once gave a fearful scream, and caught her mother round the neck as if she thought somebody was going to murder her. The mother looked up, and what do you think? The doctor keeps a large tame eagle in the garden, and the girl had seen the critter sitting on the fence. She wasn't of that scary sort otherwise, so they think the eagle must have reminded her of something she had seen before, and they all believe now that those devils on the rock carried the boy off, with nobody but his sister by."

"Do you see that round hill over there?" said José when we emerged from the cañon a little after noon. "Well, right behind there is the Franciscan convent, and that hill,

CONVENT OF SAN RAFAEL.

as it looks, is a grove of mango-trees in the convent-garden. We will get there in time for some meal or other: they're eating all day long."

"What are they doing besides eating, amigo?"

José stole a look at my face before I could suppress an involuntary smile: "Drinking? That's what you want me to say, isn't it? But no," with a sigh: "I wish my chance of going to heaven was as good as theirs. They are praying three or four times a day, and one of them stuffs his mattress with corncobs, they say—*povrecito!* And they don't charge anything for burying and baptizing; only, marriage is two dollars and a half."

"Are they attending the sick or doing anything for the poor people?"

"Yes, they do: they keep a place for poor travellers who cannot pay, and even for poor men's horses. And one of them is a physician,—the smartest man you ever saw: he has a large room full of stuffed butterflies and poisonous animals, birds, vermin, and all. You mustn't forget to see that: it's right inside of the church; they made a special partition for it."

At about four o'clock we reached the convent premises, a large garden not wholly devoted to kitchen vegetables, since the centre was occupied by a grove of shady mango-trees, and the hedge was reinforced with a row of jessa-mine and other flowering shrubs, swarming with butterflies that would have thrown a North-British collector into ecstasies. The convent itself, flanked by a church and sundry agricultural outhouses, had the substantial look of a Dutch country castle, a spacious portico and an extin-guisher-roofed balcony, and a little glass-covered turret,— perhaps the observatory of the doctor-priest.

"They haven't seen us yet," whispered José when we approached the door: "the *prelado*" (abbot) "is taking long naps after dinner. Let's ring the bell."

A barefoot boy opened the door, left it half ajar and ran into an adjoining room.

"All right," said a voice from within: "tell them to come in. But hold on! Ask them if they can chop us a little wood."

José burst out laughing. "That's Father Matias," said he, and, entering the door without ceremony, grabbed the boy by the neck before he could deliver his message. "Go back and call the father, you little monkey. *Esta un caballero, sino es á caballo*" ("This is a cavalier, though he hasn't brought his caballo along"). "He is going to pay."

"*Mil pardones!*" said Father Matias, popping out of his office and opening the door as wide as he could: "excuse the boy's stupidity. Step into this room, please: Father Hilario" (the prior) "will be down directly."

I took a seat in a cool, airy reception-hall, not over-furnished, like our Northern drawing-rooms, but provided with all the essentials of a guest-chamber, six or seven chairs, a lounge, and, near the window, a table with a couple of books,—De Vega's dramatical works and an illustrated *Natural History.*

After a few minutes the door opened, and Father Hilario made his appearance,—a short, fat man with a coquettish mantilla over the coarse habit of his order,—who made me a polite bow and inquired after the state of my health, rubbing his hands *à la maître d'hôtel:*

"Please make yourself at home, sir, while they are getting your room ready. Would an early supper be convenient, or would you prefer something warm in the mean time?"

"No such thing, padre mio," I protested. "Don't mistake me for a fine gentleman. I came to the sierra for the special purpose of getting away from hotels and fashionable suppers, and you mustn't let me interfere with the more important occupations of the worthy fathers. Your customary supper will do for me, and at any time that may suit you best."

"You are over-kind, sir: sit down, please." Then, in a more jovial tone, "*Viene usted á una casa pobre*" ("You are coming to a poor house"), "sir; but I don't doubt that you will make allowances, since your servant tells me that you camped in the sierra last night. *Mi vida!* what delight your countrymen take in those horrid mountains of ours! I wish we could export them in exchange for your beautiful farming-country in the North. You are an American, sir?"

"At present, my father, and I am proud of the name, since I have seen such a glorious part of America as this mountain-land of yours."

"Yes, yes," laughed the padre, "you are right: we should treat each other as brethren,—*Americanos libres,* all of us, whether north or south. You are on your way to Jalapa, I understand?"

"Yes, sir," getting ready for cross-examination. "I must see Fort Perote and the Rio Frio Valley while I am in the State, and Jalapa is a good central point for a foot-traveller, and the town itself is the prettiest on the eastern slope."

"That's true," switching off into the geographical topic. "They say, with the exception of Oaxaca, there is no town in Mexico with a more beautiful neighborhood. Well, I am glad you are so favored by the weather-saints. Wasn't it splendid the last three weeks?"

End of cross-examination. Want of inquisitiveness is perhaps the best side of the Spanish character from a social standpoint, as it is certainly the worst in regard to scientific affairs.

"Do you smoke, sir?" asked the padre, straddling the corner of the table and taking a package of cigarettes from his bosom.

"*Mil gracias!* I don't, for a wonder. My countrymen are great smokers now, and the habit is still gaining ground. It would become epidemical if they had your good tobacco."

"You flatter us, or rather our habit, señor. No, no! you are right, and we are wrong: it's an abominable vice. But what shall a man do? Rather learn to relish it than have others smoke all around you and make you sick. I have forty *calvitos*" ("baldies," shaven polls) "under my charge—all ages, from fifteen to seventy-five—and they *all* smoke, *pecadores*, every one of us. The saints didn't smoke, that's one sure thing."

"I don't think that St. Francis did."

"*Gran Dios*, no!" laughed the padre. "He would take the hide clean off our backs if *he* caught us at it. He used to mix all his victuals with gall, they say, wore woollen shirts in summer and a linen jacket in winter, and slept on a plank with a cross for his pillow. Well, you must make yourself comfortable till supper. You don't know farmer Pacheco—the one who has the contract for hauling wood for the Perote garrison—do you? Well, his wife died yesterday,—that is, his third wife. They say he is going to get another one before the end of the summer."

Fearing that the prelado was preparing for local gossip for my benefit, I was glad to remember the museum and the scientific convent-doctor. "You have a physician of your own here?" I remarked, apropos of Mr. Pacheco's wife.

"Oh, yes—Padre Ramon: he takes care of the whole *comarca*" (county). "We could not wish to have a better doctor."

"He is a natural philosopher too, I understand?"

"So you have heard about him? Yes, sir, he is quite a scholar: he has made a collection of natural curiosities that's really worth seeing."

"Is the doctor at home?"

"No: I am sorry to say he went out fishing this afternoon, but he will be back before supper, and we can take a look at his collection in the meanwhile."

12

CHAPTER VI.

LA TIERRA FRIA.

Up in the highlands, in the home of health —Prior.

Dogs and horses whose caudal appendages have been clipped for different generations are at last born with bob-tails, and the pathology of the human mind presents some very analogous phenomena. The spiritual tyranny of the Middle Ages, for instance, has certainly left its mark on the Latin races, for nature accommodates herself to ab-normal circumstances, and when she found that the posses-sion of an inquisitive mind subjected her children to the knife of the hierarchical vivisector, she saved them and their trainer a trouble by making an incurious disposition hereditary. The posterity of the orthodox Spaniards have, in consequence, become contentedly, and almost compla-cently, ignorant, and the difference between the science of the Anglo-Americans and that of their Spanish-American neighbors is one of kind as well as of degree. In Yankee-dom knowledge is a hobby, a passion, a recreation: in Mexico it is a trade The convent brethren of the Padre Ramon tolerated his scientific pursuits as a harmless mono-mania, but I do not think that more than three or four of the forty-two *frailes* were able to understand how a sane man could busy himself with stuffing birds and collecting minerals unless he was engaged by a museum or the assayer of a mining company.

182

"*Venga*," said the abbot, "*vamos a ver las singulari-dades*"—Let's take a look at the oddities, the extravaganzas, of the honest doctor,—a chance to utilize the fool by show-ing him off to strangers and fellow-lunatics.

Padre Ramon was certainly a versatile scientist. His museum (in a partition of the church that I should have mistaken for the cage of a staircase) comprised natural and antiquarian curiosities, relics, mechanical contrivances, busts, and several dozen oil pictures, mostly of his own paint-ing. His collection of beetles and butterflies was really splendid: he had sixty or seventy varieties of swallow-tailed papilionides, horned *scarabæi* of wonderful metallic lustre, and one specimen of the colossal atlas moth (*Sphinx gigas*), measuring eleven inches with outspread wings,—the first I had ever seen on this side of the Isthmus. A gorgeous display of fossils and minerals on a varnished oak table evinced more taste than erudition : the polychromatic crystals were arranged with a view to effective color con-trasts, but a piece of coralline rock was labelled "*Panal petrificado*," petrified honeycomb, and the skull-bone of an Aztec warrior and the canine teeth of a cave-bear were grouped together as homogeneous fragments, and described respectively as "Skull of Fossil Man" and "*Horns* of the Same." The pictures were of the modern idyllic type, Paul and Virginia promenading on verdigris-colored lawns, and landscapes that bore a strange resemblance to the fifty-cent chromos in our metropolitan variety stores.

"It can't be denied that he is a superior artist," observed the prior: "come and let me show you two pictures he painted for our church."

The one was a *Mater Ecstatica* with uplifted hands and large expressive eyes : the other was a *Temptation of Christ*, the tempted a meek saint, but a trifle too sleek after his forty days' fast,—the tempter luridly grotesque, with red proboscis and carnivorous teeth. The abbot and his friar met here on common ground. Besides the doctor's contributions, the main church contained a collection of pictorial miscellanea whose presence in a sanctuary seemed hardly justified by their artistic merit. Sundry uniformed generals and grandees from an illustrated history of Spain glittered among the beatific visions of a Mexican Tintoretto, and the department of simple woodcuts comprised a "Street-scene in Melbourne" from some illustrated English monthly, and a view of the "Riverside Military Academy" at Peekskill, New York.

Toward evening, when I was picking a few berries from the currant-hedge on the south side of the convent-garden, Padre Ramon entered the gate with his angle and a string of black pickerel, but made straight for the refectory. After supper he joined me in the garden,—a fat, vulgar-featured little monk, but with a singularly pleasant voice and an infectious laugh. His joviality was not the sly self-persiflage of certain French abbés in the presence of suspected sceptics, but the unaffected frankness of a man who felt his practical independence of his present situation.

"You can boast of a very indulgent prior," I remarked when he mentioned a recent visit to the lake region of Michoacan in company of the *padre cocinero*, the convent kitchen-master.

The doctor shrugged his shoulders. "Our gates are open," said he, "and inside parties nowadays need *algunas alicientes*—some inducements—to stay," alluding to President Juarez's abrogation of the law that made monastic vows legally binding.

"Are these concessions sanctioned in Italy?"

"In Puebla at least: our vicar-general leaves it optional with each abbot."

The prior of San Rafael seemed to have made the freest use of that privilege. There was no regular night-chapel, and, with the exception of a few detailed functionaries, the friars were at leisure after sundown, pleasing themselves as to the employment of the next twelve hours, provided they restricted their choice to indoor pastimes. Those who dis-

"DOLCE FAR NIENTE."

regarded this provision had to take their chance of finding the gates closed at their return, but the readmission of a penitent seemed to depend on the degree of his prospective usefulness rather than of his previous guilt, and in the case of valuable artisans the prior had a trick of "conniving with both eyes."

"You may have noticed that big fellow in the tree there," said the doctor, pointing to a sycamore near the gate, where a burly friar had swung his hammock: "that's the chief carpenter, one of our monks, but just as independent as you or the French consul if it should please you to pass a few weeks on our premises. He left us twice, and the last time built himself a shanty for his children and their mother in the Villa Amorosa, as they call that settlement in the bottom there, inhabited mostly by females. When his woman left him the prior offered to take him back, promising comprehensive indulgences for past and future offences, but he stipulated for a triple ration and six yards of black cloth per month, since we cannot pay him in cash; and finally we had to take him on his own terms."

"You are not permitted to employ outsiders, I suppose?"

"Yes, we are, but we cannot afford to pay them: the convent is too much in debt, and the receipts of our farms are nearly swallowed by the *mudanzas*,—the commutation-money."

"What's that?"

"The constitutional amendment of '59 suppressed all convents, you know, excepting those connected with a charitable institution; and, since we have no hospital of our own, we pay 'commutation-money,'—nominally in support of the Puebla State hospital, but in reality into the pockets of the official blackmailers, who would have us by the throat in a minute if we didn't plaster their palms. That law defeats its ostensible purpose," he added, "for it has reduced us to *passive* charities and raised the price of our hospitality considerably."

The padre's last remark made me thoughtful, and seeing José at the gate half an hour after, I took him aside and asked him to ascertain the terms of our present boarding-house as discreetly as possible. He knocked stealthily at the door and slipped into my bedroom a minute after the prior had recommended me to his patron saint.

"I'm glad you thought of that in time," he whispered. "I told them we preferred to settle our bill every morning, and the padre cocinero says that their regular terms are five dollars a day, and two for each servant, but that the prior will probably deduct a couple of reals because you have no horse. *Santissima, que sinverguenzas!* Let's get out of this; that beats the hotel prices in Aguas Calientes."

We needed no better pretext than the glorious weather of the next morning, and continued our road in the direction of Perote and the "Coffer Peak," the highest summit of the eastern coast-range. When we left the convent-gate, and again an hour before sunset of the same day, I noticed an interminable swarm of blackbirds flying in a southwesterly direction, probably northern emigrants on the way to their winter quarters in Honduras or Yucatan. Their flight was as silent and steady as that of migratory pigeons, as if fatigue or the wonders of the strange country had hushed their accustomed chatter.

On our first halt, at the edge of a precipitous cliff, we were overtaken by a troop of noisy gamins, the youngsters of the Villa Amorosa, to judge by their pure Spanish and convent-cloth jackets. One of them clambered up to our cliff, and, seeing me drink from a dripping rock-spring, asked me for the loan of my gutta-percha cup.—"Just come up here, boys, where this gentleman can see the fun," he called down to his comrades.

"What are you going to do, niño?" I asked.

"Oh, they are coming, sir: you'll see the whole lark. Padre Tito's Pablo caught a big black squirrel last Friday, and yesterday morning the creature got away and up a big pine-tree behind our house. There were eight of us after him, and when we cornered him near the top he jumped down on our roof, sixty feet straight, and never hurt himself a bit. We caught him on the chimney, but Pablo's godmother wouldn't let him keep the thing: he's bewitched, she says. But if we can't keep him we are going to have

,some fun out of him, anyhow; so we agreed to take him out here and throw him down one of these high cliffs."

" What good would that do you?"

" Why, to see the fun and to find out if he is bewitched or not. If there is any *bruxeria*" (enchantment) "about him, a thousand feet more or less won't make much difference."

The outer crags of the declivity overhung the valley of the Rio Blanco, more than six hundred feet below, and the foot of the precipice was bristling with cliffs and bowlders. The question whether squirrels can be killed by a fall could hardly be put to a severer test. the problem had a scientific interest, and a stout squirrel might survive the *salto mortale;* so, calming my conscience with these considerations and the blessed absence of Mr. Bergh, I decided to tolerate the experiment.

They had him in a pillow-slip, a full-grown *Sciurus niger,* as bulky and heavy as a moderate tom-cat, and quite as wary in his movements. He crouched for a spring when I peeped into the bag, and lowered his head, measuring the opening with glittering eyes.

" Let him look down, and let's see if he will risk the jump on his own account," said I, when his proprietor approached the brink.

The boys got around him and turned the flaps of the slip back, till the captive sat exposed at the bottom of the bag. He looked down and then back and sideways, as if comparing the chances of escape in the different directions, and finally clambered to the edge and turned half around, so as to face an open space between the spectators and the brink of the precipice. But just when we widened our circle to intercept a flank movement he took a flying leap into space, and fluttered rather than fell into the abyss below. His legs began to work like those of a swimming poodle-dog,

MOUNT PEROTE.

but quicker and quicker, while his tail, slightly elevated, spread out like a feather-fan. A rabbit of the same weight would have made the trip in about twelve seconds: the squirrel protracted it for more than half a minute. With utter disregard of the conventional laws of gravity the ratio of its descent *decreased*, till it appeared to hover in empty space, and alighted as easy as a skylark on its return from an aerial flight. The four-footed bird landed on a ledge of limestone, where we could see it plainly squat on its hind legs and smooth its ruffled plumage, after which it made for the creek with a flourish of its tail, took a good drink, and scampered away into the willow-thicket.

In leaping from a roof or tree a cat has to rely on the elasticity of its legs, which will not save it if the height exceeds a certain modicum, unless the ground below is soft or sloping; but a squirrel breaks the force of its fall in mid-air, using its tail and flat body as a parachute, for the common varieties, as well as the flying-squirrel proper, have an expansive skin joining the upper half of each leg to the body.

The children of the amorous village seemed rather disappointed at the result of their experiment, but it settled two points to my satisfaction . that squirrels cannot be killed by a fall, and that they must act some important part or other in the household of Nature, since their survival has been secured by such ample precautions. With the exception of the diving sea-gull, which can fly, swim, run, and stay under water for minutes together, hardly any other animal is so well protected against the contingencies of its trade as the fan-tailed rodent, that unites the agility of a monkey with the immunities of a bird, and supplements the winter-store-gathering providence of man by a faculty of intermittent hibernation.

Leaving the *camino real* to the right, we kept along the precipitous banks of the Rio Blanco, crossed it about ten miles above the convent, and again struck into the *piñal*, the coniferous region of the Tierra Fria, whose lower boundary rises in the coast-range to nine thousand feet, while the warm Gulf winds elevate the snow-line to thirteen or fourteen thousand, or about eight hundred feet above that of the central sierras. On northwestern slopes I noticed a slight frost on the grass, but the vegetation was less uniform than in latitudes of the same average temperature: mulberries, copper-beeches, chestnut-trees, and even magnolias, still mingled with the furs and hemlock pines, for the persistent invasion of semi-tropical germs from the neighboring Tierra Templada has here adapted some plants to the climate of Scotland which

PRECIPICE OF THE RIO BLANCO.

human art could hardly propagate in France or North Carolina. I have often thought that our attempts to acclimatize Southern trees and flowers would be more successful if we could procure our seeds from the forests of an equatorial mountain-region rather than from the borderlands of the temperate zone.

We passed a *venta*, a little wayside tavern, in the open forest where our trail crossed the Orizaba stage-road, but the *ventero* had nothing but pulque and bacon on hand, so we took dinner a few miles farther up, at the turpentine-distillery of Don Luiz Tacoma, where the shopkeeper of the casa sold us a bunch of plantains and a pailful of fresh milk, and where we witnessed another experiment with flying mammals. One of the overseers, who was taking his siesta on the porch of the shop, informed us that the proprietor had shipped six hundred barrels of turpentine to Matamoras this year, and could undersell the Yankees after realizing a handsome profit. He paid his laborers from two to three reals (twenty-five to thirty-seven cents) a day. "I am sorry that the superintendent isn't at home," said he; "he could show you a specimen of a curious sort of cannel coal which our workmen have found at different places in this neighborhood. It's jet black, and burns in chips, like sulphur; you can light it without any wood at all."

"You don't store your turpentine in a combustible building like that?" said I, pointing to a long wooden shed above the factory.

"No; that's the workmen's barracks: we have first-rate storage in a natural cave back there. All we had to do was to level the floor and fix a gate to the entrance. I haven't got the key, or I would show it to you."

"Ask that gentleman if he has ever seen a pitched bat fly," said the storekeeper.

"You are right. Look here, sir: have you ever tried to blind a bat and let him fly in daytime?"

"No: how do you do it?"

"I'll show you. Oh, Lorenzo!" he hailed one of his workmen: "tell that boy Lucas to get a couple of bats if he can climb the gate. Tell him to get two big ones, and bring the pitch-bucket here. That cave is just lined with them," he explained. "In winter-time you could gather them like grapes in a vineyard. In midsummer they are pretty scarce."

"Now, look here," said he when the boy returned with a pitch-keg and some things in his hat that looked like two pieces of flabby leather: "just notice the size of their eyes, —little black specks, that's all. What do you say now?" after anointing one of the victims with a spoonful of pitch-grease: "is there any earthly possibility now of this creature's seeing with his *eyes?* No more than if you'd chopped his head off. But now I'll show that he *can* see, after all."

We entered the shop, closed doors and windows, and flung the bat more than once against the ceiling. The third time he took wing, and began to navigate the air as steadily and knowingly as any bat or moth in the twilight of a summer day. He avoided the rafters, dodged the hams and fox-skins at the ceiling, and turned just before his wings touched the walls at either end of the building.

"That will do," said I. "I have heard something of the sort before, but I believe it now. They can see in a pitch-dark night as well as in daytime."

"Yes, but how?" said the overseer: "they don't do it with their eyes, that's one sure thing: it must be——"

"Witchcraft?" I suggested.

" No, but—what d'ye call it?—*instinto*" (instinct), said the overseer. " Yes, that's it: it must be *instinto*."

Indefinable words are useful in such cases, but I don't know if the " sixth sense" which Schwammerdam ascribes to birds of passage and carrier-pigeons is a much better explanation. I incline to the theory that the hidden sense or clairvoyance of bats is nothing but a very acute sense of feeling, that intimates the neighborhood of a solid obstacle before they come in actual contact with it. Sensitive persons walking in a dark corridor may notice that a sort of physical presentiment gives them timely warning if they are going to bump their head against a wall or pillar.

On the ridge of the San Rafael range we got a glimpse of the Val de Perote, with its yellow cornfields and sombre mango-forests. The famous fort was not in sight, but on two opposite hills, on either side of the camino real, the old commercial highway between Vera Cruz and the cities of the table-land, I distinguished the ruins of two ancient castles, La Fortaleza and Torres Negras, that bore a striking resemblance to the dismantled châteaux of Switzerland and Southern France. Among the adventurers that followed in the track of Cortés and Ojeda there were some enterprising hidalgos who hastened to fortify themselves on the hills of the New World, in the hope of reviving the age of feudal independence and romantic forays, and in the latter part of the sixteenth century New Spain could boast of some regular robber-knights—sans peur et sans *approche*—defying gods and men behind their inaccessible battlements. But they soon found that the alcaldes and friars sheared their flocks too close to leave much wool for extra-official clippers.

The last ten hours of our march had led us skyward at the rate of at least five hundred feet per mile, and an occasional chill, with a growing acceleration of the breathing process, reminded me that we had reached the region of high barometers and low thermometers, that tests the lungs of man and discovers the defects of his habiliments. Our Tuxpan converted his armhole scrape into a Scotch plaid, and I found that the upper buttons of my coat were not wholly expletive. To judge by the scale of arboreal vegetation, we were about eleven thousand feet above the level of the Gulf. The air of such altitudes is not difficult to breathe: on the contrary, it relieves asthma and pleuritic strictures. The trouble is, that it is not *filling* enough to supply the organic laboratory at the ordinary rate of respiration: it is air diluted with ether, and a lungful of it contains so little oxygen and hydrogen that the intervals of respiration have to be shortened. Hence the distress of diseased lungs, whose functions are already abnormally quickened, and cannot be further accelerated without overstraining their mechanism. The climate of the Tierra Fria, therefore, will counteract dyspepsia and all complaints that could be relieved by vigorous physical exercise, and it will almost certainly cure incipient pulmonary disorders, but it will prove quickly fatal to patients in an advanced stage of consumption

"This neighborhood used to have a bad name," observed José when we crossed a broad ravine which in the rainy season forms a tributary of the Rio Blanco. "The Orizaba stage-coach was robbed here a few years ago, and during the French occupation a troop of guerrillas, as they called themselves, had their headquarters in the outskirts of the piñal.—*Que novedades hay*" (what news?): "is the coast clear?" he hailed an old man who had hitched his mule at the roadside and seemed to be taking a rest at the foot of a gnarled mulberry-tree.

" *No hay nada*" (nothing stirring), replied the stranger. " Which way are you—— Halloo!" he interrupted himself, " where did you leave the rest of the boys, old chum?"

The guide stopped and stared. " Santa Virgen!" he burst out, " if that ain't my *tocayo* (namesake), my old tocayo, Don José Macán! Did you ever digest that dish of armadillo, Don José? Are we going to have another eating-match to-night?"

" You'll find out if you stop at my shanty to-night," laughed the old fellow. " I'll beat you at a squirrel-stew, with or without pepper, and give you odds besides. I take that gentleman for an umpire, and I hope he'll shoot you if you try to bribe him."

" Why—mi santissima!—you do not mean to say that you are still living in that same old trap, Don José?"

" Of course I do. Don't stand gaping there now, but *anda*—go ahead—or it will be another drawn game. *Anda, te digo*—just make that lazy Greaser move ahead, sir. I'll overtake you before you reach my place : it's more than four miles yet. You'll excuse me : I'm just mending my buckskin breeches."

" All right!" I laughed.

" Hurry up," the guide called back, " or we'll decide that match without you."

" Who is that ?" I inquired, when the mulberry-tree was out of sight.

" A trapper, an Irish heretic from Poland or England," said the guide, whose notions about the subdivisions of Anglo-Saxony were somewhat misty. " He used to belong to the harbor-police in Vera Cruz six years ago, but one night he disappeared, and has lived in the sierra ever since. They say *que se encaro al reves*—that he came across the wrong man, a detective, perhaps ; but *quien sabe?* It's no

concernment of ours. He is a *tigrero* now—a panther- and
bear-hunter—and the best hand we ever had in these parts

EL TIGRERO.

for catching such creatures alive : I know that the ring-
master of the Potosi arena paid him two hundred dollars
in a single year. Vermin are getting rather scarce in this
neighborhood, but he still lives on the old place, it seems,
alone with his dogs and pigs in the same shanty where I
saw him three years ago. *La Trampa*—the cage—they call
it, because it was first built for a bear-trap. We could
have camped more comfortably in a ravine near here, but
his trap is only two miles farther, and I guess he can sell
us provisions enough to take us through to Perote."

The hunter failed to overtake us, and we stopped repeatedly, doubtful if we might venture to enter the trampa
in the absence of the manager ; but on turning the flank
of a hill whose primitive vegetation was interspersed with
a few straggling apple-trees, we saw a thick black smoke
rise from a coppice at our feet.

13

"Let's hurry up," said José: "there is somebody at home, or the trampa must be on fire."

"Why, I declare! it's the old man himself!" he whispered when we reached a little clearing in front of the shanty. The mule, only half unsaddled, was hitched to a post, and his owner was sitting on his porch grinding corn or coffee in a little hand-mill.

"How on earth, or under the earth, did you get ahead of us?" laughed the guide, starting back as if he had seen a ghost.

The trapper put his mill down and leaned forward to shake my hand. "You came by way of the old limekiln, didn't you?" he inquired, without answering his tocayo's question.

"Yes, certainly: isn't that the right way?" said the guide.

"I thought so: just like a mule, following the trail he is used to, no matter if it's six miles out of the way. Didn't you see that the Perote *arrieros* had laid out a new road over the hill? You might have saved at least half a league. Well, make yourself comfortable," said he, "and excuse me a minute: I believe I hear my cow down in that bottom."

We slung our baggage to different harness-hooks on the porch, and put our terrier under a hen-coop, to propitiate a pack of obstreperous hounds at the rear of the shanty.

"He says we missed the right road: did we, José?"

"Nonsense!" growled the guide. "The truth is that he himself has taken a roundabout way and galloped ahead of us."

"Why?"

"I don't know, but I believe that the old chap is a little sensitive about strangers coming here unawares, before he has fixed things up a bit. He seems to have had a pretty

good education in some respects, but if his folks ever taught
him to handle a scrubbing-brush and a piece of soap he
must have forgotten all about it."

" Has he ever been married ?"

" No : that's just what's the matter with him, for what
can you expect of an old bachelor keeping house with a
litter of pigs? The miners in San Carlos used to tell some
tough stories about his place: they said that one of his dogs
died of a broken heart from having to live in such a pigsty.
He's a smart carpenter, though : he has enlarged his trap
considerably : this porch is new, and he has a good roof
now, I see."

LA TRAMPA.

The trampa was a rude log cabin, built around and into a
huge limestone bowlder, a vertical cleft in the rock having
been fashioned into a chimney, while a sort of rock-cellar

with a lattice door at the other end of the bowlder served the purpose of an outhouse.

"That's his larder," said José, "and he keeps it full. He's living pretty high for a hermit."

"What 'eating-match' was that you were quizzing him about?"

"Oh, he was beaten that time, but not fairly: they pitted him against a fellow who had an unnatural appetite, a regular hunger disease, that obliged him to stuff like a hog-tapir. My tocayo here had made a standing bet of fifty dollars that he could out-drink and out-eat any native Mexican at any kind of tipple or meat they might fetch along; and three years ago the miners heard about a strange Indian in the Pintado settlements who had been driven away from his native village on account of his appalling appetite. He could digest anything from a bushel of wild chestnuts to a roasted alligator; and when they found out that he could even go a broiled armadillo, it struck them that they might risk fifty dollars on such a champion, for if a man is in his natural condition an armadillo-steak works him like a dose of *arovano* (*nux vomica*), you know. So they procured half a bushel of horse-chestnuts and three fat armadillos, and asked your landsman if he would undertake to roast them as a supper for two, and stake his championship on the result.

"He said that he had never tried armadillo before, but that he was sure he could stand it if any native Mexican could. Well, sir, that night there were about sixty Indians around this shanty, and some twenty *Blancos*, the engineer of our blast-furnace acting as umpire and I as one of the seconds. The meat and things were weighed and portioned out on different dishes; and at first I thought the Indian was losing ground, but when my tocayo commenced on his second platter of steaks he turned about sixteen different colors and asked me to go down to the spring for a pitcher of cold water.

"I do not know what happened next, for just when I reached the spring I heard a fearful hurrah, and two minutes after the old man came tearing down the road like a cavalry horse, and the crowd was cheering and laughing like lunatics. The confusion was too great to get a sensible account of the last round: all I know is that they had got the fifty dollars. The next morning I came by here and found the door locked, but the old man was in bed, for I heard him grunt like a four-footer."

When the trapper returned with a pailful of milk we took supper on the porch, but after sundown the wind seemed to set from the direction of the Orizaba ice-fields, and drove us one by one into the interior of the trampa. The narrow chimney had the advantage of dividing the atmosphere of the shanty into a torrid and a temperate zone, so that the natives of different latitudes could select their favorite climate.

Don José M'Cann, the "vermin" exterminator of the Rio Blanco, was a countryman of the snake-destroying saint, but he had been more than sixteen years in the Western hemisphere, during which time he had passed over nearly every republic of North and Central America, and lost all traces of his Milesian descent, being in manners and appearance a perfect Mexican, and had almost forgotten his native language. He had been in California, Arkansas, and Texas, and preferred Western Arkansas to any other part of the United States, but not to the South Mexican highlands.

"A man who can rely on himself can be more independent here than anywhere else in the world," he said; "and if he's a hunter or a farmer he wouldn't be ruined by

competition. You could not find a better climate, either,—
too far south for a cold winter, and too high up for a warm
summer."

"Wouldn't you like the foot-hills better yet?" I inquired ; "with less snow and ice and more wild fruit?"

"I don't know, sir. The nights are rather chilly up
here, but the day-weather suits me exactly; and there's
one great advantage. you can *digest meat*, and the low-
landers can't, unless they content themselves with sparrow-
hawk rations. I could eat a roast boar every Friday, and
have as good an appetite as ever before the end of the week.
They call me a glutton and a drunkard, but since I have
lived up here I have never 'been sick longer than ten or
twelve hours. A man who had a mind to diet for his
health could outlive Old Nick in this sierra. A fellow
doesn't know what the next day may bring, but if I should
get seriously sick I would just lock my door and open the
windows, and rely on the mountain-air to do the rest, without any priest or doctor nosing round me."

"You are self-reliant in everything, it seems, but don't
you find it rather dull work,—in the long winter nights,
for instance ?"

The hermit picked a coal from the embers and lighted
his pipe. "No, sir," said he. "You wouldn't think so
if you had ever tried it for a winter or two. But an old
Mexican hunter asked me the other day if I wasn't *afraid*
to live alone; and that's nearer the point, though it seems
a foolish question to ask a man with two rifles and four
dogs, and no money hardly about him. Trusting yourself
with your own thoughts is just like going to an Indian
ball : a fellow may see more than he has bargained for.
There are things that never show themselves till you are
alone, but if you once make up your mind that there is

no harm in them, you find out that they are pretty good company."

"Well, I suppose a man may get used to lonesomeness as to anything else."

"Yes, but that's not what I mean, sir. He may get so 'used' to it that he will be sorry he didn't begin sooner. Have you ever been in the army, sir?"

"Why?"

"Because an old soldier would know from experience that I am right. If a man has to go on post it may rile him to be waked in his best sleep, but if he has been out for an hour or two, especially on picket-guard or in a dark, calm night, where he can dream with his eyes open, it's ten to one that he will be sorry to hear the relief come round: it's like being interrupted in a pleasant conversation. It makes time pass you don't know how, and much faster than before sunset, because in daytime a man can never be entirely alone."

"According to that, it would not interfere with your comfort if they should lock you up and keep you in solitary confinement?"

"Yes, it would: I like fried trout and open-air exercise. And, to say the truth, there is something else: a man wants to have a pet. It would make people happier if they all knew that, especially if they knew that it needn't be a human being. I'm better off with my dogs."

"At least if you count upon gratitude."

"Yes; and they ain't bad company, either. You have no idea how they get used to you if you are alone with them for weeks together: the worst of it is that it comes so awful hard on a fellow to lose a creature of that kind. I bought a fine Scotch deerhound in Baltimore in '66: I had him nearly eight years, and I tell you, sir, I felt like shooting myself when I lost him. The Greasers poisoned him, because he wouldn't let them come near my smoke-house at night. No square, straightforward poison either, for it took him a whole week to die: it just went through me like a knife to hear him whine, and perhaps I ought to have put him out of his misery, but I was thinking of all the scrapes we had helped each other out of,—we had frozen and starved together all over Texas and Arkansas,—and I couldn't kill him while there was a ghost of a chance of his pulling through."

The voice of the old rough became inarticulate at the recollection. He had spread the dog's couch at the side of his own bed, and patted his shaggy coat till he lay silent and motionless. But late in the evening, when the logs in the fireplace had almost flickered their last, the hound raised his head and placed it upon his master's arm, looked into his eyes and sank back dead,—like the last pressure of a human hand, "a 'farewell' mutely spoken, but not easy to forget."

My companions had ensconced themselves in a recess of the chimney-corner, and snored a quartet with two asthmatic pigs under the board floor of the shanty, and for a while I hesitated between the popular night-air superstition and a private antipathy or prejudice against heated dormitories; but after a look at the crowded floor I unbuckled my blanket-roll and spread my couch on the moonlit porch. The intermittent breath of the night-wind swelled or muffled the voice of a waterfall, and at larger intervals the silence of the upper piñal was broken by a sudden scream: it was the hour when the panther-cat descends from the crest of the hemlock-fir where she lurks during the day, and the pine-marten leaves its hidden nest to steal along the branches and surprise the slumbering birds. Our dogs

ignored such noises, but attested their watchfulness by a
sotto-voce growl when the lower valleys echoed the gallop
of a nocturnal rider,—perhaps a belated gambler or a minor
returning from the rancho of his dusky *amante*.

The next morning the mountains were shrouded with a
persistent fog, and our host accompanied us across the plateau to the brink of a declivity, where, in accordance with
his prediction, we emerged from the clouds into the sunshine
of the eastern slope.

"Well, compañeros, now you can't miss your road," said
he: "if you follow this creek you'll strike the camino at
the river. From there you can take the Perote trail across
the San Inez range; but if this fog should overtake you,
you had better follow the camino and stop at Mr. Urban's
place for supper. By the by, sir: there you can see the
benefit of mountain-air: he's a pretty old buck, but his
father is living in the same house, and if you go out in the
yard you can see his grandfather chopping cord-wood. He
does that every evening, and won't let anybody else come
near the wood-pile. His son is eighty-two, and he must
be at least twenty years older, but he still earns his rations
and shows them that he knows it if there are garbanzas for
dinner. And that's just the way I am going to live a century or two," he added. "In my younger days I had a
different plan, but this is the best: a man has to try a good
many dishes before he knows what really agrees with him"

"You wouldn't try any more armadillo-steaks, then?"
suggested his tocayo.

"Hush up, you *sanducho*, you skinny swamp-ape setting
up for a guide! I could just demoralize you with a single
kick. Good-by, sir," said he, "and don't forget that there
is freedom in the Tierra Fria if the crusaders down in
Potosi make things too hot for you."

The immunity of mountaineers from physical and political diseases may be referred to the same cause,—the ruggedness of their territory, which keeps invaders out and health in.   On level ground pedestrianism has to be pursued to a considerable length before it can rank with the health-giving exercises, but if it includes uphill work, it becomes a substitute for the most elaborate course of hygienic gymnastics, and the only reliable charm for exorcising the demon of dyspepsia.

Eastern Mexico, like the Atlantic slope of our own republic, is favored by a humid climate, which manifests itself in the variety and exuberance of the arboreal vegetation.   Near the junction of the Inez range with the Sierra de Perote our trail skirted the great Piñal de Loreto, a coniferous jungle of sixty or seventy leagues, whose thickets gave me an idea how many trees to the acre even a rocky soil can produce where the aggregated growth of centuries has never been touched by the earth-desolating axe.   There were no creepers, no brambles, and but little underbrush, but the pines stood so close together, and crowded their neighbors with such a maze of lower branches, that their visible interspaces extended rarely beyond a fourfold row of trees.   A flock of turkeys that crossed our road only twenty yards ahead of us vanished instantly, like rabbits in a quickset hedge, and, viewed from a ridge of higher ground at a horizontal distance of about half a mile, the single tree-tops could no longer be distinguished.

The neighboring Val de Loreto was the home of the Amozocs, a race of warlike Indians who committed inhuman cruelties among the settlers of the Tierra Templada, and after having been expelled from the lower valley took refuge in the thickets of the piñal, from which they made frequent raids into the next haciendas, and once even sacked the town of San Augustin, near Puebla. In 1812 the governor of Vera Cruz ordered a general *razzia* against these marauders, but it is said that a remnant of their tribe still lurks in the inaccessible mountain-jungles of the Rio Mesillo, and that hunters and miners have occasionally seen the smoke of their wigwams from the heights of the Sierra Madre. No government surveyor has ever carried his quadrant into this wilderness : like the swamps of Eastern Yucatan, the piñal is *pays de ninguno,*—nobody's land,—exempt from taxation, not included within the *comarca* limits of any State map, and never visited by custom-house spies and begging friars,—the abode of the puma, the pine-grouse, the bush-panther, and who knows of what other guests?

When we came unawares upon the cliffs of the eastern slope a black eagle shot out of the rocks at our feet, uttering a curious whoop, not unlike the coughing boom of the bull-bat, as they call a certain species of nighthawk in Northern Georgia. Though it seemed most unlikely to find unfledged eaglets at this time of the year, we clambered all over the cliff in the hope of discovering the nest, misled by repeated shrill squeaks and twitters, till we found that these sounds emanated from a heap of bowlders farther down, where a colony of *marmottos,* or mountain-weasels, had their burrows. These little mountaineers build themselves commodious nests, and fill them with nuts and grass-seeds at the approach of winter, but their domestic peace seems to be disturbed by chronic family feuds, perhaps in consequence of their polygamous habits, for the champion marmotto of each community keeps house with a whole harem of young females, after driving his rivals into remote bachelor holes.

I noticed that in descending the eastern slope the coniferous region is succeeded by a belt of nut-bearing trees, especially of the genus *Juglans,*—walnuts, pecans, and hick-

ories,—while in the West the corresponding altitudes
produce chiefly thorn-trees,—mesquites, hackberries, and
acacias,—besides different thorny shrubs. In regions of our
earth whose climate has been deteriorated by the outrages of
man upon the vegetable kingdom it seems that by a curious
by-law of Nature all larger plants become spinescent,
as if to protect them from the hand of their ruthless destroyer. From the dwarf cactus to the gigantic boudæx-
tree, the plants of the arid West are bristling with spikes
and thorns like vegetable hedgehogs, and the *palo verde*, a
shrub of the North Mexican desert, shows no leaves at all,
the green bark answering their purpose, but is covered from
the root up to the extremity of the smallest twig with an
armor of thickest, formidable spines.

The sun had disappeared behind a cloud-bank in the
southwest when we reached the camino real on the eastern
flank of the mountains that overhang the Val de Perote.
The ramparts of the Sierra Madre rise abruptly on either
side with a majestic sweep, barely allowing room for the
clambering pine-forests that fringe the crags at their feet,
and, viewed from a ravine of the opposite mountains, could
hardly be suspected of enclosing a more fertile valley than
the cloud-capped hills around the Andalusian Vega. But
from the brow of a hill about a league west of the castillo
a wide and magnificent view opens over the northern districts of the State of Vera Cruz and the beautiful valley of
Perote, with its lakes and shady haciendas. The horizon
is bounded by the Sierra de Loreto, once the stronghold of
the long-invincible Atuozacs, and the Peak of Perote, one
of the highest in Eastern Mexico, rises immediately on the
right. The town resembles a long straggling village, and
contains few buildings of more than one story, but the
fortress-hill that towers above the terraces of its southern

suburb like a huge Acropolis gives it an antique and, I might say, Oriental appearance.

The fortress of Perote used to be called the New Spanish Gibraltar, a comparison which only the isolation of the

VAL DE PEROTE AND THE OLD FORT.

mountain could justify, but the rock is certainly steeper and much higher than the *soi-disant* inexpugnable fortress of Ehrenbreitstein near Coblentz, and the southern declivity, from which a bridle-path closely resembling a staircase winds down to the valley below, could easily be made as inaccessible as the sheer precipices on all other sides. But the

ories,—while in the West the corresponding altitudes produce chiefly thorn-trees,—mesquites, hackberries, and acacias,—besides different thorny shrubs.   In regions of our earth whose climate has been deteriorated by the outrages of man upon the vegetable kingdom it seems that by a curious by-law of Nature all larger plants become spinescent, as if to protect them from the hand of their ruthless destroyer   From the dwarf cactus to the gigantic bombax-tree, the plants of the arid West are bristling with spikes and thorns like vegetable hedgehogs, and the *palo verde*, a shrub of the North Mexican desert, shows no leaves at all, the green bark answering their purpose, but is covered from the root up to the extremity of the smallest twig with an armor of thick-set, formidable spines.

The sun had disappeared behind a cloud-bank in the southwest when we reached the camino real on the eastern flank of the mountains that overhang the Val de Perote. The ramparts of the Sierra Madre rise abruptly on either side with a majestic sweep, barely allowing room for the clambering pine-forests that fringe the crags at their feet, and, viewed from a ravine of the opposite mountains, could hardly be suspected of enclosing a more fertile valley than the cloud-capped hills around the Andalusian Vega.   But from the brow of a hill about a league west of the castillo a wide and magnificent view opens over the northern districts of the State of Vera Cruz and the beautiful valley of Perote, with its lakes and shady haciendas.   The horizon is bounded by the Sierra de Loreto, once the stronghold of the long-invincible Amozoes, and the Peak of Perote, one of the highest in Eastern Mexico, rises immediately on the right.   The town resembles a long straggling village, and contains few buildings of more than one story, but the fortress-hill that towers above the terraces of its southern suburb like a huge Acropolis gives it an antique and, I might say, Oriental appearance.

The fortress of Perote used to be called the New Spanish Gibraltar, a comparison which only the isolation of the

VAL DE PEROTE AND THE OLD FORT.

mountain could justify, but the rock is certainly steeper and much higher than the *soi-disant* inexpugnable fortress of Ehrenbreitstein near Coblentz, and the southern declivity, from which a bridle-path closely resembling a staircase winds down to the valley below, could easily be made as inaccessible as the sheer precipices on all other sides. But the

construction of a new highway around the northern base of
the sierra made the *fortin a cornejal*,—a rook-tower, a fort
in the wilderness,—and in 1835 the arsenal, together with
a large part of the garrison (and even the name of El Castillo,—The Castle, *par excellence*), was transferred to the
Presidio de San Carlos, half a league northeast of Perote,
a clumsy quadrangle, whose proximity to the junction of
two principal highways should not have overruled the
strategic objections to its position in an open plain.

At present the old fortin is only used as a prison for
political culprits and soldiers of the regular army on trial
for capital offences.   It is the head-quarters of the *preboste
capitan*, the chief executioner of the Mexican army, and
from the activity of this official the Indians of the neighboring villages call the fort "La Matagente," the man-
slaughter-house.

On the ridge of the hill some merchants of Perote and
Vera Cruz have their summer residences, and their pleasure-gardens soften the aspect of the stern battlements with
a background of evergreen foliage.   The fort itself I recognized by the tricolor of the Mexican republic, though on a
meadow at the foot of the mountain we saw a similar and
larger flag, and behind it a body of men, which I took for
a brigade of soldiers drawn up in close marching-order.
But on crossing a viaduct over the ravine of a mountain-
creek I noticed that the uniforms of the supposed brigade
were largely mixed with serapes, and even with the white
rebosos, or head-shawls, of the Mexican matrons of the
upper classes.

"What is it?" I asked when we met a trooper who had
watered a couple of horses at the creek—"*que hay?* another execution?"

"No," said he; "only a foot-race.   Cardena's circus is

in town, and one of our *muchachos* has challenged their champion runner and wrestler. The *desafio* is for ten onzas (about one hundred and sixty dollars) a side, and they are just mowing a meadow for a race-course."

Enthusiasm is contagious. I had intended to dismiss my guide on the same evening, and take the stage-coach to Jalapa and Potosi, but we all stayed till the following morning to witness the result of the desafio.

The presence of a crack regiment of cavalry at Perote and their weekly prize-drills had fostered a spirit of gymnastic emulation, and the citizens had organized different rifle, race, and bull-ring "teams," which frequently tried conclusions with the matadores of the garrison. Two brothers of the neighboring village of Tresmontes, Luiz and Juan Vegos, had scored so many victories in these local contests that, like the Maccabees, they had come to think themselves invincible, and when the circus gymnasts tried to astonish the natives one of the brothers had the boldness to challenge the wrestler, Gil Rivas, an athlete of national reputation.

The desafio was threefold,—wrestling, running, and spear-throwing, a favorite game of the mounted lancers,—the victor in more than one match to claim the stakes; and by making interest with the umpire the Peroters had carried the shrewd proviso that the contest should begin with the foot-race.

The next morning was cloudy and disagreeably close, but the population of the comarca turned out *en masse* to see their champion put his head in the lion's mouth. The competitors seemed not fairly matched. Gil Rivas was a broad-shouldered, fine-looking gymnast, a native of the warlike border State of Nueva Leon: his rival was a mere *mozo*, a clean-built but slender lad of eighteen or twenty;

but the Peroters had conferred with a council of veteran strategists, and were resolved that the big frontiersman should not have it all his own way.

The benches of the circus, supplemented by barrels and planks, formed the stage, and after pacing the race-course

THE FOOT-RACE.

and choosing their sides the champions deposited their slippers at the umpire's stand and dashed off with a fair start, the mozo barefoot, the circus-man in his stocking feet. At the half-mile post the latter led by at least six yards, but after that the mozo redoubled his speed, and when they

passed the stake Don Rivas seemed to be a trifle behind.
But that might be on account of his fluttering scarf. The
goal-keeper pronounced it a *concurso*—a dead heat. The
same on the second trial: the mozo hung back for the first
four or five hundred yards, and then overtook his rival
without any visible effort. The third time he took the
lead, but relaxed on the home-stretch till his competitor all
but overtook him. Concurso again. Mr. Gil's comrades
looked glum: they began to suspect the mozo's stratagem;
but the fair Peroteñas, who were not in the secret, and the
garish belles of the circus, rose in groups, waved their
mantas, and cheered their respective favorites at the fourth
start.

"*Anda, Don Gil! Viva! viva!*" "*Anda, Juanito, por
mi amor, muchacho!*" they screamed, in intense excitement.

But Don Gil needed no such stimulus to do his utmost,
and Juanito could not afford to gratify his fair friends just
yet. His confidants chuckled behind their scrapes. Three
more heats resulted in concursos, till the athlete's white
jaqueta became gray with dust and perspiration, while his
rival's shirt and skull-cap looked as dry as his demure
countenance. The circus-men put their heads together, and,
seeing the umpire getting uneasy, the mozo's friends whispered a word in his ear when he returned to the stand the
next time.

At the seventh heat Juanito let the gymnast forge ahead
till the contest seemed decided, when he suddenly flung his
cap down, went away like the wind, and won the race by
four or five yards, though Don Gil, seeing him come, had
finished with a magnificent spurt in the hope of saving his
lead. Shouts and vivas rent the air, for all Perote now
saw what the sachems had known long ago,—that their

champion was dallying with his antagonist in order to exhaust his strength before the second match.

But the athlete had his revenge. After a rest of ten minutes and a glass or two of *pulque helado*, the men stood up to each other in front of the stage, and with a sudden dodge Don Gil caught the youngster round the waist, and was about to force him on his knees when the Peroters set up a general shout of foul play,—" *No esperó el señal!*" The circus-man had not waited for the proper signal, but grabbed his man unawares. The athlete grinned, and permitted his rival to regain his equilibrium, and then stood still, waiting for the *señal*. But Juanito was on his guard this time, evaded the waist-grip and disengaged his neck by screwing his head through, using his chin as a lever and his nape and occiput as a sliding fulcrum. After trying in vain to get a body-hold from below, Don Rivas changed his tactics and complicated his evolutions by feints and an aggressive use of his knees; but Master Juan could not be tripped, and repaid his adversary's thrusts by butting his stomach. During the first six rounds Rivas had no fair chance to bring his superior strength into play: the mozo's head proved untenable, and he obviated all attempts at his waist by a movement which French wrestlers call *jeu de à coude*,—elbow-parrying. His chin-and-nape trick seemed to answer a variety of emergencies, and he might have succeeded in protracting the match beyond the regulation time of forty minutes if his long impunity had not betrayed him into occasional offensive manœuvres. Stimulated by the applause of his countrymen, and perhaps by an injudicious suggestion of his second, he changed his position before the seventh round, and at the word " *Va!*" had his man round the leg, and attempted to trip him by jerking his foot up and throwing himself back with his full weight. Catch as catch can, strike where you please, but don't kick, is the rule of the Mexican wrestling-ring.

Don Gil seemed to yield, but in stumbling forward bore down upon his aggressor in a way that obliged him to clutch his arm in order to save himself from an underfall. In the next moment he had him round the waist, and, disengaging his right arm with a sudden wrench, he bent the mozo backward till his knee-joints gave way, and in spite of his desperate writhing and plunging the youngster was prostrated on his native soil in front of his black-eyed inamoratas.

That made them even, and the possession of the ten onzas now depended on the result of the third match—*echar lanzas*, javelin-throwing—an exercise which the six lancer regiments of the regular army and the use of the hunting-spear among the half-savage Indians have made very popular in Mexico. The target was the skull of a goat stuck on a short pole—distance, sixty yards. By agreement of the seconds the athlete used a short heavy spear of polished boxwood, while the mozo preferred the government regulation lance, which had won him weekly victories on the parade-ground of the castillo. Their proficiency in the use of these archaic implements would have won the applause of a Turkestan robber-knight and thrown Maurice Thompson into ecstasies.

The mozo's friends were confident of victory, and even his former rivals, the soldiers of the garrison, cheered uproariously when he knocked the target down at the first throw. But the frontiersman showed that he had not lived among the Comanches in vain, for at the end of the first two rounds each *lanzero* had scored one square hit and one "graze," and when the attendant *chulos* returned them their missiles the spectators leaped from their seats and crowded to the front with utter disregard of civil rights and female privileges. The ring-master vociferated, girls clambered on the shoulders of their gallants, and even the priests and foreign residents were in a state of fierce excitement. Juanito declined the first throw, so did his rival; but before the seconds had found their dice-box Don Gil had changed his mind and stepped to the front, spear in hand, with the sangfroid of an old stager.

His javelin touched but failed to stir the target, and the silence became breathless when the mozo squared himself for the decisive throw. He paused on hearing his name called: his second had seen his arm tremble, made his way through the crowd with a bottle of *aguardiente,* and offered him a glass *por darle firmeza*—to steady himself if his nerves should be in need of it. But Juanito, smarting under the sting of his late defeat, declined the offer with an impatient gesture, and again poised his lance. His hand trembled visibly, and once more his second challenged him, but before any one could interfere he leaned back and let drive.

The lance darted through the air with an audible whizz, a little too high, as it seemed, but coming down in a flat curve it struck the jawbone of the strange target fair and square. The skull spun round like a top, and when it fell the men of Perote rushed upon their champion like a crew of Sumatra pirates, snatched him up and dragged him away: regardless of his modest protests, of the shower of bouquets and the pouting of disappointed lips, they rushed him off to the rear of the circus-tent, where the manager had left a splendid roan stallion as security for the payment of the ten onzas, and amidst shouts that were echoed by the cliffs of the Sierra Madre they lifted him up and upon the horse, which, though wild with terror, could not stir a leg in the crowd that pressed around it in a compact mass. " Did he

like the horse? Would he prefer it to the cash?" The
owner valued it at twenty-five onzas, but the collection was
taken up in a minute, and the multitude surged back, drag-
ging horse and rider along till they stopped in front of the
stage, where they surrendered their victim to the mad mu-
chachas.

The population of Perote and Tresmontes was crowded
together within a space of forty yards around the stage—
merchants, muleteers, priests and soldiers—in a confused
mass, all shrieking and gesticulating like Donnybrookers,
laughing, bragging, and cheering, and shaking hands with
all the friends and relatives of the victor.

A troop of ragged Indians that had come from the mountains at the northern border of the comarca were standing
together in the rear rank, and the enthusiasm of the poor
devils gave me an idea what the rapture of gymnastic competition must have been in a country where every male adult
was an athlete at a time when men did not think it necessary to despise earthly things for the love of heaven.

The sages of that time inclined to the view that this world
has been created for its own sake—nay, that it might just
be possible to enjoy paradise on this side of the grave—and
our system of ethics takes alarm at the mere mention of such
heresies; but we have begun to rediscover a truth which
was familiar enough to those Nature-taught heathens—
namely, that the highest moral and physical well-being
cannot be attained separately, but must go hand in hand,
like thought and action, or will and force; and I hope that
the time will come when every school-house shall have its
gymnasium and every village its arena, for only then can we
celebrate our recovery from the Semitic pest, which has
turned our proudest forests into deserts and our noblest men
into monks. The ancient Greeks reckoned their dates from

the institution of the Olympic festivals, and their re-establishment would indeed mark a new era in the history of a world which had so long forgotten that God is the Creator of our bodies as well as of our souls.

What nation will inaugurate that revival?

CHAPTER VII.

THE VALLEY OF OAXACA.

Mariners who reach this strand
Will renounce their native land
TASSO *L'Orto d'Armida.*

THE most enviable homesteads on earth are generally
supposed to be the suburban villas of some Eastern capitals,
whose environs have been reclaimed by Nature, and thus
combine the peace and the verdure of a rustic solitude with
the opportunities of a great commercial metropolis, as the
gardens of Castellamare near Naples, or the Val d'Arno,
which Chateaubriand calls an "Arcadian faubourg, and for
the abode of an independent human being the most desira-
ble site." But that claim might be disputed by some of
the mountain-regions of our continent, which enjoy the
abundance of the tropics together with the immunities of a
higher latitude, and compensate their inhabitants for the
absence of a few artificial luxuries by a lavish and gratuitous supply of their daily natural wants.

The happiest situation of this kind is perhaps that of the
terrace-land which the agents of Maximilian selected for
the reservation of a Swiss colony on the heights of a plateau
that overlooks the incomparable Valley of Oaxaca. The
Rio Verde, which drains this valley, empties into the Pacific
near the upper isthmus of our continent. Eight hundred
miles northwest of torrid Panama the American mainland
contracts to one-fiftieth of its breadth between Baltimore
and San Francisco, and the traveller who disembarks at

FALLS OF THE RIO VERDE.

Alvarado, on the Gulf of Mexico, can reach the Pacific coast after a leisurely ride of two or three days. The climate, therefore, is insular, the sun of South Mexico tempered by the breezes of two oceans, while the excessive moisture is moderated by the elevation of the central plateau. West and southwest of the isthmus and along the spurs of the Sierra Madre the lowlands of Tehuantepec spread their swamps around, and the lower forty miles of the Rio Verde lead through the depths of a forest-region whose annual rainfall exceeds seventy inches, and whose exuberance of animal and vegetable life would make it a Garden of Avalon if mosquitoes and perennial thunderstorms were compatible with an abode of the blest; but within easy reach of this wonderland of tropical marvels and treasures the *Llanos Ventosos*, or "Wind Plains," of the Sierra de San Miguel rival the summer climate of the Maritime Alps, and derive their moisture-supply less from the clouds than from the dew of the cool, clear nights and the unfailing springs of the Central Sierra.

I crossed this region in the summer of 1876, in the midst of the rainy season, and was astonished at the contrast of the cloudless heights with the reeking atmosphere of the Tierra Caliente, whose mists and showers were even then confined to the lower two thousand feet, the undulating plains and the slopes of the foot-hills, while all above was serene and dry as an October day in the southern Apennines. From the cliffs of the Llanos Ventosos the wanderer looks down upon an ocean of clouds and driving fog, which boils up from a thousand valleys and far-stretching coast-forests, and often submerges the island-like summits of the foot-hills; but if the spray of the misty sea should sprinkle the rocks at his feet, he may ascend to higher and drier ground, as the rambler on a rocky beach retreats from the rising tide. Hazy white cloudlets drift over the surging fog, gloomy vapors bulge up from the jungles and stand like looming hills on the horizon, and in August and September this cloud-panorama seems often as immeasurable as the azure vault above, but its upper limits are always clearly defined, and while the sun remains above the horizon the peaks of the Sierra de San Miguel are rarely dimmed by a shadow.

Our steamer left Acapulco in a thick squall, and all along the coast from Cape Lopez to Tehuantepec the land was

veiled by a shroud of rain-clouds till toward sunset, when
the horizon partly cleared, and between the gray-green
coast-hills the vapor could be seen rising from the valleys
as the white steam from our boiler-valves; but far beyond
the coast, beyond the cloud-bank and beyond the horizon
itself, the blue heights of the Sierra Madre stood revealed
like the aerial forms of another world. When the setting
sun gilded their crests the effect was strange indeed—a
long-stretched, sombre fog-bank crowned with gleaming
pinnacles, mountain-capt clouds instead of cloud-capt mountains.

We reached the offing of Tehuantepec at ten o'clock on
the following morning, and, as the mail-skiff of our steamer
looked rather overloaded, I stayed behind and asked them
to engage a shore-yawl. The weather was oppressively
sultry, and when our engines ceased to puff we heard the
growl of an approaching thunderstorm. Before the boats
returned the coast wind spattered the deck with big drops
of rain, but my baggage was handed down as soon as the
yawl came alongside, and I had to follow. Two minutes
after, the squall broke upon us with a torrent of rain and
spray that drenched me to the skin in less than ten seconds.
Our outrigger was torn into shreds, the boatmen crouched
under the thwarts, denouncing the shortcomings of their
patron saint in the most unequivocal terms, and for more
than twenty minutes we were unable to face the storm. At
length, taking advantage of the varying wind, we readjusted
the remnants of our jib-sheet, and managed to reach the pier,
as wet as if we had come up from the bottom of the Pacific.

I went to the agency of the Tabasco mail-coach, and,
finding doors and shutters closed, inquired for the *alcalderia*,
the city mayor's office. My business being semi-official,
the deputy alcalde put his "house and services at my dis-

position," but warned me that I should have to prepare for some delay, as no conveyance of any kind had crossed the flooded Tierra Caliente for the last ten days, and there was no saying if the diligencia would resume its regular trips before the end of the month. But further inquiry elicited the fact that the Trans-Continental Stage Company still despatched a weekly coach from San Miguel in the Sierra Madre, which might possibly be reached by taking a coast-boat to Guatalco, from where the trails through the Tierra Caliente were less subaqueous than in the immediate neighborhood of Tehuantepec. I could not learn the precise day on which the stage would leave its present western terminus, but I preferred to wait in the Sierra Madre, where a delay of a few days would give me a long-desired opportunity of visiting the Swiss settlement near San Miguel. Guatalco is nothing but a wharf with a few abandoned harbor-sheds, so I was advised to engage a guide and carrier at Tehuantepec. The latter was soon found, but the few professional *caminadors* ("way-makers") of the little town confessed their ignorance of the Guatalco trail, and disinterested parties, as well as my landlord, assured me that I had better rent a week-room and wait for the next diligencia or mule-caravan than tempt the dangers of an unknown road in the worst week of the rainy season.

I was on the point of adopting their plan when I learned that a Swiss colonist, who had been involved in a suit before the probate court, was still boarding at one of the down-town posadas. He proved to be familiar with a quite practicable trail, and very anxious to return if he could come to terms with the authorities. It appeared that the son of a Swiss ranchero at San Miguel had been apprenticed to a Tehuantepec harness-saddler, and when, after the death of his father, his mother sent one of her neighbors to bring

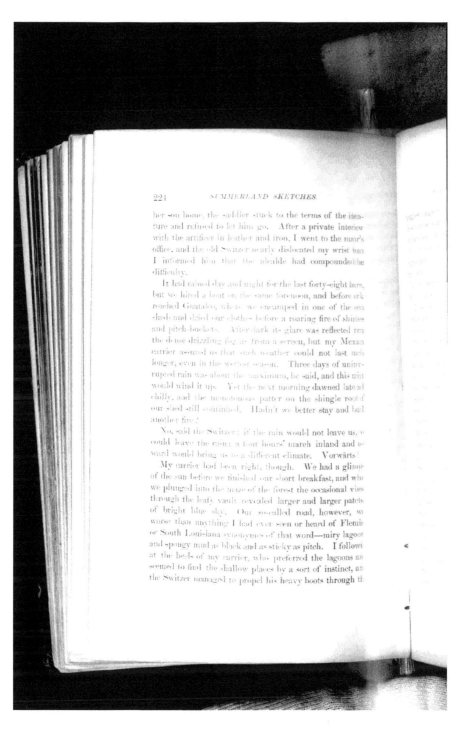

her son home, the saddler stuck to the terms of the inden-
ture and refused to let him go. After a private interview
with the artificer in leather and iron, I went to the man's
office, and the old Switzer nearly dislocated my wrist when
I informed him that the alcalde had compounded the
difficulty.

It had rained day and night for the last forty-eight hours,
but we hired a boat on the same forenoon, and before dark
reached Gnatalco, where we encamped in one of the corn
sheds and dried our clothes before a roaring fire of shingles
and pitch-buckets. After dark its glare was reflected from
the dense drizzling fog as from a screen, but my Mexican
carrier assured us that such weather could not last much
longer, even in the wettest season. Three days of uninter-
rupted rain was about the maximum, he said, and this one
would wind it up. Yet the next morning dawned late and
chilly, and the monotonous patter on the shingle roof of
our shed still continued. Hadn't we better stay and build
another fire?

No, said the Switzer; if the rain would not leave us, we
could leave the rain; a four hours' march inland and upward would bring us to a different climate. Vorwärts!

My carrier had been right, though. We had a glimpse
of the sun before we finished our short breakfast, and when
we plunged into the maze of the forest the occasional vistas
through the leafy vault revealed larger and larger patches
of bright blue sky. Our so-called road, however, was
worse than anything I had ever seen or heard of Flemish
or South Louisiana synonymes of that word—miry lagoons
and spongy mud as black and as sticky as pitch. I followed
at the heels of my carrier, who preferred the lagoons and
seemed to find the shallow places by a sort of instinct, and
the Switzer managed to propel his heavy boots through the

teghest quagmire; but his boy, after losing his shoes five
or six times, slung them across his shoulder and splashed
on barefoot. We kept through a comparatively open forest
of cottonwood- and tulip-trees, with a dense jungle on our
right-hand side, while on our left the land sloped toward
the bottom of the Rio Verde, which is here about five
hundred paces wide, and during the rainy season fills its
muddy banks to the brink.

These lower coast-forests abound in gigantic trees, whose
fruits are only accessible to the winged and four-handed
denizens of the forest, but farther up the river-shores are
lined for miles with a dense growth of wild-growing plantains, of which the natives distinguish four varieties under
as many different names. The fruit of the largest, the
cuernavacas ("cow-horns"), attains a weight of seven pounds,
and resembles in shape the crooked pod of the tamarind
rather than the cucumber-shaped little bananas which
reach our Northern markets. They ripen very slowly, and
often rot on the tree before they become eatable, but the
Mexicans cure them over a slow fire of embers and green
brushwood, after which their taste can hardly be distinguished from that of the finest yellow bananas. Palm-
trees mingle here with the massive stems of the cottonwoods,
talipot palms and the *palma prieta*, whose nut might become
a profitable article of export, having a close resemblance to
a filbert. The plum-clusters of the mango can only be
reached by a bold climber, as the trunk rises like a mast,
often perfectly free from branches for eighty or ninety feet,
and the chief beneficiaries of this region are still the macaws
and squirrel-monkeys; but farther up Pomona becomes
more condescending, and the ancient Gymnosophists, whose
religion restricted true believers to a diet of wild-growing
tree-fruits, would have found their fittest home in the

terrace-land between the lower twenty miles of the Rio
Verde and the foot-hills of the Sierra de San Miguel.
Plum-bearing bushes abound from June to September with
red, yellow, and wax-colored fruit; the mora, or wild mulberry-tree, literally covers the ground with its dark, honey-
sweet berries, the crown of the piño palm is loaded with
grape-like clusters, which, struck by a cudgel, discharge a
shower of rich acorn-shaped nuts; guavas, alligator-pears,
mamayos, chirimoyas, and wild oranges display flowers and
fruit at the same time, and under the alternate influence of
heat and moisture produce their perennial crops with unfailing regularity; the algarobe (*Mimosa siliqua*), a species
of mezquite not larger than an apple-tree, yields half a ton
of the edible pods known as carob-beans or St. John's
bread; the figs of the gigantic banyan-tree furnish an
aromatic syrup; the trunks of the *Robinia viridis* exude an
edible gum; and from the vine-tangle forming the vault
of the forest hang the bunches and clusters of forty or fifty
varieties of wild grapes, many of them superior to our
scuppernongs and catawbas, while the amber-colored *uva
real* rivals the flavor of the finest Damascene raisin-grapes.

A forced march of ten hours through fens and silent
virgin woods brought us at last to the hummock region:
the plain swelled into mounds and the currents of the sluggish bayous became more perceptible. The higher levels
showed vestiges of cultivation. we crossed dikes and ditches,
a neglected fence here and there; and where the larger trees
had been felled grapes and liana figs covered even the
bushes and hedges in incredible profusion. A troop of
capuchin-monkeys leaped from a low mango-tree, and two
stumbling youngsters who brought up the rear in the scramble for the high timber would have tempted us to a chase
if we had not been anxious to reach less malarious quarters

before night. The neighborhood of the great swamps still betrayed itself by that peculiar miasmatic odor which emanates from stagnant pools and decaying vegetable matter, and in the recesses of the forest fluttered the slate-colored swamp-moth, the ominous harbinger of the mosquito. The tipulary pests were getting ready for action: their skirmishers, the *sancudos* and *moscas negras*, had already opened the campaign, and became sensible as well as audible in spite of the rapidity of our march. One of the twilight species, the *mosca delgada*, a straw-colored little midge, bites like a fire-ant,—a mischievous, and, it seems, unpractical, freak of Nature, since the superfluous virulence of its sting must certainly interfere with the business facilities of a suctorial insect.

"Halloo! here is the corduroy road: we are near the Casa Blanca now," cried the boy, who trotted ahead of us wherever the thickets were not too cruelly matted.

"A hacienda, I suppose? Couldn't we get there before night?"

"Yes, a fine country-seat—Mr. Lacerda's place," said the senior Switzer: "there is land belonging to it all the way up to San Miguel. Still, I would advise you to give the casa a wide berth. The owner is on his last legs, dropsical and decrepit, and the place is now bossed by a set of scandalous shrews. Miss Nancy Lacerda and her mother were up in our village last year, and my uncle Fritz lodged them in his parlor and treated them to the best his place affords,—anyhow, never charged them a cent, I am sure,— and how do you think they paid us? By ridiculing his poor old Swiss jacket and slandering our girls for not wearing *rebosos*" (a veil-like head-dress). "Confound their tongues! No, no: I would rather sit in the stocks all night than trust myself in that den of venomous vixens."

Seeing I looked disappointed, "Never mind," said he, "I'll get you to a fine *trapiche*—a cotton-gin—before night: none of your tumbledown *remolinas*, but a mill with a strong roof and planed floors, all in good order except the machinery. It was built by a man from Texas, who bought land in this bottom twelve years ago, but was gone before we came here. 'The rancho of the crazy American,' they used to call the place. He couldn't agree with his neighbors, they say, and hedged his place in, threatening to shoot any one at sight who should dare to cross his fence. No doubt we should hear a different tale if we could see the man himself."

"No mosquitoes there, I hope?"

"No, not in the loft. That's the best of it; they never bother you in a high, open building, unless there are higher trees close by—maybe on account of the draught, for a good breeze blows them away like smoke, you know. The Greasers say they never go higher than twenty feet above the level ground, because the upper air belongs to St. Hubert, who does not tolerate witches and gnats in his department."

The evening mist rose from the saturated ground and the woods began to darken "*Dios mio!*" grunted the carrier, slapping his neck left and right: "*ya vienen*—we are in for it: here they come"

Yes, they were upon us. the nocturnal host of the Fly-god was in the field, and a humming cloud of invisible pursuers tracked our march like the ghost of a bloodhound. We kept on through bushes and brambles, across anthills and fallen trees, till the boy was getting blown and foot-sore, but when we tried to rest, sitting or standing, the whining falsetto of the little vampires increased rapidly to a fierce buzz that soon made us take to our heels again.

Our guide, who had pressed forward in silent haste, began to peer around in a way that made me a little uneasy till a full hour after sunset, when we stumbled upon a bramble-covered clearing, and a regular Appenzell view-halloo whoop reassured my mind: "Z'Gott, Herr Landsman, we found him! Now for the trapiche!"

The cotton-gin loomed at the farther end of the field, and was taken by storm over piles of muck and scattered fence-rails. Seeing no ladder, we clambered through the pivot-hole in the ceiling of a musty-smelling machine-shed, but in the open loft above we found a delicious breeze, and —St. Hubert be praised!—not a single mosquito.

The carrier threw himself upon his pack with a sigh of relief, and we squatted around the hatch to cool off before we opened our mess-bag.

From the hills on our right came the perfume of blooming tamarisks, and from the jungle below a cool lake air, and at times strange voices of the wilderness—the hoarse bark of a cayman, answered by the shriek of swamp-geese in the canebrakes of the Rio Verde, and in the distance now and then a queer rustling sound, like the shaking of a tree butted by some heavy animal. Bats were circling above our heads in the moonlight, and our advent seemed to have excited the curiosity of a troop of flying squirrels, who uttered their chirping squeak now on the roof, now in the branches of a neighboring live-oak tree. After removing a layer of seed cotton that might harbor scorpions or centipedes, I spread my blanket near the hatch and made myself comfortable for the night. My feet still smarted, though I had pulled off my stockings as well as my boots; yet I could not regret the hardships of a march which had brought us to such an encampment. The portador was taking his ease in the centre of the floor, where the night

15

wind played with his long hair, while the Swiss boy had
fallen asleep on the mantle of his countryman, who was
sitting in the open louvre, smoking his pipe in measureless
content. The air up here was delightfully cool, and with
the buzz of the legions of Beelzebub still ringing in our
ears the sense of security itself was more than a negative
comfort.

Baron Savarin, who wrote a treatise on the art of enjoy-
ing life, should have added a chapter on the happiness of
contrast A snug cottage in a stormy November night, a
shade-tree on the Llano Estacado, the silence of the upper
Alleghanies after a "revival-meeting" in the valleys, a bath
in the dog-days, would rank above all the luxuries of Paris
and Stamboul if unbought enjoyments could ever become
fashionable.

The moon set soon after midnight, but we managed to
readjust our luggage by the light of greased paper-spills,
and entered the gates of the foot-hills before the watch-call
of the nighthawk had been silenced by the réveille of the
iris-crows. A keen land-breeze, tumbling the mists through
the fens of the Tierra Caliente, gave promise of a bright
day. What wonderful perfumes the morning wind brews
from the atmosphere of a moist tropical forest-land!—
scents that haunt the memory more persistently than the
echo of a weird song. No latter-day nose could analyze
these odors and trace them to their several sources; but,
with or without an attempt at further classification, they
might be primarily divided into sweet, and pungent aromatic smells, the latter prevailing in the coast-jungles, the
former in the mountain-forests. A few of the first named,
the spicy scents, are so peculiar that, once identified, they
can be easily recognized: here, for instance, the effluvium
of the musk lianas, whose flowers diffuse a sort of odorous

diapason, which predominates even through the bouquet-medley of the South Mexican flora.

As the white streaks in the east assumed a yellowish tint, the paroquets in the crests of the piño palms saluted the morning with sudden screams; the multitudinous voices of a crow-swarm approached from the coast-forests; two and two, and in a series of pairs, the macaws came flying across the sky; and in our near neighborhood the startling cry of the *chachalaca*, or jungle-pheasant, went up from an hibiscus-thicket. Softly first, then louder and louder, the *calanda*, the mocking-bird of the tropics, intonated its morning hymn, and the fluting curlew rose from the grass like a skylark; but a sweeter sound to our ears was the murmuring of a little brook at the roadside: we had reached the region of rocks and swift-flowing waters.

Of reptiles, as of Red Republicans, it may be said that they are least dreaded in the countries where they most abound. While a New England boarding-school virgin goes into epileptic spasms at the aspect of a blindworm, the young Mexicanas surround themselves with a variety of ophidian pets, and view a freckled tree-snake and a gay butterfly with equal pleasure or equal unconcern. A little barefoot girl that met us on her way to the spring, put her toes caressingly on the smooth hide of a green-and-white speckled *vivora mansa* that wriggled across the road; and our barelegged portador kicked dozens of good-sized bush-snakes out of our path after noticing that they frightened our young travelling companion. More than ninety per cent. of all South American snakes are as harmless as lizards, and the four or five venomous varieties are well known and easily avoided.

I will here add a word on the dreaded venomous insects of the tropics. The ant and mosquito plagues of the coast-

JUNGLES OF THE RIO VERDE.

jungles can hardly be overestimated, but the virulence of their larger congeners is frequently and grossly exaggerated. The chief insect-ogres of sensation romancers and fireside travellers are three: the scorpion, the tarantula, and the centipede, either of whom can rival the homicidal prestige of Victor Hugo's octopus. But I may confidently appeal to the verdict of any personal observer who has passed a few years in the African or American tropics when I assert that these supposed express-messengers of Death are not more venomous, and are far less aggressive, than our common North American hornet. I doubt if the sting of

twenty tarantulas could cause the death of a healthy
child, and I am quite sure that a poison-ivy blister and
the bite of a fire-ant are more painful than the sting of a
centipede. An hysterical lady may succumb to the bite of
a common gadfly, but I hold that only *co-operative* insects
—termites, wasps, humblebees, etc.—could ever make away
with a normally-constituted human being.

A swarm of vociferous iris-crows appeared in the sky
overhead, and before they had passed the woods were wide
awake all around. The humming-birds were on the wing,
the wood-pigeons repeated their murmuring call in the
taxus-groves, and from the lower depths of the forest came
the chattering scream of a squirrel-monkey. The rising
sun was hidden by the tree-tops of the eastern valleys when
we halted on the summit of a rocky bluff, but the mountain-
mists had disappeared, and the vistas on our left afforded a
dazzling view of the sun-lit foot-hills and the valley of the
Rio Verde. The river is here crossed by a rope-ferry a
little above its junction with a tributary that drains the
glorious valley of Morillo and an Alpine group whose
wooded heights stand in my memory like a vision of Gana-
desha, the mountain-park of Indra's Paradise.

The air of these woodlands is the antithesis of our
Northern workshop atmosphere. There is a feeling of delight—our lost sixth sense, I am tempted to call it—which
gratifies the lungs rather than the olfactory organ if you
inhale the morning breezes, oxidated, and perhaps *ozonized*,
by the first influence of sunlight on the aromatic vegetation
of these hills—a delight which, like the charm of harmo-
nious sounds, reacts on the soul, and awakens emotions
which have lain dormant in the human breast since we
exchanged the air of our Summerland home for the dust
of our hyperborean tenement-prisons.

The hum of insects soon mingled with the bird-voices of our forest. To and fro, in fitful flight, flashed the *libellas*, the glitter-winged dragon-flies, and a few large papilios flopped lazily through the dew-drenched foliage. No gnats up here, but thousands of tiny, honey-seeking wasps and midges, and bright-winged grasshoppers that rose with a fluttering spring when the first sunbeams reached the damp underbrush. Ants hurried about their daily toil, and when we ascended the next ridge we saw various kinds of lizards flitting across the road or basking on the wayside rocks, one of them a sort of dwarf iguana, of a moss-green tint, on which protective color it seemed to rely for its safety, as its movements were as sluggish as those of a toad.

As we kept steadily uphill, the sun seemed to mount very rapidly, and, peak after peak, the summits of the upper sierra rose into view. Zempantepec, La Sirena, and the Nevado de Colcoyan towered above the rest, the latter at least four thousand feet above the snow-line. Few prospects on earth could efface the impression of that panorama. In the Sierra de San Miguel our continent reproduces the Syrian Lebanon on a grander scale. Septimus Severus, who vacillated between his throne and the Elysian valleys of Daphne, would have renounced the empire of the world for the mountain-gardens of the Val de Morillo, and the giants of the cypress forests on the southeastern slope of the sierra dwarf all the cedars of Bashan and Hebron. The largest, though not the tallest, of these trees, the cypress of Maria del Tule (twelve miles south of San Miguel), which Humboldt calls the "oldest vegetable monument of our globe," has a diameter of forty-two feet,* a circum-

---

* The celebrated "cypress of Montezuma," near the Mexican capital, measures only thirty-eight feet in *circumference*.—*Vide* Humboldt's "Views of Nature," p. 289, n. 12.

ference of one hundred and thirty-six feet near the ground
and of one hundred and four six feet higher up, and

CYPRESS OF MARIA DEL TULE.

measures two hundred and eighty-two feet between the ex-
tremities of two opposite branches. Yet this tree has many
rivals in the Val de Morillo and near the sources of the
Rio Verde, where groups of grayish-green mountain-firs
rise like hillocks above the surrounding vegetation.

On our right extended the orange-gardens of Casa
Blanca for two miles along the base of the hill to a deep
ravine, reappearing on the other side, where their white-
blooming tree-tops mingled with the copses of a banana-
plantation. Farther up, euphorbias and hibiscus prevailed,
and the upper limit of the foot-hills is marked by the paler
green of the cork-oak forests that cover the slopes of the
sierra proper. In the northeast this sierra becomes linked
with the ramifications of the central Cordilleras, and connected with our ridge by one of the densely-wooded spurs
that flank the plateau of the Llanos Ventosos. The rocks

at our feet belonged therefore to a mountain-chain that might be called a lineal continuation of the Gila range in Arizona and Nueva Leon. But what a difference in the climate and scenery! There, arid rocks and thorny ravines; here, dense mountain-forests, deep rivers, a saturated atmosphere, and springs on almost every acre of ground. The very brambles in the rock-clefts were fresh with dew, and the sprouts of the broomfurze looked like wildering asparagus. The ravines flamed with flowers of every size and every hue. An agent of a London or Hamburg curiosity-dealer might make his living here with a common butterfly-net. On any sunny forenoon an active boy could gather a stock of Lepidoptera that would create a bonanza sensation among the collectors of a North European capital: the rhododendron thickets of the upper Rio Verde are frequented by gigantic varieties of *Nymphalis, Vanessa,* and *Parnassius* which would retail in Brussels at from two to ten dollars apiece.

The sun rose higher, but not the thermometer, and when we clambered up through an orchard of scattered cherry-trees I am sure that the maximum temperature in the shade did not exceed sixty-five degrees Fahrenheit. We had reached the Llanos Ventosos, the air-plains of San Miguel, the playground of the four winds of heaven, where sun-strokes are unknown, though the mists of the rainy season never cloud their deep-blue sky. Down in the coast-jungles the Rain-fiend was at it again: dark-gray showers swept visibly along the shore, while the foot-hills simmered under the rays of a vertical sun. But up here the air was dry as well as cool: the edge of the plateau is at least six thousand feet above the level of the Pacific, which is in plain view from Punta Piedra to the downs of Tehuantepec.

We entered the village about two P.M., and my companions conducted me to a little frame house, where I was hospitably received by the Indian gardener and the daughters of Pastor Wenck, the minister of the Protestant part of the community, whose brother in Tehuantepec had entrusted me with different letters, with a note of introduction. The pastor had harnessed his mule an hour ago to get a load of Spanish moss from the foot-hills; so I left my carrier in charge of the Indian gardener and sauntered out into the village.

Neubern (New Bern) de San Miguel—or Villa Cresciente, as it was originally called from its situation on a crescent-shaped bluff—was founded in 1865 under the happiest auspices, the charter of the colony including such inducements as exemption from taxes for the first five years, free roads and schools, gratuitous seed-corn, farming implements, etc., to indigent immigrants, and attracted a considerable number of the very best agriculturists from Tyrol and Southern Switzerland. But after the collapse of the imperial government a waning moon would have been the fitter emblem of the Crescent Village: its privileges were abrogated, and many of the disappointed Bauern returned to their native countries. Still, the appointment of a few half-Indian officials is the only positive grievance of the colonists, and the advantages of their climate and situation might well reconcile them to greater inconveniences.

At a distance of only sixteen degrees from the equator, the average temperature of the coldest and warmest months differs less than spring and summer in the United States, so that the September weather of Geneva or Innspruck is here as perennial as a sea-fog in Newfoundland. During a residence of seven years Pastor Wenck has chronicled four thunderstorms, twenty-two common storms, two hoar-frosts (both in November), one sultry day, and two hundred and eight short showers, leaving a balance of two thousand two hundred and ninety-two days of *himmelswetter*—heaven-weather—as he called it, alternating with cool nights whose dew indemnifies the fields for the scantiness of the annual rainfall. Yet the denizens of this Himmel-land come in for a first-hand share of all the luxuries which a compensating Nature has lavished on the inhabitants of the sweltering Tierra Caliente.

Forty or fifty varieties of tropical fruits come to their tables in a freshness and sun-ripened sweetness quite unknown to our Northern markets; their builders may select their material from groves of mahogany, iron-wood, American ebony, greenheart, euphorbia, and other timber trees of the coast-swamps; cacao, vanilla, gums, and frankincense can be bought at half trade-prices, and an excursion of ten miles will take them to a region where the pot-hunter can fill his bag day after day without fear of ever exhausting the meat-supply, where the adventurous sportsman may try his luck and the mettle of his dogs, and where the naturalist can revel in all the wonders of a tropical terra incognita.

At six P.M. Pastor Wenck returned with a cargo of Spanish moss for mattresses and other domestic purposes, a bundle of broom-brush, and the following little extras: a rabbit, a six-pound cluster of yellow grapes, a handkerchief full of rare orchids, a rhinoceros-beetle, a lot of wild yams, and two swamp-turtles. He could have shot a batch of nest-pheasants, he said, if he had not been short of ammunition, for down in the foot-hills his dogs treed a young puma, and he exhausted his shot-pouch in a vain attempt to dislodge the little dodger. Venison was a drug in this market, he told me: his Indian neighbors frequently offered a fat *cimaron* (bighorn sheep), an agouti-antelope, or a brace of turkeys for the privilege of using his carpenter tools or hand-mill for a few minutes. Irish potatoes need a good deal of hoeing and artificial irrigation, and fetch four reals (forty-eight cents) per bushel, but most other vegetables are as cheap as whortleberries in a Georgia swamp. As all foreign residents agreed that pulmonary complaints are not only rare, but quite unknown, on the Llanos Ventosos, the following price-list may interest Northern invalids who would like to try the Sierra de San Miguel for a winter or two:

Rent, per month, of an unfurnished cottage at Neubern	10 reals	= $1 20
Indian boy of all work, per day	3 medios	= 18 cents
Saddle-horse, "	2 reals	= 24 "
Guide, "	4 "	= 48 "
Milk, per quart	1 medio	= 6 "
Eggs, per score	1 real	= 12 "
Pigeon-eggs, per score	1 medio	= 6 "
Butter, per pound	3 medios	= 18 "
Flour (wheat), per bushel	4 reals	= 48 "
Flour (maize)	1 real	= 12 "
Olive oil, per quart	3 medios	= 18 "
Calmet-seed oil, per quart .	1 medio	= 6 "
Mutton, per pound	1 "	= 6 "
Rabbits, per half score	4 reals	= 48 "
Pigeons, " "	3 "	= 36 "
Turkeys, apiece	3 medios	= 18 "
Pheasants, "	1 real	= 12 "
Brown beans, per bushel	3 medios	= 18 "
Lentils, "	5 reals	= 60 "
Sweet potatoes, " .	3 medios	= 18 "
Brown sugar, per pound	1 medio	= 6 "
Mangos (large plums), per bushel	5 medios	= 30 "
Grapes, best quality, "	5 "	= 30 "
Oranges, "	3 reals	= 36 "
Bananas, best, "	3 medios	= 18 "
Honey, per pound	1 medio	= 6 "

The Valley of Oaxaca abounds in game; red deer, elk, otters, turkeys, and pheasants can always be met in their favorite haunts, panthers, pumas, and three varieties of bears frequent the jungles; and perfectly wild black cattle, shyer than deer, are occasionally seen in the forests of the foot-hills. Still-hunting and *emboscados*—lying in ambush near the springs and salt-licks—are the favorite methods; the great difficulty with hounds, besides the thickness of the jungles, being the abundance of *vermin*, as an Arkansas hunter would say—of small quadrupeds whose scent confuses all but the veteran finders. Mr. Wenck had a couple of acclimatized deerhounds that would track a panther even through the thickets of the Tierra Caliente and follow a deer for days; but the scent of a capuchin-monkey never fails to throw them out: the peculiar rank odor of a *gato pardo*, or palm-cat, seems also to have an irresistible attraction for canine nostrils.

A species of stout chickenhawk is trained by the Oaxaca Indians as falcons, and the hamlet of Villarica, near Amatlan, is famous for its bird-fanciers, among whom the "gentil craft of gerfalconry" has been handed down, with all its mysteries and by-laws, perhaps from the retainers of one of the Spanish robber-knights who infested these mountains in the sixteenth century. They train them to catch pheasants and woodcocks, and even *gazapos*, or mule-ear rabbits, on the upper table-lands; and Mr. Wenck told me about a half-breed falconer of the neighboring village of Las Tunas who, with the aid of two co-operating hawks, once filled an order for a dozen parrots in a single forenoon. His birds captured nine macaws and twenty-two paroquets, nineteen of them "rough-caught"—*i.e.* torn into pieces—but of the rest seven were apparently uninjured, and five at least in a salable condition.

INDIAN FALCONER.

I was obliged to decline the invitation of an American speculator who had purchased a promising silver-mine in the upper sierra, and wanted to show me his new hydraulic rock-blaster; but Mr. Wenck insisted that I must stay till the next evening and see the festival of Santa Lucia at the neighboring Dominican convent of Las Tunas.

The following morning my Swiss travelling-companion from Tehuantepec lent me his saddle-horse, and the pastor managed to pack his family of six children, together with sundry baskets and boxes, into a two-wheeled cart padded and cushioned with hay; and, leaving the house in charge of the Indian gardener, we proceeded in a northeasterly direction on a tolerably good country road. After the village there was a long, gradual ascent of about a league, with the deep valley of the Rio Verde constantly in view on our left, while the rising hills on our right were covered with woods and orchards. Wherever we passed a clearing we got a glimpse of the snow-capped sierras in the northeast, and now and then of a glittering double peak a little farther south, somewhere in the central sierras of Guatemala. After an hour or two of slow riding and lively talk, Mr. Wenck drew up on a level plateau where the road turned sharply to the left and downhill.

"If my eldest son shows any turn for business," said he, "I shall buy him this land and a silk-culture outfit. There are whole forests of wild-growing mulberry-trees in the valleys all around, and with the summer climate of Southern France it would be strange if we could not raise all the silkworms we want. Labor is cheaper here than in Languedoc, where food and winter-houses are a heavy additional expense. In New Orleans raw silk brings five dollars a pound: here I do not think that the producer's expenses, including transportation to Vera Cruz, would amount to fifty cents. I have a mind to try it myself if I should ever resign my charge."

"So you have not lost faith in the prospects of the colony?" I asked.

"No, but I should stay for better or worse," said he. "My relations in Lucerne want me to come home, but I know that even in the valley of the Engadine I should be haunted by a homesickness after this Switzerland of the tropics."

We stopped for dinner at Las Cascadas, the country-seat of Captain Remely, a Tehuantepec merchant of German descent. The house, built in 1810 by the Spanish governor of Oaxaca, is charmingly situated near the lower falls of the Rio Verde, and the present proprietor has turned a portion of the old orchard into a botanical garden, with a little Zoo, whose inhabitants, with few exceptions, run at large like domesticated animals.

The irregular groups of tropical trees and flower-bushes gave the garden a park-like appearance. There were huge old taxus-trees, whose hollow branches were garrisoned by swarms of paroquets: orange-groves, where sloths and squirrel-monkeys could get free luncheon at all hours of the day; and a great variety of palms, many of which my Swiss cicerone could only distinguish under their Spanish names. The trunks of different tall cocoanut-trees were almost overloaded with a tangle of luxuriant grapevines, that hung like a mantle from a height of sixty feet to the ground; and it struck me that viticulture would be as profitable as the silk business in this valley.

"It has never been tried," said Mr. Wenck. "The natives get all the fresh grapes they want out in the woods, and only few of them are enterprising enough to sell them in the form of raisins. They do not care much for grapes, anyhow."

"Don't they drink any wine?"

"Not often: they have other tipples. There is a disgusting kind of poison-herb growing in the swamps,— *cicuta* they call it, a sort of water-hemlock,—and a simple decoction of a handful of the fresh leaves is enough to intoxicate the toughest toper. If you try it for the first time, a spoonful is enough to make you seasick, and a glassful might kill you; but they, somehow, get used to it, and prefer it to rum and pulque. I have often thought that *any* poison may become a 'second nature' and a 'tonic;' and if a man must needs stimulate himself, he might as well get his tipple in the next poison-swamp, instead of buying it across the counter."

At least an inexpensive way of going to pot; but, like opium, *cicuta* seems to have the further advantage of inducing a peaceful kind of delirium, while hashish and alcohol affect the temper as well as the senses.

The zoological department of the park comprised nearly all the felines and quadrumana of Southern Mexico, besides birds and a variety of reptiles and curious rodents. If Mr. Remely's captives objected to their treatment, they showed a strange want of enterprise, for the ring-fence that enclosed the park was low and full of loopholes; but I suspect that a congenial climate and a liberal food-supply would reconcile most wild animals to a smaller and less agreeable prison than a forty-acre lot of woods and orchards.

DON CARL'S PETS.

They seemed, indeed, to have made themselves at home, agile squirrels, as well as sluggish water-hogs and defence-less monkeys, not less than the larger carnivora. A coyote bitch suckled her litter of black-muzzled puppies under a bush close to the main gravel-path, and the capuchin-monkeys had multiplied till many of the young ones had to be drowned like supernumerary kittens. Mr. Remely's eldest son, a poor cripple of nineteen or twenty years, was

at present the only Caucasian inhabitant of the casa, and
could not enter the park in daylight without becoming the
centre of an excited group of four-handers and reptiles.
They wound around his crutch, clung to his legs, and
often impeded his progress so effectually that he had to
surrender at discretion, and wait on the next garden-bench
till the *monos chicos* had filched the last nut from his
pockets and the bear had satisfied himself that there would
be no meat for supper this evening. A young boa wound
around his waist when he showed me the she-bear's den,
and seemed to enjoy the warmth of his under-garments
like a nest-squirrel. But an old armadillo on a bundle of
reeds in the corner rolled himself up at our approach, and
contracted his body with the tenacity of a hedgehog.

"We have had this chap more than four years," said
Don Carl, "but I do not know if you will believe me if I
tell you that nobody ever saw him eat yet. The carrots
we leave near his couch disappear and his excrements ac-
cumulate periodically, so we know that he *does* eat; but,
like a grand Brahman, he conceals the act from all mortal
eyes. I believe he would starve to death if you would sit
up with a lantern and watch him."

Besides the capuchin- and squirrel-monkeys and a few
good-sized *sapajous* (*Ateles paniscus*), they had a large
coaita, or spider-monkey, from Guatemala, who seemed to
prefer the society of man to that of his hairier Darwinian
brethren. He approached us like a mendicant with outstretched paw: the gardener, Don Carl told me, had taught
him to shake hands, and his notions of the efficacy of that
function were somewhat transcendental. Being a native of
the lower tropics, he was rather sensitive to cold, and on
rainy winter mornings used to crouch under the gateway
and shake hands with all visitors, as if to solicit their in-

terference in the obnoxious meteorological proceedings.
On the roof of a tool-shed we found a good-natured little
sloth, who permitted me to tickle his neck and turned over
on his back like a playful puppy, parrying my fingers with
his long claws. A sloth is indeed rather awkward than
sluggish · the peculiar formation of his limbs makes him
almost helpless on level ground, but on his native trees he
is active enough for all practical purposes, and an old cinnamon bear is a much fitter emblem of laziness. The one
in Mr. Remely's park used to squat at the foot of a shady
copper beech, embrace the trunk with his fore paws, and,
pressing his forehead against a projecting root, remain immovable for hours together, brooding over dreamy me-
mentos of the Tierra Fria, whose temperature enabled him
to prolong such blissful torpors for weeks and months.

Don Carl's gardener introduced me to an interesting little
pet, a gray lynx, with restless yellow eyes and an evident
penchant for practical jokes. They kept him in the open
tool-shed, and as we entered he turned his head with a
sudden interest in the construction of a patent lawn-mower
behind his couch. But as I approached, his right paw
stole out from under the hay, he humped his back and with
an abrupt spring alighted on my breast and had his paws
around my neck in a minute. The guffaw of the old Prussian guaranteed the peaceful intentions of my interviewer,
who cocked his head, and, with his left ear touching my
chin, eyed me in a serio-comical way that almost upset me
with laughing before I could get rid of him.

"I wonder how you can keep this little bouncer away
from your chickens and things," said I when I recovered
my breath, "if you leave his door open?"

"God have mercy upon any of them if they touch my
chickens!" said the Prussian. "No, sir: I'm pretty safe

as far as that's concerned: they know I would skin them alive. We had a young pointer pup that got into the garden once in a while, and used to worry the pheasants, but I cured him in just twenty-four hours."

" What did you do to him ?"

" Well, sir, I caught him on top of a lame old cock-pheasant that I meant to kill anyhow; so, instead of whipping the dog, I opened his jaws and crammed the cock in as far as I could, and then tied a twelve-yard wash-line around his muzzle, bird and all. With the rope I had left I tied his four legs into a bunch and threw him out in the hot sun. Chawing the bird only made matters worse for him, for he bit through into its bowels, and with that mess in his mouth he had to lie in the broiling sun for full eight hours, all night and four hours the next morning, till I released him a little before noon. I do not think he will forget the day of the month. The mere sight of a pheasant sets him galloping as if the devil were at his heels. I once caught old Mr. Cinnamon nosing around a pen where we kept a litter of young water-hogs, but I cured him by sticking a pitchfork into his ribs whenever he came within ten yards of that pen."

" No wonder you can ' cure' them, if you have a list of such remedies."

" Yes, sir, you can break the most obstinate brutes of almost anything if you just show them that you are in downright earnest. I wasn't here two weeks before they found out who was ringmaster of this circus. I can break them of all their bad habits—with one single exception, so far as I know: no human power or ingenuity can cure a capuchin-monkey of squealing if you take hold of him I tried it, and gave it up after killing about fifteen of them."

"You did? They had reasons for squealing, then, I should say."

"Yes, but I tried them with fair means too—coaxed them, fondled them, let them starve and came up with my hands full of tidbits,—all no use. they licked their chops, but the moment I touched their starved carcasses the squealing began. I grabbed some of them and choked them till their eyes and tongues started out of their heads, but the minute they got wind enough they used it for squealing instead of breathing. There was no doubt of it that they did know what I choked them for, but they would rather die than live and not squeal."

"Don't you think an animal's bite is dangerous if you torment it that way?"

"Not a monkey's, sir; but carnivorous brutes can give you a dose of gangrene with a mere scratch. I think it's the putrid flesh and stuff sticking to their claws and poisoning your blood if they just rip your skin. But monkeys are subject to hydrophobia, it seems We had a case of that kind a year ago with the mate of our big spider-monkey. She was the best-natured creature in the lot, but one morning she went tearing around the park like a wild-cat. It was some kind of a fit, we thought, but when we were at dinner in the casa she rushed into the room and upon my little poodle-dog, and bit him to death in less than a minute. It struck us then that she must be mad; and I can tell you, sir, I wished that there had been more than one door to that room or no wire-screen at the windows. She was crouching in the open door, ready to spring, and we had no gun handy, and hardly knew what to do. Don Carl turned as white as chalk, but didn't say a word, and I was satisfied as long as he would not ask me to put that monkey out. We saw then that Greasers are

not all cowards. Our old mestizo woodchopper went around
the table and got a cider-jug in the opposite corner, swung
it up and walked towards the door with his teeth set. The
monkey did not seem to like his looks, and drew back a
little, maybe to brace herself for a spring; but in the next
second the jug came down like an axe, and we had to own
our mistake if we had thought that hydrophobia was incurable. Don Carl was puzzled for a new set of skull-
bones when he tried to stuff that monkey."

LIMESTONE CAVES OF THE
SIERRA HONDA.

There were four half-
grown panthers and five
very young pumas, who had all been captured in the rocks
of the Sierra Honda, whose limestone caves seem, indeed,
to be used as a lying-in establishment by all the female
carnivora of the isthmus mountains. The cavernous limestone crops out in a massive stratum at the head-waters of
the Tehuantepec River, and follows the ridge of the sierra
for more than twenty leagues to its junction with the east-

ern Cordilleras. The whole intermediate mountain-range abounds with unexplored caves, and must be actually honey-combed, if we are to believe the Indian tradition of a hidden passage from Amatlan to Villalta, on the eastern slope, by a continuous rock-tunnel, in whose lateral ramifications the satraps of Montezuma concealed their treasures when the Spaniards overran the province of Tehuantepec.

About four P M. we remounted, and reached the convent of Las Tunas an hour before sunset. At least two hundred horses were haltered outside in a row, and, seeing nothing but strange faces, Mr. Wenck drove through the lodge-gate in the hope of meeting one of his village Indians or finding a place for his mule in the convent stables. The gate-posts, the veranda, and many trees were decorated with flags and huge bouquets in honor of Santa Lucia, the convent's patron saint and a far-famed adjutor of orthodox invalids. The *funcion* was an annual festival, and it was hoped that the liberality of the visitors would this time meet the expenses of a new corona and chaplet, of which, as a placard near the contribution-box informed us, the saint was in pressing need. A continual low tolling of the bells seemed to ring out a standing invitation to the faithful, who, indeed, had answered the summons in numbers which must have been swelled by quotas from different adjoining counties.

The convent park was crowded with devotees and sight-seers; the squaws of the Indian villages had mustered for dress-parade, and noisy swarms of children on the grass and in the trees gave the funcion somewhat of the mirth of a Sunday-school picnic. My padre Abad had squeezed his ample proportions into a garden-chair under a magnolia-tree that rose from the centre of a round table as from a flower-pot, and the shade of the lawn, with its hillocks of

fresh-mown hay and sprawling friars, seemed here so inviting to our mule that she came to a full stop. Before
we could set her agoing the hospitable Dominicans had removed the tail-board of our cart, deposited our baskets and
buckets on the table and our youngsters on the garden-
bench. When I rejoined them after a stroll through the
park one of the padres had buttonholed Mr. Wenck about
the loan of an Appenzell rooster which he wished to enter
at the next Mitla cocking-main, while the abbot helped the
children of the heretical parson to open their lunch-basket
and trotted one of the flaxen-haired girls on his knee. He
complimented the pastor on the purity of his Spanish pronunciation,—*muy singular por un estranjero*, quite unique
in a foreigner,—urged him to address the assembly, pre-
tending to scout his objections, and between his arguments
flirted with the young lady on his knee till she boxed his
ears. But when her little brother provoked a jeremiad
from paterfamilias by dropping the semi-fluid contents of
the butter-bowl on his coat, the old celibatist grinned, and
a sly twinkle of his roguish eyes made me fear that he
meditated a mischievous sally. The physiognomy of his
nose betrayed a penchant for sarcasm, and the opportunity
to indulge it might seem tempting, if not even recommended
by a sense of duty. But presently the grin gave way to
a good-natured smile: he had concluded to forbear—no
sufficient inducements to spoil an evening like this.

They expected a popular preacher from Mitla this evening, but in the mean while the assembly was indulged in a
soirée dansante and musical exercises, in which even the
choir-boys were permitted to join on condition that the
dances must be confined to *rondas*—strictly decorous roun-
delays. Near the chapel, now ablaze with flowers and
flounces, the father kitchen-master had a little pavilion,

where he dispensed iced orangeade and *dulces* at a penny a plate, and retailed a lot of splendid grapes for a mere song —often in the literal sense, for the choir-boys repeatedly filled their hats without asking his permission.

Some of the *mozos* outside fired off their musquetoons, and when the moonlight broke through the tree-tops a troop of Indians from Amatlan mounted the veranda and formed a semicircle to make room for a *gitana*, a female vocalist, who stepped to the front and sang "La Virgen del Pilar" in a ringing contralto and with such electrifying pathos that almost at the first notes the chatter was hushed all around and the monks rose and stared at her in amazement and admiration. An officious usher slipped around to obviate noisy demonstrations, but the applause could not be wholly suppressed, and if she had repeated the song the canonized queen of the festival might have found a dangerous rival.

A simple *hacha azul*—a blue torchlight fed with alum and odorous gum—sufficed, however, to attract a large part of the crowd to the opposite end of the park, and near the lodge-gate the young bucks thronged around a "wigwam swing," a stout rope terminating about eight feet from the ground in a bunch of rings which could only be reached by a lucky jump; but after four or five athletes had got a good hand-hold the light-weight champions clung to their legs, and the bundle of yelling aeronauts was set agog by means of a drag-rope He who let go first had either to pay a fine of a penny or assist in swinging the next batch. When one of the bundles had dropped from simultaneous exhaustion, a young Catalan Hercules, the shepherd of the convent farm, caught the two bottom rings at the first jump, and offered a bet that he would hold as many men as could hang on to his legs and arms directly or by proxy, with the

THE WIGWAM SWING.

sole proviso that the padre Vicario, a monastic Falstaff, should be made to keep his hands off.

The convent church stands at the very edge of the plateau, and from the lodge of the gatekeeper we could see the lights of the city of Oaxaca, and farther back the long-stretched cloud-belt of the Tierra Caliente, illuminated now and then by a flash of sheet-lightning. But the peaks of Colula on our left were glittering cold and clear in the pale moonlight, and the zenith of our own table-land was as cloudless as ever. In the intervals of the coast-lightnings only the faint forest-perfume of the night wind suggested the neighborhood of an ocean of tropical vegetation.

Torches and Chinese lanterns were now lighted in the park and around the terrace of the main building, where the choralists had assembled after surrendering their pavilion to the lady visitors. The presence of a number of well-dressed mozos from Chimaltepec proved that the popularity of the patron saint was not confined by the comarca limits; and, to judge by their frequent visits to the contribution-box, Santa Lucia's chances for a new head-dress began to brighten. But when the choir was reinforced by a guitar-player from Amatlan, the enthusiasm of her devotees became a trifle secular, and if the expected preacher had called the meeting to order just then the vanity of all earthly things would have been a rather unpopular text. Nobody inter-fered . the abbot himself clicked his plate like a castanet, and averted his attention with the utmost bonhomie if an unmindful dancer happened to pass the boundary between ronda and fandango by a step or two.

The true Semitic *askesis* can flourish only in a desert country, where the idea of a better world to come is within reach of our imagination, and where it is less difficult to renounce an earth which, after all, might be—our only chance. But here the very monks declined the risk of the experiment. The "vale-of-tears" theory is untenable in the Valley of Oaxaca.

CHAPTER VIII.

THE DELTA OF THE SUMASINTA RIVER.

Here they are free here they find shelter-places,
Beyond the reach of their remorseless foe.
RÜCKERT *The Children of Nature*

On the eastern slope of Mount Atlas there is a valley which for many centuries has been the freehold of the Beni Hammadin, a tribe of independent Arabs who boast that Allah has built up their mountain-ramparts for the special purpose of protecting their liberty against the ambition of the padishah. Perhaps they are right, for it really seems as if Providence had taken precautionary measures against all plans of universal empire, since even the power of man over the brute creation has been restricted within liberal but probably unalterable boundaries. Earth will never be all enslaved No diver has yet invaded the algæ-pastures of the northernmost ocean, and no hunters will ever follow the white bear to the Ultima Thule of his arctic domain nor molest his black brother in the depth of the tropical coast-jungles.

In the swamps of Maine and Oregon, whose lagoons are alternately bridged by frost and evaporated by midsummer droughts, snakes and bears might be permanently exterminated; but in Florida an enterprise of that kind would require a Chinaman's patience, combined with super-Yankee ingenuity; and in Southern Mexico even Orion and St.

Patrick would prefer day-wages to a job contract   Travellers, for instance, who have visited the State of Tabasco, southeast of Vera Cruz, will admit that the difficulty of detecting the proverbial needle in a haystack would be mere child's play compared with the problem of discovering a fugitive wild animal in the fens that skirt the Rio Zelades or the Great Sumasinta, whose delta can only be crossed by water-ways, the shore-thickets being absolutely impervious to man and all his locomotive contrivances.

The Sumasinta, or Usamasinta—the shoreless river, as it may be called in the lower sixty miles of its course through the Tierra Caliente—was formerly the great highway between the southwestern Gulf coast and the Pacific slope of South Mexico and Guatemala, but the weekly steamers from Panama to Vera Cruz have made that circuitous route the quicker as well as the cheaper one, and the traffic of Northern Yucatan has found new harbors in Sisal and Campeche   For travellers from Palenque or San Carlos to Southern Yucatan, however, the old Sumasinta mail-barge is still Hobson's choice, and from Guatemala to San Carlos nearly so, the alternative being a canoe-trip with Indian oarsmen and night-camps in the mosquito-jungle. In the summer of 1875 the exigencies of the government troops in Southern Yucatan had pressed all the Sumasinta mail-boats into the transport service on the lower river, and, having reached the Guatemala frontier a day after the departure of a merchant's *conducta* which had engaged the available canoes, we were obliged to make our way through the shore-forests as far as Lagunas, twenty miles farther down, where the influence of my clerical fellow-traveller procured us a passage on board of a raft-faluca, a flat-boat with provisions for a logwood-camp not far from the junction of the Sumasinta with the Chiatlan, the latter river,

THE SWAMPS OF THE SUMASINTA.

according to reliable report, being still navigated by the government mail-barges. The faluca was rather over-

loaded, though skiffs and side-rafts added to her breadth
of beam, but with our bramble-torn shins and gnat-bitten

THE RAFT FALUCA.

faces a seat on a coffee-bag pile in the shade of the mat sail
seemed comfort itself; and our content was enhanced by
the discovery that we had reached her just in time, for seven
leagues farther down the banks began to disappear: the
stream had turned into an island-studded lake. A map
showing the terra-firma boundaries of the river would represent the Sumasinta as a monster stream, measuring from
fifteen to twenty miles from shore to shore; but, more properly speaking, it might be described as a river meandering
through a swamp-archipelago, or rather through woods that
have adapted themselves to a permanent state of inundation.
Here flourishes the mangrove: bogs and good-sized islands
are entirely covered with its sap-green copses, hung around
and, as it seems, supported by offshoots that send sprouts to
the ground like the aërial roots of the banian-tree; palms

rise from the thickets wherever the alluvium has accumulated above high-water mark ; and here and there a majestic copal-tree guarantees the stability of one of the wooded
islets whose jungle vegetation would not secure it against
being torn from its moorings and swept away like driftwood by the next freshet. The river itself—*i.e.* the current—often loses itself in the mazes of the archipelago,
divided perhaps, and as it were absorbed, by an open cypress forest, and reappearing farther below at the end of a
large lake or sweeping like a mill-race through a strait between two large islands. The river-pilot knows and avoids
these rapids on account of the snags that often clog the
channel in unforeseen places, and keeps through the open
lagoons, steering his way between wooded headlands and
pond-weed shallows, and reefing his sail where the ripple
of the current or a projecting branch suggests subaqueous
obstructions.

" *Fé de mi santo !*" our shipmaster would exclaim whenever we approached a driftwood pile, " *otro mal punto*"
(another dangerous point). " May the saints overlook our
sins! *Cuidad !*" with an uneasy glance at his rough-and-
ready negro pilot. " Take care, man : don't spit in the
water. It's unlucky, I tell you."

" Hang those fools ! Starboard, I say ! Bear on that
rudder ! *Tenga !* easy now : confound you for a set of——"

" Don't swear, man, till we get out of this trap—don't !
That tongue of yours will be the ruin of us. *Cuidad !*"
and so on till the *mal punto* was passed and saints and
sinners resumed their cigarros.

" D'ye see that log sticking out of the mud across there?"
said the pilot, when we passed through a sedgy lake near
the mouth of a sluggish tributary. " Well, boss, two years
ago there was an island there as large as Morgan's Bar near

Galveston harbor, and last October the river swept it clean away, trees, jungle, and all,—fifteen acres of it I should say,—though it hadn't been rainier than usual, either. I have known this river to rise seven feet in forty minutes without any warning: if a fellow was going to settle on one of those islands, he might get a free passage to Campeche some fine night."

Among the various theories by which the natives account for these sudden freshets, the most plausible ascribes them to the bursting of some large upland lake. Between Elisario and the Guatemala frontier the Sumasinta is flanked by large lagoons, some of which, in the dry season at least, are true lakes,—i e, inland waters with smaller or larger affluents, but without any permanent outlet. In the rainy season, however, the tributary creeks become torrents, and, after swelling their lake till its banks give way, discharge their accumulated waters into the next river valley like the deluge of a cloud-burst. Whole forests of trees and brush-wood are thus swept away and scattered over the delta-islands, where they either take root in the new alluvium or blockade the skirts of the forests with mountainous heaps of driftwood. Indirectly, too, these floods help to make the jungles of the lower Sumasinta the most impregnable thickets on earth by stimulating the vegetation of the under-brush into a rankness which can hardly have been exceeded by the fern-forests of the Triassic period. Wherever the jungles are periodically submerged the fertilizing sediments favor the growth of the *hicdaselvas*, or swamp-liana, a thorny creeper that spreads along the ground from bush to bush, and knits even a strip of willows or canebrake into a formidable hedge.

Though abounding with game, the Sumasinta jungles are therefore no hunter's paradise, and the *feræ naturæ* have no safer asylum on the western hemisphere. Hunting, in the literal sense of the word, is out of the question. A rifle-artist may kill a jaguar at his drinking-place or bag a peccari or two while the herd crosses the river, but neither a Texas trapper nor the hardiest wild Indian could here follow his game to its cover: there is no chance of pursuit, and but rarely time for a second shot. The scattered settlers keep watch-dogs, and, at the most, permit them to tree a raccoon or a wild-cat near the clearings, for out in the swamp they are useless. In the water they would fall an easy prey to the alligators that infest even the smallest lagoons, and in the bush a dog might keep a wounded deer at bay for days together before his master could reach him. A pot-hunter has to content himself with waterfowl, and the pleasure of exploring the thickets for the mere sake of adventure would be more than outweighed by the grievous mosquito-plague.

We made our first landing at one of the larger islands, and, finding the poop-cabin insufferably close, followed the crew ashore,—to camp, but not to sleep like those case-hardened natives. The negro pilot sat nodding over his camp-fire, extracting solace from a pipeful of N. C. "Rebel Comfort," and my companion, the padre Cristoval, tossed and grumbled till midnight before he at length fell a-snoring under his woollen blanket, though he had preached two years at the hammer-works of the San Carlos copper-mines, where he could certainly have studied the art of sleeping under difficulties. I had bandaged a torn Mexican hat with the shreds of a silk handkerchief and drawn it over my face like a hood, but after a long and vain attempt to breathe through the interspaces my patience and the strings of my head-dress gave way together, and I concluded to sit at bay for the rest of the night, renouncing Nature's

17

sweet restorer for the sweets of revenge upon my winged
tormentors. How I envied the snoring Franciscan at my
feet! The current in the canebrake murmured strange
lullabies, and the soughing of the night wind in the tree-
tops sounded drowsy and sleep-inviting; but it wouldn't
do: the blanket threatened me with suffocation, and with
my head unprotected I would not trust myself to nap for
fear of awakening *exsanguis*. The morning chill hardly
abated the fierce buzz around me, but to my delight our
craft got under way with the first twilight, and the clouds
overhead seemed to veil a vertical sun, when a shower at
length awakened me from a trance-like slumber in some
crevice of the luggage-pile.

I have often wondered if the human hide can become
mosquito-proof, and I believe that our tropical red-skins
become hardened against at least the *after-effects* of a gnat-
sting,—against the venom that distinguishes the bite of most
winged insects from that of a flea. By a many thousand-
fold repetition of the doses their epidermis becomes, as it
were, inoculated with the poison and ceases to be affected
by its virulent stimulus. They feel a mosquito-bite only
as we should feel the puncture of the smallest needle-point,
and old swamp-rangers may at last get callous to even this
mechanical irritation, as blacksmiths get indurated to flying
sparks and Bedouins to a sand-storm. This *anœsthesis* and
the fur, feather, and scale armor of wild beasts are Nature's
preventives, and probably superior to the best artificial
remedies. A sweltering night makes it doubtful if a mos-
quito-bar is the lesser evil, and the peace obtained by fetid
ointments is certainly too dear bought. Experimental phi-
losophy, however, has devised a more comfortable, though
not quite infallible, expedient. Mosquitoes, like mildew
and miasma, hug the ground, the bogs and the rank under-

growth of the tropical forests, and rarely rise more than thirty feet above the next water-level. Acting upon this discovery, the ranchero of the Tierra Caliente builds himself a platform on trestlework or swings his hammock in the top of a tough-wooded tree, and sleeps in peace high above the vexations of the lower world—provided that the night wind does not disappoint him altogether. In absolutely calm nights the gnats somehow get on the track of their victim, and may treat him to a surprise-party even in the top of the highest tree.

They avoid the open water, at least in daytime, and gave us a chance to study the varying scenery of the river-shores. *Secas*, or dry-land isles, alternate with aquatic forests, the latter predominating: on our left, for many leagues, the woods were inundated, if they had ever been out of water at all. Below Lagunas the average water-mark does not vary much in the different seasons, the pilot told me, though freshets which subside as quickly as they come are most frequent between June and December. The submergence of their lower trunks rather agrees with the majority of tropical trees, and seems to be no serious inconvenience to their wild inhabitants. Squirrels and palm-cats disported themselves in the upper branches, and when our faluca skirted a mulberry-grove a monkey of the genus *Mycetes* descended to the water's edge, paddled the scum out of the way, took a good drink, and clambered leisurely back into the screening foliage.

Wherever the current was opposed by the broadside of an island the wash had accumulated hillocks of driftwood, and on one of these piles—a good-sized island itself—we saw an animal which I at first mistook for a beaver, but which proved to be a large swamp-otter (*Lutra palustris*), light brown with a snow-white belly, and a whisker-like fringe of bristles around its mouth. At the approach of our raft it rose on its hind legs, eyed us keenly, and slipped into the penetralia of its hole, where it probably reared its young, more secure than a fox in his subterranean burrow. No human force, as we are, could have forced a passage through sixteen acres of tangled logs and brushwood intertwisted with the roots of creepers that had sprouted in the bottom of the rubbish heap and overspread the pile with a mantle of bright green leaves. We passed numerous floating logs, some of them bestridden by sea turtles on their return trip from an expedition to the sand banks of the upper river, where they deposit their eggs before the end of the rainy season, and, trusting their incubation to the sun and good luck, commit themselves to the current, which sooner or later will carry them back to their haunts in the Bay of Campeche.

The rivers of this swamp region abound with skate-shaped flying fish, whose aeronautical propensities seemed to be excited by the splash of our oars or perhaps by the gambols of two fresh-water dolphins that had accompanied the tahpa from our last landing, but gave our anglers a wide berth. Our shipmates regarded their escort as an omen of a lucky trip. "Si no saltan el timon" unless they should jump across the rudder, which would presage a dire catastrophe; and it seemed really as if they had brought us good weather, for the threatening clouds had so far let us off with a single brief shower. A continual cackle of gannets mingled with the chatter of our mestizo crew, and now and then a pelican swept by with its grunting squawk. More than once on turning some lando headland we came suddenly upon a conventicle of waterfowl that took wing with a simultaneous rush, and once a splendid black heron rose from the skirts of a canebrake almost under our thwarts and flopped away over our heads with a noise that sounded like a clapping of hands in the air.

Toward evening the sun came out for a moment and glistened upon a large expanse of pond-weeds on our left. It looked like a meadow in the middle of the lake, a level and dense tangle of green tendrils with yellow flowers, frequented by a swarm of small yellow butterflies. But at the edge of this lacustrine lawn we found four fathoms of water, and the flowers, a sort of water pimpernel (*Nymphæa capilaris*), must have had their roots at the end of an equally long stem. The strange flower-patch measured about half a mile in circumference, and in the centre, in a small pond of open water, we saw a crested moor-hen with her chickens diving around and exploring the vegetable borders of their little reservation. They too were safe; only a winged pursuer could have followed them to their aquatic asylum; wading was out of the question, and the tangled weeds would have impeded the progress of a boat as well as of the best swimmer.

After twelve leagues of alternate rowing and sailing we reached, two hours before sunset, the landing-place, the wigwam of Corrientes, at the mouth of the Rio Negro, where we had to wait till the falúca returned from the logwood-camp, about fourteen miles up-stream on the banks of the muddy tributary. Corrientes had been one of the regular landings of the government mail-barges, which now were temporarily withdrawn from this part of the river, and we were now only twenty miles from the mission of San Gabriel, whence the Chiatlan boats would carry us to our destination. A government courier who had joined us at Lagunas grumbled considerably at the delay, but the luggage of the padre Cristoval included a mule and a large wooden box, and I would rather not have trusted my own

trunk to a dug-out canoe; so there seemed nothing for it but to await the return of the faluca.

The station dépôt was a wretched shanty, but farther up we found a weatherproof log cabin and a little Indian wigwam, where we bought grapes and fresh turkey-eggs. Our purveyor also kept hogs, and informed us that he had to feed them on cayman flesh, since the last freshet had played the deuce with this year's nut- and acorn-mast, except on the opposite shore, where some of the islands were above high-water mark.

"My starved hogs would swim the river unless I pen them up," he said; "so I have to choose between letting the alligators have my pork and feeding my porkers on alligator meat."

"Do you shoot them?" we inquired.

"Can't afford it, caballeros. times are hard, and powder and shot are very high hereabouts. I spear them."

"We should like to see it, but it must be a rather ticklish job in that little dug-out of yours?"

"No, no: I spear them ashore," he said. "There is not much risk about it, except of losing my harpoon. It's only half a mile up the river, and we can be back in time *por otra cena*—for a second supper."

"No horse-thieves around here?" asked the cautious Franciscan.

"*No hay cuidado:* your worship's mule will be perfectly safe here," laughed the old Indian. "My daughter and her cousins wouldn't steal him, and there is nobody else on the island just now: our bucks have gone up the Rio Negro turtle-hunting."

Said bucks and our cayman-hunter belonged to the tribe of the Pintos, a horde of independent fishers and hunters who formerly ranged the hill-country between Yucatan and

Guatemala, but have now retreated to the coast-forests of Eastern Tabasco, where they defy all attempts at conversion and civilization. Their neighbors, of the race called the white by prescriptive right, accuse them of anthropophagous habits, a charge too uniformly preferred against all pagan Indians to have any practical significance. I believe that they are quite as moral as, and a great deal more intelligent than, the Christian plantain-eaters of the northern Tierra Caliente.

Half an hour before sunset we followed our guide to the landing, where he took a harpoon and a stout club from the shed of the station dépôt, and led us to a narrow jungle-path that kept along shore and across different log-bridged bayous. In a baglike piece of matting he carried a coil of tarred lariats and a little sucking pig, whose grunts of discontent rose to a shriek whenever the bag-carrier accelerated his pace. A sort of swamp-fog had settled over the woods when we halted behind a coppice of taxus-trees near the shore at a point where a projecting sand-bank formed a little river-bay. The Pinto cast a searching look across the water, and, motioning us to stand back, deposited his cargo in a bush and proceeded to business. Selecting an overhanging bough about six yards from the water's edge, he stripped it of its leaves, girdled the squealer with a double hitch of his lariat and suspended him in the fork of the bough at a height of about four feet from the ground. He then uncoiled a longer and stouter lariat, and fastened one end to a tough but elastic sapling and the other to the handle of his harpoon. An indescribably offensive smell deterred us from examining a little box which he had left on his poncho behind the taxus-hedge. He opened it, took a twisted string of bombax wool from his girdle and greased it with the contents of the box, a yellowish viscid substance whose composition he seemed unwilling to disclose. "It belongs to the station-master," he said: "I don't know where he gets it." Its effluvium seemed a mixture of musk, putrid meat, and something resembling the pungent odor of sal-ammoniac. He tied one end to the next bush, and weighting the other with a piece of wood threw it into the river.

"What's that for?" we inquired,—"a bait?"

"Yes, a nose-bait," said he · "the pig is for the eyes and ears, and now comes the grub-bait," taking one more bundle from the matting, a rag containing three chunks of half-roasted meat "That will make him mount the *barrera*," he chuckled. The barrera (barricade) between the taxus-thicket and the water's edge was a long sand-dam, capped with a row of gnarled logs. Toward the water the dam sloped very gradually, while its landward front was abrupt enough to check the speed of a retreating reptile.

After depositing the tidbits at equal intervals between the beach and the ridge of the barrera, the hunter stimulated his pig with a kick that ensured its vocal co-operation for the next ten minutes, and joined us in our ambush, spear in hand. The sun had set some time ago, but the air was still oppressively sultry—not a ripple on the bay, save where little fishes played duck-and-drake upon the surface or a louder splash suggested the advent of the much-baited saurian.

"It's getting dark," said one of my Mexican companions at last, breaking a long silence: "this seems a poor place for cayman-hunting."

The Pinto raised his hand, but made no reply, looking immovably in the same direction.

"Do you see one," asked the padre.

"There are four or five of them heading this way," whispered the hunter: "one was close by here a minute ago, when that other gentleman began to talk. Speak low, please."

" Where, in the name of——"

" Hush! here he comes."

At the lower end of the dam a dark object rose slowly from the water till its upward and shoreward motion revealed the lower outline of the shapeless protuberance. The Pinto was right: that was the head of an old cayman, or coast-alligator, distinguished from the northern variety by a flatter tail and receding lower jaw. He mounted the beach opposite the lower extremity of the barrera and waddled around the dam, raising his head every now and then to reconnoitre the bushes on his left. He either had not yet seen the pig or meant to approach it from the land side.

" *Mala suerte!*" muttered the Pinto—"confound the luck! He is bound to spy us if he gets through that bush. If he keeps on I'll have to try him at long range."

The cayman hobbled across a fallen tree and the harpoon rose: another step forward would bring him in sight of our ambush. But no: he stopped and listened, and as if his guardian spirit had whispered a word in his ear he suddenly turned, dashed through the bush, and waddled back into his native element

" A lost game," said the courier: " he has seen us."

" Keep quiet," whispered the hunter " No, no, he's all right: he has seen the pig; only that tree bothered him. He's going to try from the other side, just where I want him."

But minute after minute passed without a sound or sign of our departed visitor. While we listened we heard a loud triple splash on our left, a quarter of a mile up-stream.

" Did ye hear that?" whispered the Pinto " There are

three or four of them in that little bayou up there. *Pura terquedad*—sheer contrariness of the miserable thick-skulls; but never mind, I shall get even with some of them "

" We had better go there now," I suggested : " it will be dark in ten minutes "

The Pinto hugged the ground and raised a warning hand · "Keep quiet ! here he comes again. I thought so," he chuckled : " he's smacking his chops. The old pork-thief believes he has found a free sausage-shop this time. I wonder what he will think of himself in five minutes from now ?"

The cayman had emerged directly in front of us, and could be seen through the lower branches of our coppice with his belly squat on the ground and his upturned jaws at work upon the first chunk of roast bait

" I believe I have seen that chap before," whispered the Pinto in my ear. " Yes, it's the same one-eyed old sinner. He owes me two pigs, but he's going to pay his debts. I'll whack it out of his brain-box before that river has run another furlong But let us keep very still now : not a word, gentlemen. We'll get him sure this time."

The pig had suddenly stopped squealing, and the general silence was only broken by the doleful squawk of a tree-frog over our heads.

The cayman had gobbled the second chunk and advanced upon the dam, but stopped short at sight of the third and largest morsel He cocked his head, and his solitary eye assumed a puzzled expression. Who was the unknown benefactor? No answer to the mute enigma,—nothing but the monotonous call of the tree-toad. Never mind : No 3 followed its predecessors. On top of the dam he stopped once more, and glared at the pig in surprise and apparent mistrust of his own senses. It might seem incredible, but there it was, an actual living pig within easy reach, obvious even to a one-eyed cayman. Should it be a trap? He looked sideways and turned his head. Nothing stirring: the very air seemed to stagnate—Nature's voice reduced to the monotone of the tree-toad. The coast was clear. Still—— He seemed on the point of sliding back, but suddenly, as if ashamed of his own misgivings, he jerked his tail up, leaned forward, and plumped into the sandy hollow behind the barricade.

The Pinto sprang up, and the cayman turned like a shot and headed for the dam, and up it with super-reptilian energy; but the gnarled logs delayed him for a moment, and in that moment the iron went crashing through his scaly hide, and the pent-up emotions of the Pinto found vent in an exultant yell. The spear stuck. "Mil caraxos! I got you this time!—Look out! here he comes!"

Jerked back by the tension of the lariat, the captive came floundering through the bush, making the leaves fly around his switching tail, and several times plunged forward with an impetus that would have snapped the rope like a trout-line if the elasticity of the sapling had not broken the force of his spring. The Pinto had seized his club, a stout cudgel of hackberry wood, and jumped around his reckless prisoner with anathemas that would have appalled any other heart; but the intrepid saurian only redoubled his efforts till the rope caught in the root of a bush, complicating the difficulties of his situation to a hopeless degree. He was at the end of his tether, and, seeing his opportunity, the Pinto dealt him a whack across the head that laid him sprawling on his back. The second blow made him rear, with his jaws full of broken teeth, and the third and fourth squirted a mixture of blood and brains from his nostrils. The cayman had paid his debt.

We slept in peace that night, as the tight walls and narrow windows of our cabin favored a successful application

SETTLING OLD SCORES.

of the smoke-pot process, which consists in evicting the
winged tenants of an apartment with a potful of smoulder-

ing leaves, and preventing their return by screening the
apertures with a double sheet of gauze. Common leaves
or dry moss answer the purpose very well, but the creoles
of the lowland tobacco-plantations use by preference the
sobras or sweepings of the curing-houses, and breathe the
densest nicotine fumes with all the gusto of an old toper
sniffing the alcohol effluvium of a wine-cellar.

I believe that the gift of sleeping is a distinct faculty
which can be cultivated without the aid of such palliatives
of insomnia as gluttony and alcoholic debauches. Our faluca was not expected before noon, and, finding the morning
air agreeably cool, I returned to the cabin after breakfast
to invite the Franciscan to a stroll through the woods, but
found him snoring in a corner where he had fallen asleep
among the remnants of his frugal repast. Sauntering
along the beach, I met the Pinto with a big shoulder-bag
containing a section of the captured alligator, whom he had
chopped up *in situ* like a log; and on my return to the
station dépôt I found our courier hobnobbing with the
wigwam belles, who had brought in a jugful of pineapple
cider from an outlying cottage. There were three of them,
—a stout wench of eighteen or twenty, with a red-lined
reboso or head-shawl and a sort of dalmatica, sack-like, but
more sensible than the strait-jackets of the North Mexican
country-girls; and the twin daughters of the station-master, a little taller than their stout cousin, as they called her,
but perhaps younger in years, and evidently so in social experience. One of them, who shook my hand with the zeal
of an old acquaintance, was "barefoot up to the neck," as
good Bishop Heber described the toilette of the Bombay
nautch-girls, but wore a sailcloth imitation of her cousin's
reboso trimmed with copper tacks and capped by way of
climax with the rowel of a Mexican spur. Her somewhat

smaller sister preserved her sangfroid in the costume of the Nereids. They acquainted us with the current gossip of the wigwam. Pepita, she of the spur-bonnet, informed me that her aunt Inez contemplated the purchase of a milch goat, and that her brother Pancho would probably win a prize in the next sculling-match; and they were just describing the visit of two American logwood-choppers during the late freshet when the approach of Father Cristoval set them agog with curiosity and surprise. What! a *padre*, a monk, without a cross and without an acolyte! Was he going to preach like the missionary from Campeche? Would there be a gift-distribution of rosaries and pictures?

"Ye fell barbarians, what are you doing?" laughed the padre. " *Coquelando con las pelladas canibales*—flirting with the sansculotte cannibals?—And you, niña, don't you know it's wicked to wear a head-dress like that? How is a poor stranger going to resist a red-lined reboso with forty spangles?"

Pepita giggled.

"You are right," said the stout wench: "she ought to know better than to put on airs about that bonnet,—a person in her circumstances, not having a shirt or shift to her name!"

Pepita grinned.

" *Y mira*," continued the wench—"look here! She stuffs her braids with sow-bristles to make them look fuller."

"That will do now," said the courier: "you are only envious."

"Envious about what? That bonnet of hers? There is nothing enviable about it. She got those tacks out of an old mule-saddle, and the red lining is all a sham. *Mira!* she fringed it with a bit of red yarn to make it look lined

like. Humbug! Look here! nothing inside but greasy
canvas!"

Pepita snatched her bonnet away, and—paradox of the
female mind!—the same maiden whose equanimity could
resist the most glaring defects of apparel had blushed
crimson through her dusky skin at a discovered deficit in
fripperies.

"*Ay, que seas maldita, cabrona*—shame on you for a
malicious vixen!" she hissed, and whisked away, with her
still nuder sister at her heels.

The padre shook his head: "What a state of affairs for
a Christian country! The governor of Tabasco ought to
be tarred and feathered, together with all his breechless
backwood apes. Heaven defend me from the African sav-
ages if they are any worse than our Pintos!"

"Why doesn't your holy order reclaim them?"

"We tried to," said the Franciscan, "but they are the
most *inconvertible* of bipeds. It's impossible for a white
man to follow them in all their wild wanderings, and the
casual proselytes relapse into barbarism as soon as they are
out of sight. They are called *Pintos* because they used to
paint their bodies like barber-poles, you know; and one of
our missionaries converted a whole village of them up on
the Chiatlan, and thought he had cured them of that paint-
ing mania, but when he revisited their place after a year or
two he caught one of his vicars dancing in a coat of yellow
ochre and copal varnish."

When I repacked my trunk the courier came in and
asked me for the loan of my pocket-knife to cut a piece of
scarlet cloth out of the lining of his poncho. While crossing a brier-patch behind the wigwam, he said, he had found
the twins rolling on the ground, drenching the grass with
tears, which the duty of a cavalier required him to dry.

Just before the faluca reached her landing the sisters slipped into our shanty, all smiles and thanks, to inquire if we could spare them a needle and a little black thread. They had resolved, *en petite comité*, to elaborate a bonnet that should burst the midriff of their envious cousin.

Below Corrientes the Sumasinta becomes broader and deeper, often expanding into a placid lake whose waters reflect the varying hues of the firmament and the different tints and shades of the shore-vegetation. The shell-banks at the mouth of the Rio Gordo glittered like snow, and seemed to stretch inland and northward for a considerable distance. The birth-land of this tributary abounds with lakes, some of them flanked with dangerous quicksands, and one of its upper affluents, the Rio Pinto, drains an almost unapproachable wilderness. Turtle-hunters who have ascended the Rio Gordo in their small sailing boats report that even in the dry season its banks consist of a black vegetable mud more yielding and treacherous than quicksand, while the thickets are infested with panthers and jaguars, who here have become almost wholly arboreal in their habits and prey upon monkeys and various kinds of gallinaceous tree-birds. Our shipmaster, who had visited this region, assured me that where sloths and monkeys are scarce the jaguar will attack the camps of the roving Indians with reckless ferocity, and can often be captured by baiting a trap with a human corpse. A half-breed hunter, he said, who had thus avenged the death of his brother, was himself poisoned by a scratch of the captured man-eater, and would have died if his comrades had not amputated his arm at the shoulder.

The weather of the past twenty-four hours had been too fine to last, and twelve miles below our last landing we were caught in a thunderstorm that drove us shivering and chattering into the hindmost corner of the poop-cabin, while our naked oarsmen continued their work with aggravating complacency. The padre, as usual, took refuge in Dreamland, and the courier in a tobacco-cloud. "Never mind," said he: "we are only six miles from San Gabriel now: the major will comfort our souls with butter-pancakes and hot coffee."

"The major? Commander of a military station, I suppose?"

"No: he is a man of peace and somewhat hunchbacked, but commander-in-chief of the port, for all that. He has kept a ship-store at the mission for the last seven years, be-

MISSION OF SAN GABRIEL.

sides a tavern and the station dépôt. His family are the only white people in the settlement, and of course the redskins have to keep in the rear rank."

"Was it ever a regular mission?"

"Oh, yes: the priests had a school and a chapel there, but during the Indian rebellion of 1858 and '59 their converts gave them the slip, and monks know better than to work for their own living. They went back to Campeche, where their order has a large convent. Their chapel is used for a storehouse now. The whole place is a curious old wigwam, growing out of the water like the swamp-oaks around it. It will be pitch-dark before we get there, but if we leave to-night you must take a look at it while they light their pitch-pan."

Like many of his countrymen, Major Casales rejoiced in the advent of a stranger as an Oregon backwoodsman hails the arrival of the Eastern mail with the accumulated news of the last three or four weeks. His emotion on ascertaining that two of us came directly from the headquarter States left us no doubt that we were really welcome. He oversweetened our coffee and double-buttered our pancakes in his eagerness to learn the result of the Diaz manifesto and the presidential counter-proclamation. Was Diaz popular with the army? Would the United States support Tejada? He bustled in and out with empty pots, wrong dishes and half-cooked dishes, inviting us to help ourselves and obliging us to make the freest use of that permission.

Our store of current news having been drained to the last drop, we learned that the courier's impatience had been superfluous, and that we should have to wait here for a full day, as the barge was not expected before the next following night. The Yucatan insurrection was spreading, the major informed us, and the government officials hereabouts had a lively time of it, but his private business was dull: the upper-river traffic had come to a full stop, and even the turtle-hunters had made themselves scarce for fear of being pressed into the " volunteer service," as the State governors were pleased to call their forced levies. The agricultural prospects, too, were rather dreary: the banana crop was rotting on the stem, and the continual rains would probably result in another freshet and ruin his oak-mast.

But Don Casales had evidently laid something by for a rainy day. His private table was sumptuous, and the furniture curiosities of his parlor, if not in the very best taste, demonstrated certainly the ability to indulge it. After pancakes and politics we strolled out on the veranda to see the bright sheet-lightning that illuminated the sky from end to end every other second, and the major's conversation proved that the light of knowledge can enter by the ear-door as well as by the eye-window. He had to sign his name by proxy, but expressed himself with clearness and fluency, and seemed well informed on most points of contemporary interest. "Where I was brought up," he said, "books were only known from hearsay, and I confess that there was a time when I thought I could afford to despise them, but I gradually discovered that without a school education even the smartest man runs a handicapped race. I use every chance to impress that fact on my boys," he sighed, "but, as usual, they follow my example rather than my advice. They don't seem to know what paper is good for, except to make into shot-gun wadding: fishing and boat-adventuring are all they care for."

The environs of San Gabriel seemed indeed to favor the ascendency of these foibles. The vicinity of the coast was felt in the heavy throb of the Gulf-tide beating against the foundation-piles of the building, and in the open water farther up the splash of leaping fish was loud and incessant. The open bay in front of us seemed to extend for several miles southwest, but in the east the electric flashes revealed a long row of wooded islands,—sombre hillocks with rounded outlines that suggested the prevalence of palm-forests. As often as occasional brighter flashes were followed

by a roll of thunder the echo was answered by the distant voices of a flamingo-swarm in some reed-meadow of a mist-shrouded lagoon in the north,—el Lago de Patos, at the outskirts of the great Rio Gordo swamp. This swamp, Mr. Casales told us, was supposed to be the retreat of a gang of pirates who infested the coast between Sisal and the Bay of Carmen, and who reached the sea by some northeastern channel of the Rio Gordo. Logwood-cutters who visited the lower affluents of that river had often seen the smoke of their camp-fires rising from the heart of the jungle-wilderness in the north, or heard the report of distant rifle-shots in the stillness of the winter nights. The Lago de Patos communicates in the east with a large sedgy forest-lake whose islands would furnish an almost inexhaustible supply of valuable timber if the dangerous shoals that obstruct the channel could be dredged or avoided by a canal from the Rio Gordo to the south corner of the timber-lake

The breeze from the direction of this archipelago, though moist and not quite free from a certain swamp-odor, was agreeably cool and promised a refreshing night. A little flower-garden on our left sweetened the air with the odor of gillyflowers and blooming oranges, which seemed to have attracted a swarm of nocturnal honey-hunters: moths of all sizes and forms buzzed around our ears or blundered with a dull thud against the panes of the corner window. Down in the canebrake a water-fox whimpered like a whining child, and where the garden adjoined the rank shore-forest two wills-o'-the-wisp danced around a rotten tree with that peculiar cold-white flicker that differs from fire as moonlight does from sunshine. Here they were the only lights of the night,—no beacon-fires, no flaming factory-chimneys or harbor-signals, near and far. The

horizon was dark all around, but there was a charm in that
very solitude, and I could conceive that a native of this
island-world would be loath to exchange its wild freedom
for the comforts of a more populous country.

Señor Casales had lived here for the last eleven years.
He was an observer, in his own way, of Nature's physical
and moral phenomena, and though he had managed to live
in peace with his neighbors, and had rarely ventured beyond
the premises of the mission farm, his memoirs of the last
decade would have furnished the material of a curious chronicle of the wilderness. One night about the end of the rainy
season he was awakened by the furious barking of a little
terrier, and, descending into the yard with a lantern, found
that a big black wolf had swam the river and was culti-
vating the acquaintance of his mastiff bitch. He went
softly up-stairs, got a gun, and shot the shaggy Leander
before he discovered his danger. The major had seen bear-
tracks on the sandy neck between his peninsula and the
mainland, and used to keep a heavy trap chained to a mulberry-tree in a thicket behind the mission farm. A few
months ago it was dragged away by some unknown animal,
the chain being broken close to the root of the tree, while
the surrounding bushes were trampled down and the tree
itself stripped of its tough bark in different places. All
the hunters who frequented his store assured him that no
bear could have torn that chain. What could it have been?

Some equally mysterious two-legged guests had visited
the mission,—hirsute desperadoes who answered no questions and asked none, except about the price of tobacco and
flannel shirts, and were permitted to depart in peace after
settling their bill, or fugitive Indians who sought and obtained aid in the name of the common father of all nations.
One morning, while the rain was coming down like a

waterfall, a canoeful of armed men sought shelter in his boat-house. The strangers mounted the platform of his warehouse, but declined his invitation to enter the store. They bought a bag of navy biscuit and some dried meat, paying in advance, and asked the lady of the house to get them some dinner while they waited under the wharf-shed. A mess of mutton and sweet potatoes was boiling and almost done, when the men suddenly hurried to their boat and pushed off, after throwing a handful of copper coins through the window. They were out of sight when the major stepped out on the wharf, but he saw the government mail-barge approach the landing from the opposite direction.

The swamp-pirates, whose vicinity was a source of constant uneasiness to the delta settlers, had never damaged him in his property, perhaps for the same reasons that induce a fox to spare the hen-houses in the near neighborhood of his burrow; and only once he had cause to believe that some unknown party or parties had visited his place with burglarious intent, and would have robbed him if they had not been baffled in an unexpected way. On a high shelf behind his counter he keeps a cage containing a more or less happy family of squirrels and opossums and two monkeys, a capuchin and a young ceboo (*Ateles paniscus*), and one night, between two and three A.M., he heard the latter animal screeching with all its might, and soon after hurried footsteps on the veranda in front of his store. His Indian-of-all-work rushed in from an adjoining room, and all the male members of the household rallied *en masse* with guns and lanterns; but the nocturnal visitor had vanished. The store-door, however, stood wide open, and the major was positive that the lock must have been picked, as he kept the key in his bedroom. The would-be marauder had left a track of dirty boots between the wharf and the store, but as there were no marks on the counter, he could not have hurt the monkeys or even touched their cage, and the alarm-cry of the little ceboo is therefore a curious instance of the manifestation in a quadrumanous animal of an instinct which in general may be said to be confined to one species of mammals and a single genus of birds,—the canines and the goose. All other domestic animals witness the plunder of their master's property with perfect uncon-

A PINTO PATRIARCH.

cern, and even the sagacious horse may be abducted by midnight thieves without betraying its fears by the slightest sound.

We took a bath next morning in a tolerably limpid bayou between two flood-gates warranted alligator-proof. The water I found by actual measurement fifteen degrees cooler than the air in the shade of an adjoining caucho-grove. There was a grayish-white mist on the river, and the morning wind was saturated with that peculiar swamp-odor which on the lower Mississippi is thought to be symptomatic of the deadliest malaria. The delta of the Sumasinta, however, is almost free from climatic diseases. The major took us to the cabin of a reputed centenarian, a Pinto patriarch, who remembered the great Indian rebellion of 1798, and whose father had cultivated maniocs on the upper Sumasinta before any white man had penetrated to the highlands of western Tabasco He was mending the trimmings of a rawhide saddle apparently coeval with himself, and behind the cottage a young Indian was engaged in skinning a boa which his grandfather had killed with a common cudgel. The old man answered our greeting with a cheery " *Buena suerte á mis caballeros,*" but bewailed the shameless rapacity of a swarm of palm-squirrels who still entered his larder by an undiscovered hole. He had caught one of them a few nights before, he said, anointed him with turpentine-grease and set him on fire—*por enseñarles crianza* —to teach them manners; but they were carrying on as bad as ever.

His countrymen have practically relapsed into paganism, having in some cases exhausted the patience of their wouldbe converters by sheer passive resistance, disregard of holy days and church ordinances, and persistent neglect of their cornfields. The "mission Indians" were in the habit of smuggling their boys away as soon as they could run, permitting the padres to support the young squaws during the age of uselessness,—*i.e.* from infancy to the middle of their teens,—after which they managed to follow their brothers. When the monks abandoned the mission many of the fugitives returned and emphasized their satisfaction by a three days' bonfire that lighted the midnight skies for many miles around.

The Franciscan missionaries have virtually abandoned them to their fate. In their wigwam meetings the sachems studiously discard the Spanish language, and some of the

SKINNING A BOA.

old squaws set a bad example by substituting the ancestral paint-pot for imported calicoes. They burlesque the Sabbath by mock masses with war-dance entr'actes, and the

immigra... from the land of snow
...sweet poi...ns cease to be sweet in any
With the ...rest exception, the Ameri-
...ir ardent ...uors neither as intoxicants
...urposes," ...t rather as fluid spices,—
...ich, like ...pper and ginger, facilitate
...in a tropic climate.

...urned in ...e course of the afternoon,
...ntinued o... trip on board of the Rio
...mail-barg...of eighty tons to Carmen
...Gabriel ...e Sumasinta expands into
...Lago de ...rminos,—"the terminating
...the sweet...ater lagoons,—a brackish
...ds are tw... a day submerged by the
...Caribbea... ea. The shores here recede
...nd the ta...led thickets that cover the
...almost, o...wholly, uninhabited, a para-
...water-sna...es. Hunting ceases to be
...r-trappin...would not repay the danger
...ingles.

...the cloud in the east parted, and a
...ked down ...on a dismal expanse of water
...ks. Low-...iling clouds drifted seaward,
...rfowl pas...d us with rushing wings, but
...ed into si...ce by the vast dreariness of
...y the nigh...eron croaked in the distant
...near and f... from the seaweed shallows
...e mist-shro...ed fens of the Gulf-islands,
...rk of the ...ast-alligators. In the night-
...eir deep-m...thed groans sound in your
...l significan..., and I believe that even the
...ed our feel...g of relief when the signal-
...harbor gle...ed through the morning mist

trees behind the mission are covered with hieroglyphic inscriptions which can hardly have been dictated by a spirit of Christian reverence, the emblem of the cross being frequently combined with a more ancient symbol which the sculptors of classic Italy also used rather too freely in their graphic extravaganzas. A stone image of San Gabriel which had disappeared from the mission chapel was at last discovered in the cabin of an Indian hunter, looking very much as if it had been doing duty as a whetstone.

But the Pintos have hardly consulted their material interests in neglecting the agricultural lessons of the good padres: the cornfields are covered with weeds and the irrigation-ditches clogged with mud and driftwood. The hammock wigwams cultivate manioes and perhaps a few plantain-trees, but the Pintos of the delta are mostly carnivorous. We met two young bucks with a boa which they had shot in the taxus-swamp—"*por guiso de Domingo, señores*"—for a bit of a Sunday-stew. Boa flesh is oily, semi-transparent in thin slices, and has a musky flavor, but is perhaps not more indigestible than our eel pies and pork fritters. In point of diet, indeed, a practical philosopher cannot be blamed for suspecting that nature and habit are interchangeable terms. Liebig demonstrates with the most plausible logic that Hindoos *must* be vegetarians,—that they have to abstain from meat on pain of disease and physical degeneration; but in still more torrid climates the Ethiopians and South American swamp-Indians devour all the meat they can get, and seem, physically at least, not much the worse for it. Nobody, however, can doubt that the lethal effects of alcoholic intemperance are swifter and more incurable in a tropical country. Neither inherited vigor of constitution nor open-air exercise can save the native of an equatorial region from the consequences of habitual intoxication, and bibulous immigrants from the land of snow soon find that their sweet poisons cease to be sweet in any sense of the word. With the rarest exception, the American Spaniards use their ardent liquors neither as intoxicants nor for "medical purposes," but rather as fluid spices,—peptic stimulants, which, like pepper and ginger, facilitate the digestion of fat in a tropical climate.

Our boatmen returned in the course of the afternoon, and at sunset we continued our trip on board of the Rio Gordo government mail-barge of eighty tons to Carmen harbor. Below San Gabriel the Sumasinta expands into a bay known as the Lago de Terminos,—"the terminating lake," the end of the sweet-water lagoons,—a brackish estuary whose islands are twice a day submerged by the surging tide of the Caribbean Sea. The shores here recede to a hazy distance, and the tangled thickets that cover the littoral swamps are almost, or wholly, uninhabited, a paradise of bears and water-snakes. Hunting ceases to be profitable: even bear-trapping would not repay the danger of tempting such jungles.

After midnight the clouds in the east parted, and a waning moon blinked down upon a dismal expanse of water and gray sand-banks. Low-sailing clouds drifted seaward, and flights of waterfowl passed us with rushing wings, but voiceless, as if awed into silence by the vast dreariness of the scenery. Only the night-heron croaked in the distant swamp, and from near and far, from the seaweed shallows on our lee and the mist-shrouded fens of the Gulf-islands, came the hoarse bark of the coast-alligators. In the night-time especially their deep-mouthed groans sound in your ears with a direful significance, and I believe that even the stolid sailors shared our feeling of relief when the signal-lights of Carmen harbor gleamed through the morning mist

and the shrill crowing of a cock announced the vicinity of
human habitations. An uninhabited wilderness may be
sublime and even attractive: an *uninhabitable* one is always
dismal.

Carmen harbor, at the mouth of the Sumasinta, is a veritable city of the sea, rising from a substructure of trestle-

CARMEN HARBOR.

platforms, pontoon-bridges, and anchored hulls, and the
sluggish canal which forms the principal street reminded
me of Tasso's description of the Porto di Brondolo and its
sombre river:

Corre la Brenta al mar, tacita e bruna,

a town of swaying wharves and bilge-water odors. There
is a navy-yard here, and the harbor is the halfway station of
the Vera Cruz and Sisal packets. Our captain hinted that
the tide would probably delay us for a couple of hours, but a
private interview with his clerk seemed to have oiled the
angry billows, for we contrived to reach our pier half an
hour before the arrival of the east-bound steamer.

In spite of mosquitoes and mud-banks, long delays and
laconic dinners, I think that a trip from San Carlos to

Carmen will reward the enterprise of travellers who do not judge the byways of our continent by Mr. Baedeker's standards. The littoral forests of the upper river are not essentially different from those of the northern Gulf-coast, but at the lower landing the explorer may study Nature in her strangest forms, and the inaccessible thickets beyond can at least teach him one oft-forgotten truth,—namely, that the earth was not made exclusively for the sake of man.

CHAPTER IX.

YUCATAN.

Why left they this eternal home of Summer,
To seek a land whose flowers must yearly die?—SILVIO PELLICO

FIFTY leagues east of Vera Cruz the passengers of a homebound French steamer sight land again: first, the square-cut ridge of a coast-range that rises like a wall above the edge of the northern sky, and soon after the jagged peaks of an inland sierra far behind the southern horizon of a blue-green archipelago of coast islands. Viewed from a sufficient elevation, the eastern gates of the Gulf of Mexico would resemble the projecting piers of a double breakwater at the entrance of a fortified harbor, and the inland scenery north and south would make it difficult to distinguish the highlands of Cuba from those of Central Yucatan. Their confronting shores, however, would present the striking contrast of a rock-bound coast with the jungles of a broad and swampy estuary; and this contrast has probably decided the different destinies of the two countries. The island with its inviting harbors has attracted a continual swarm of Spanish conquerors and colonists, while the swamp-protected peninsula enjoyed the same immunity from town-and-tree-destroying invaders which has preserved the forests and ancient cities of Siam.

Even the fanatical iconoclasts who transformed the rest

290

of New Spain after the image of the mother-country have spared the monuments of Chichen and Uxmal, and the western pueblos of the Mayos belong to the few tribes of the aboriginal population whose rights have to some degree been respected by their Caucasian conquerors. Since the expulsion of the Spaniards in 1821 these pueblos have thrice seceded from the Mexican confederation, and the last time (1846–52) maintained their independence for nearly seven years, and only rejoined the union on terms which the Mexican dictators have rarely ventured to violate. The presence of a French armada in the Bay of Sisal overawed them for a few years, but after the restoration the authority of the governor was openly defied, and in 1874 I was sent to Campeche as a member of President Lerdo's *mision de reforma*, a commission of inquiry which was to confer with the delegates of the different pueblos with a view of ascertaining the cause of their chronic discontent

At the suggestion of the new governor the commission was divided, and as the race-prejudices of my medical colleague made him thoroughly indifferent to the result of the expedition, I was offered the choice between the eastern mountain-districts and the southwestern lowlands between Campeche and the Sierra de Belize. I decided for the western or lowland region, partly for the sake of the famous ruins, which might be reached by a short détour from our prescribed route, but chiefly in the hope of collecting data for the solution of a mystery which gives a special interest to the ethnological problems of our southern continent,— viz., the enigma of the almost universal degeneration of our race in the tropical latitudes.

Is there any objective necessity for it ' Are snow-storms and long winter nights really essential conditions of our well-being? In spite of a staggering array of *ex post facto* arguments, our instinct revolts at the idea that perennial fruits and flowers should be incompatible with human happiness. The analogy of the oldest and youngest, highest and lowest, forms of animated Nature proclaims the fact that light and warmth are the chief sources of all organic prosperity. In the tropics the cereals of the North reappear as palms, ferns as fern-trees, woodbines as giant creepers; the type of the wild-cat develops a tiger, of the adder a boa, of the lizard a crocodile, of the sand-spider a tarantula: the size, the strength, the beauty and longevity of plants and animals are found to increase as we approach the equator, and none of them seem the better for having to wring subsistence from a frozen soil. Does man alone make an exception? Or are we rather justified in suspecting the agency of abnormal circumstances,—of baneful habits whose effects require the influence of cold air as an antidote? The question, methinks, deserves a share of the attention which is still wasted on archæological squabbles, for its solution would elucidate the oldest and darkest of all biological problems. At present we must admit that the ruling races of the earth have lost—or rather voluntarily abandoned— their Southern garden-home, though its climate was not always unfavorable to the growth of the manly and industrial virtues.

Uxmal is the American Nineveh, and in Yucatan at least the decay of an ancient civilization cannot be explained by the exhaustion of the soil. The vegetation of the riparial forests is rankly, unmanageably exuberant, the ruins of the hill-country are covered with tanglewood as the monuments of Syria with sand, and the fruit-crop of a large variety of indigenous trees is absolutely perennial.

On our return from Merida we stopped at the Baños de San Joaquin, and the proprietor of the mineral springs

treated us to a lunch of apricots and *datiles frescos*—new
dates—whose flavor might have satisfied an emir of Bele-
duljerid. The hedges were still full of wild oranges, and
the storekeeper of the hacienda had bananas, sweet oranges,
and fresh figs for sale at a season of the year when our stores
of domestic fruits have mostly dwindled to frozen crab-
apples. Yucatan is famous for its semi-annual banana-
crops, and the second or winter harvest is often more
abundant than the first if the rainy season ends before
the beginning of November.

Seven miles south of San Joaquin the road and our *tropa*
divided: Lieutenant Perez and an American teamster, the
outrider of our cavalcade, agreed to accompany me to
Uxmal, while the rest continued their way to Campeche,
where the Christmas and New Year's festivities promised
abundant pastime till after the return of our colleagues
from the eastern circuit. Lieutenant Perez, the adjutant
of the military commissioner, was a Cuban refugee, who
seemed to have forgiven and forgotten the wrongs of the
isla heroica, though a Spanish sabre had left an indelible
memento on his face; while Nick Fisher, our guide, who
had lost a team of mules and a "valuable buck nigger" at
Murfreesboro', was still very severe on the Abolitionists.
He had followed Kirby Smith to Matamoras, where he had
found employment in an American restaurant, and, after trying his luck in various Mexican seaports, had finally strayed
to Sisal and exchanged the spit for a muleteer's goad,—vulg.,
"caracho-pole,"—having found that the close resemblance
of the climate to that of an unmentionable region would be
completed by a kitchen-fire. In less than five years he had
become personally acquainted with every teamster and
tavern-keeper in Western Yucatan, and had visited Uxmal
thrice and Chichen sixteen times, mostly as guide to Euro-

pean or Yankee excursion-parties. *El Pecador*—the Sinner
—his comrades called him, a nickname which had originated
in his own unlucky attempt at translating his patronymic,
but which in the eyes of the natives might derive additional point from his persistent and undisguised heresy.

Southeast of San Joaquin extends a chain of sand-hills
which we hoped to cross during the cool of the forenoon,
but at a ford of the Rio Becal, hardly three miles from the
cross-roads, we were detained for nearly two hours by the
senseless obstinacy of my companion's mule, which waded
the deepest part of the river with unflinching steadiness,
and then refused to proceed through the shallow water near
the opposite bank. We had to return to the western shore
and distribute the lieutenant and his baggage among the
sensible quadrupeds; but the stubborn brute, though now
unloaded and unsaddled, declined to make any concessions
in return, till the Pecador, losing his patience, tied her legs
crossways, and, after felling her to the ground, hitched the
entire *mulada* to their fallen sister and dragged her across
like a carcass of beef. Priessnitz, the founder of hydro-
pathy, holds that a bath, in order to be a perfect tonic,
ought to be followed by a *haut-reiz*, a skin-stimulus; and
the correctness of his view was triumphantly illustrated by
the application of a double-twisted cowhide after we got
our patient to terra firma. The bland alacrity of that mule
during the remainder of the trip was something unprece-
dented in the experience of her owner.

We had to face the *arenal* in midafternoon now, but the
" sand-region" proved better than its name. the plateaus
were tufted with mimosas and tamarisks, and in the ravines
feather-willows and bulrushes indicated the presence of
moisture. A descent of three hours brought us back to
the rolling woodland of the vega, where furlongs and miles

of our road were shaded by dark-green euphorbias, sloth-trees, and open groves of *algodoncras* (*Hibiscus odoratus*), whose cotton-like blossoms still covered the lower branches, while the tree-tops near and far were festooned with the flaming flowers of a variety of epiphytes, yellow bromelias, and pale-red Amphilidæ or fire-orchids. In Cuba and the littoral forests of Northern Mexico the new year's vegetation is characterized by a more vivid green and the absence of fruits and full-blown flowers, which have been stripped by the storms of the rainy season, but in Yucatan even the October showers alternate with weeks of cloudless and intensely warm weather, and the cool season—November to February—deserves that name only comparatively, the noon temperature during the Christmas week rising frequently to 105° Fahrenheit in the shade. As the climate of the Central American highlands resembles an everlasting spring, that of Yucatan may be called a perpetual midsummer,—sunny, agreeable mornings, and sultry, or else dry, clear, and superheated afternoons. If the foreign residents of the coast-towns bewail the perennial excess of caloric, the flora and fauna of the wild interior are certainly not the worse for it. The first Spanish settlers cleared large tracts of ground for the cultivation of *henequen*, or Sisal hemp, and after exhausting the soil by a succession of uniform crops abandoned their plantations as barren sand-fields,—*arenals* as they are here called,—and on these barrens, dusty limestone plateaus some of them, the noontide heat is often almost suffocating; but the river-bottoms and the virgin woods of the southwestern lowlands flourish in an evergreen luxuriance which refutes the widespread opinion that heat *per se* is a characteristic concomitant or a cause of aridity. The highlands of Northern Tartary rival those of Dakota in barrenness as well as in the severity

of their winter climate, while the equator in its range
through two continents and three large islands does not
touch a single desert nor any country that ever suffered
from a scarcity of water. Nor can sand-wastes be said to
impair the fertility of adjacent woodlands: on the contrary,
the forest encroaches upon the desert; and it is my delib-
erate opinion that if Asia and Africa could be delivered
from the tree-destroying animal miscalled *Homo sapiens,*
and left in the healing hands of Nature for half a millennium, the spread of arboreal vegetation would restore the
lost Eastern Paradise to its pristine glory. In torrid Yucatan hundreds of square miles have thus reclaimed themselves, and the arenals of Belonchen and Macoba, having
been left to their fate three or four generations ago, are now
covered with a tall second growth of timber trees.

With the exception of the nomadic Tabascanos, the inhabitants of Yucatan are chiefly agricultural, and their non-
carnivorous habits manifest themselves in the remarkable
tameness of birds and smaller quadrupeds. Bushcocks and
quails were dodging around in the weeds almost under the
hoofs of our mules, and only the larger *abutardas,* a species
of bustard (*Otis tarda*), deigned to take wing for a moment
when we approached their favorite haunts in the tall grass
of the hibiscus-groves. A graceful bird of the heron kind
was cleaning his pearl-gray plumage in our next neighborhood when we halted at a little creek for the benefit of our
mulada, and two black squirrels kept chasing each other
round and round a hollow fig-tree whose gigantic branches
overshadowed the dell of the streamlet from bank to bank.
High overhead a pair of parrots were fluttering about the
tree-top with frightened screams, but not on our account: a
tree snake had made its way to a branch immediately above
their hollow nest, and they foresaw the moment when the

safety of their young would depend on the strength of their untried wings.

"SAUVE QUI PEUT."

"Look here!" said the lieutenant: "what do you call that, close to the triple fork up there? It's too large for a squirrel: it must be some kind of black tree-bird. Do you see it moving?"

Stepping back, I distinguished a round protuberance that might be an excrescence of the tree or the rump of a half-hidden animal. With the exception of the wedge-tailed woodpecker, birds do not cling to the main stem of a tree. It must be a raccoon or a cluster of bats, I thought.

"I see it plainly now," said the guide: "it's a *hormiguero*" (tamandua, or little ant-bear). "He's picking ants out of that hollow branch."

"No, no," insisted the lieutenant: "it must be a bird. A hormiguero is larger, and would show his long tail."

"He'll show it mighty quick if you will lend me that rifle for a moment. Thank you.—*Queda*, Paquita!"

The mule stood stock-still, but somehow the shot went a trifle too high, tearing the bark about an inch above the nose of the doubtful entity.

"Yes, you are right. I see his long snout now," said Don Perez. "You scared him, anyhow."

The report and the bark-explosion under his nose had caused the ant-bear to clasp the tree with a convulsive grip, but in a shock of surprise rather than of fear. Unconscious of any offence against mankind in general and the specimens present in particular, he failed to realize the fell significance of the phenomenon, and, after sniffing and squinting around the bullet-hole, turned his head and eyed us in a way that seemed to solicit a clearer statement of our intentions. Was it a practical joke, or had we tried to furnish him a business-opening to the ant-colonies of the interior tree? The next second might have solved his doubts, but better counsels prevailed, and we left him hugging the tree and his charitable illusion.

Riding slowly along the brink of a deep gully in the hope of finding a suitable camping-place, we saw a thick yellow smoke rising from a clump of taxus-trees about a mile farther down, and I thought I heard the peculiar howling bark of an Indian dog.

"There are no ranchos hereabouts," said the guide: "it must be a gypsy-camp, wandering Indians,—*Tabascanos*, as they call them. I'll bet my mule that we shall find a spring or something in that hollow: those chaps have a good nose for drinking-water."

After inspecting the ravine near the camp and finding

our hopes of water abundantly realized, we decided to "ranch" a little farther down in a grove of wild fig-trees (*Adansonia*), whose leafy roof in case of rain would protect us against all but the heaviest showers, and certainly intercept every drop of dew. Like the elm in the North, the Adansonia is here the shade-tree by excellence, and can dispute the prize of beauty and usefulness with any palm. The figs of the wild tree are insipid, being leathery, dry, and somewhat deficient in saccharine elements, but they make excellent mast, and a single full-grown *higuera* sheds yearly from eight hundred to twelve hundred bushels of its small grayish-green fruit, besides the large quantities eaten by tree-rats, monkeys, and birds.

We had blankets enough to dispense with a fire, and could enjoy the full luxury of the gradual decrease of caloric as the night wind swelled from an intermittent afflatus to a steady breeze. Bats, night-cicadas, and moths fluttered around our heads, but no mosquitoes: the highlands of Central Yucatan offer no congenial habitat to the miasma-loving pests. Heat alone cannot breed gnats, any more than it can raise clouds from an arid soil. The mosquito is not a native of any special latitude: his home is wherever the sun shines on a mixture of stagnant water and decaying vegetable matter. Like watering-place doctors, the gnats of the northern swamps have to suspend business during the frost season, but they make up for lost time: the summer-garden of Beelzebub, the great mass-meeting ground of all his fly-fiends, is not in the jungles of the Punjaub nor in the fens of the lower Senegal, but on the beaver-meadows of Sault Ste. Marie, Michigan, where hunters and woodchoppers have to wear gauze veils in July, though the winter temperature sinks forty degrees below zero.

"Hadn't we better sleep by reliefs?" I heard the lieutenant say when my eyes had already closed business for that day. "This camp needs a sentry: those red devils are prowling around our mules, if I am not much mistaken. Yes, there are two or three of them sneaking around the trees back there," said he after a while. "Listen! you can hear them talking. I saw one quite plainly a while ago with something like a stick or a bow in his hand."

"I'm going to find out what they want," said the guide, rising from his couch; "but our mules are all right, you may depend on that. The Tabascanos have no use for them: they are tramp-Indians—not a cavalryman in the tribe."

The reconnoissance was brief and satisfactory. "I thought so," said he: "the poor devils are hunting *cachiporras*" (frugivorous bats): "they swarm around fig-trees after dark. One of those chaps has got four of them already, and would have his bag full, he says, if he hadn't been afraid to disturb the caballeros. They will soon have enough, anyhow: that's what they built that fire for."

"Por Dios! to eat them?"

"Of course they will: the Tabascanos will eat grubs and caterpillars, and prefer them to the best fruit in America. They have a nickname for the Yucatan Indians that means *monomozos*" (monkey-boys), "because our red-skins live on monkey-food,—bananas and pineapples, and such-like."

Before we broke camp the next morning the Tabascanos passed us in single file, carrying bundles of dried meat and household stuff, on their way to the hunting-grounds of the Rio Belize. Males as well as females wore a full head of hair, divided in three or four tails that hung down to their girdles or fluttered in the breeze like the standard of a capitan pasha. Prejudice aside, it does not look bad if the hair is kept well back, and is perhaps the best head-gear in a tropical climate, since it keeps the scalp cool by evaporating the perspiration, which is condensed or checked under an air-tight hat.

TABASCANO INDIANS.

After breasting a steep bluff we kept along the ridge of the Cerro de Macoba, the backbone of Central Yucatan, a hill-chain of calcareous spar with deep woodlands on either side. The limestone-mounds before us enclosed broad arenals entirely devoid of vegetation, and long before noon the air became hazy and tremulous with heat, the outline of the eastern horizon grew indistinct, and the large barrens ahead glittered now and then with the wavy water-hues of a transient mirage.

El Pecador had led the way in silence for a couple of miles, when he drew rein in the chequered shade of a mimosa-tree and came to a full right about. "Just turn your head this way, doctor," said he,—"eastward, or east by northeast, I should say. Don't you smell something?"

"What do you mean?"

"Something like plum-pudding, I mean. Do you know what day this is?"

"What day of the month? Last Monday was the twenty-first— Why, you are right: this is the twenty-fourth of December, Christmas Eve and Plum-pudding Night! What shall we do about it?"

"I'll tell you what we can do. There is a string of ranchos on the Rio de Belonchen, about six leagues ahead, where we can buy all the material for a stunning Christmas stew,—beans, bacon, potatoes, eggs and all. Now, I know a fine spring in the river-bottom, with plenty of shade, where we could make a night of it if the gentlemen will agree to let their dinner go. We can reach the river at four o'clock if we keep on at a decent trot."

The motion was carried by acclamation, and our mules went ahead as if they sniffed the river from afar, while Simoncito, our groom, wore a six-inch grin reflecting visions of *garbanzas con jamón y chili colorado*. Our *programme de cuisine* was settled in all its details when we dismounted in a shady dell in the Belonchen Valley: Don Perez was to accompany me on a fuel-forage in the lower river-bottom, the Pecador to canvass the ranchos with a pocketful of coppers and a couple of bags, and the *mozo* undertook to effect the loan of a large *olla*, or earthen pot, which he remembered to have seen at the rancho of an acquaintance.

The Pecador returned last, but his efforts had been exceedingly productive,—too much so, in fact, for the capacity of the olla, which was medium-sized and rather too flat for a blazing fire. Still, a two-gallon *dosis* of brown beans and yams, with eggs, lard, and onions, would meet all immediate wants, and the bliss of anticipation had reconciled us to the imperfection of earthly things in general when we lifted the earthen pot from the ashes. While the mess cooled off we decided to collect a dessert of yellow grapes from the vine-mantled trees in the river-bottom, and all hands were set to forage, the mozo being left to guard the palladium and get the dishes ready. I had nearly filled my hat with the contributions of a single sycamore-tree when I heard a loud scream from the direction of the spring, and my blood ran cold with a horrible misgiving even before I had understood the meaning of the shrieks which were soon echoed from the lower end of the dell: "El cochino! the hog! the hog! Santissima! she's upset the pot! *Transó la olla!* there goes our supper!"

"Sic transit gloria!" Overpoweringly tragic, but true. A big sow, attracted by the savory steam, had strolled up from the canebrake, and while the mozo was filling a tin pail at the spring she had made a rush for the main stake, upset the olla, and spilt its contents on the ash-strewn ground

We stood around in that deepest sorrow which despairs to find relief in words, when the lieutenant arrived from the farther end of the grove, his eyes dilated with terror, but not realizing at first sight the full extent of our bereavement. "Oh, the brute! What!" seeing the empty pot, "nothing rescued, nothing at all? upset the kettle altogether" *Quarenta mil caraxos del vivo—*" I must elide the climax of the anathema.

"There now!" laughed the Pecador: "isn't it clear that

a man cannot get along in this country without the *lengua Castellana?* I should like to know what other language could have done justice to an occasion like this?"

"Por amor de los santos, lend me your shot-gun, Don Felix!" whimpered the mozo. "we have to get even with that brute. Thank you. I'll run her down, if it takes me all night. Here—"

But in the next moment the Pecador had him by the shoulder· "Hold on there! Put that gun down, young man. I hope that none of us will ever see another Christmas Day if that sow is going to get off with a spoonful of small shot. I'll make her pay the full value of that supper."

"What are you going to do? Roast her alive?"

"Never you mind. I'll make it hotter for her than any fire this side of Halifax. Hand me that cowhide."

He crushed his hat down, bridled his beast with a hitch of the halter, and galloped away in pursuit of the fugitive sow, whose career had subsided into a lazy trot as she neared the river-bank. She allowed him to approach within a hundred yards before she looked round, but, finding he was on her traces, she gathered herself up and dashed away at full speed along the shore of the stream. He overtook her at the mouth of a little influent, and if grief interferes with eupepsia I do not think that hog ever digested its best supper.

Our loss, after all, was chiefly one of time: beans, lard, and eggs enough were left to fill the olla once more, and the success of our grape-forage could assuage our chagrin at the absence of yams. Soon after sunset the vibratory boom of a kettledrum sounded across the valley· the Indians of the river-ranchos were going to celebrate the Holy Night with a *gran juncion* of bonfires, music, and chants,—

perhaps an echo of the old Mexican Sun-festivals, which ushered in the winter solstice for centuries before the golden astrum of the teocallis was superseded by the wooden cross. But the original significance of these *beal-fires* has long been forgotten : what the troopers of Grijalva and Montejo attempted in vain the legionaries of St. Francis have thoroughly accomplished. From Sisal to Cape Vigia the agricultural Yucatecos have accepted the yoke of the cross, and their intolerant treatment of the pagan Ustecs and Tabascanos has frequently been

LYNCHING A LUNCH-FIEND.

the cause of inter-Indian wars which enabled the Caucasians

to hold the balance of power in spite of their numerical
insignificance. At present the resistance of the Gentiles has
almost entirely ceased, and local insurrections are promptly
suppressed by the orthodox natives without the assistance
of the general government. In the district of Izamal and
Valladolid there are Indian *curas* and Indian inquisitors
who enforce the statutes of the Church with the proverbial
zeal of new converts, and have aided the Franciscan missionaries by translating portions of the Bible into the vernacular of their respective tribes, though the ostensible purpose
of the gospel has hardly been furthered by the barbarous
methods of their propaganda   In many of the larger pueblos
the assessment of tithes and school-taxes is farmed out to
Indian *colectores*, who do not hesitate to sequester the household valuables of defaulting sceptics, and secure the con-
nivance of the ecclesiastical authorities by reclaiming apostates and deserters without extra charge.   On the upper
Belize the Ustee rancheros used to evade the wrath of their
spiritual guardians by taking *en masse* to the woods and
rocks, but after the introduction of West Indian bloodhounds
by their *fermeir-général* the danger of unbelief has ceased to
be a controverted dogma.   The *Voz de Mexico* mentions a
"collector" of El Cayo so famous for his skill in reclaiming
dissenters that in the winter of 1873 he was sent to the Rio
Zelades, in the eastern part of the State, where the infidels
were openly defying their pastor, and declined to marry or
be given in marriage after the rite of an infallibly expensive
Church.   The collector went down with two assistants and
a picked pack of his four-legged propagandists, and was
soon able to report a rousing revival.

Passing through the rancheria the next morning, we saw
a characteristic specimen of the "colored curate" (*cura
prieto*), as the Yucatecos call their indigenous clerics,—a

RECLAIMING AN APOSTATE.

fat, powerful mestizo, who strutted at the head of the procession under the canopy of a long-handled cotton umbrella upheld by his acolyte. He carried a Bible and a little bunch of bulrushes, probably a sort of aspersory. Our mozo knew him personally, and described him as a severe disciplinarian who had been known to exact a fee of " cien fanegas" (about sixty bushels) of maize for baptizing an illegitimate papoose. On taking

holy orders he had also assumed the patronymic of his
defunct Caucasian predecessor, Pedro Santerra, whom he

DON PEDRO SANTO.

imitated in his habit of spicing his sermons with **Spanish**
sesquipedalities. "Don Pedro Santo" his unregenerate
neighbors used to call him.

Half a league southeast of the rancheria we reached the
camino real from Campeche to Uxmal, and by an easy
ascent of seven miles the ridge of the Cerro de Macoba,
here the watershed between the Gulf and the Caribbean
Sea. In the far southeast we had a glimpse of the Belize

coast-jungles now and then, a light-blue expanse spangled with water-bright streaks and dots; nearer by, the valley of the Rio Bacala, winding between densely-wooded hills; and on our left, the Cerro de Izamal, whose plateau abounds with ruins that antedate the oldest aboriginal traditions. The table-lands of our higher ridge, too, somehow suggested the idea of former cultivation: curious long-drawn furrows, though full of brambles and stones, bore a decided resemblance to boundary-ditches, with the earth heaped up at either side; a pile of rocks at the brink of a deep ravine reminded us, not without reason, perhaps, of a buttressed *tête de pont;* and the gradual descent of the winding slopes seemed too regular to be quite accidental. With woodlands on either side, our ridge was very sparsely timbered: the plateau seemed naturally arid, and the Spanish muleteers had aggravated the evil by their condemnable habit of using the wayside shade-trees for firewood: the most frequented highways of New Spain are lined with tree-stumps and the charred vestiges of innumerable camp-fires. In certain respects the Latin races are our superiors in hygienic insight, but their conformity to the health laws of Nature is subjective rather than objective. Cleanly in his personal habits, the Spanish creole tolerates all kinds of nuisances in and about his rancho: he permits his land to become a desert or a seed-plot of malaria, but counteracts the consequences ·by dietetic precautions.

Frugal, in the original sense of the word, meant literally to live on fruits in distinction to carnivorous habits, which the ancient Italians discountenanced as a dietetic aberration , and this literal kind of frugality is no bad plan in the tropics. We halted for refreshments at a wayside *renta,* and heard to our dismay that the ventero had only tortillas and oranges for sale; but we found no reason to repent our

lenten fare   The sun seemed to have lost his power for
mischief this morning; the roasting of our skin did not
affect the department of the interior; our orange breakfast
had made us caloric-proof   Besides being the most digestible articles of food, fruits seem to have the property of
lowering the temperature of the system, as it is increased
by meat and all kinds of fat; and I have often found a
fresh-plucked pineapple or orange from twenty to thirty-
five degrees cooler than the surrounding air under the
shadiest trees.   Plants seem to possess a power for producing
cold analogous to that exhibited by animals of producing
heat, and even in the midst of a large desert the cool ex-
halations of an isolated forest will draw rain from passing
clouds which withhold that blessing from the thirsty sand-
fields around.   Insects, too, seem somehow able to maintain a comfortable temperature under a blazing sun : at ten
o'clock the flint buttresses on our ridge felt as hot as oven-
plates, and the lizards in the shade of the cliffs lay gasping
with open mouth, but the insect world seemed to celebrate
a holiday, the manna-mesquites swarmed with wasps and
beetles, and the flower-tufts of the dusty-green cassias
sparkled with hovering butterflies.

A winding ravine brought us to the valley of the Rio
Macoba before noon, and, after stopping at different unpro-
ductive ranchos, we found the right one and replenished our
mess-bag with a store of cakes and bananas.   There was no
lack of drinking-water in the creeks, but we had set our
heart on reaching a little eminence with a magnificent clump
of trees that had been a conspicuous landmark for the last
four hours.   Our perseverance met its reward : no draught
of spring-water could be more refreshing than the air that
received us on entering the tree-shade : the sudden change
equalled the thermal contrast at the mouth of a deep cave.

CHRISTMAS IN YUCATAN.

The family of a poor ranchero were eating their Christmas dinner at the foot of a giant fig, and rose with exclamations of welcome: "*Buenos dias de Dios, caballeros!*—a happy

Christmas to you! What fine weather you have brought us! Dismount, amigos : *hay campo por dos pueblos*—there is room here for a cityful."

We needed not much urging, and in a few minutes the good *ranchera* had revived the embers of her camp-fire, and proceeded to warm our tortillas with a sauce of onions and clarified butter.' They declined our invitation to share our repast, but showed their good-will by joining us at the second course, and our combined efforts soon produced an imposing pile of banana-peels. While we enjoyed our Christmas siesta the ranchero's muchachos combined pleasure with business by chasing the big yellow butterflies that visited the honeysuckle festoons of our shade-trees, the tally being kept by their little sister, who announced each capture with screams of delight and derision of the unsuccessful competitor. Their father's farm was crossed by the camino real to Uxmal, and visitors from the strange country called Inglaterra had often paid as much as twenty cents for a single butterfly,—the day's wages of a stout peon for a flimsy and almost imponderable insect! But fun, to be unmixed, must be unprofitable, and the young entomologists soon devised a change of programme. On the opposite bank of a deep ravine grazed a troop of young mules, led—or rather misled—by a wary old donkey who had retired from business to enjoy the evening of his life on the sunny slopes of the cerro. In a bush near their pasture, but overhanging the ravine, a colony of black hornets had built a conspicuous nest, a grayish-white spheroid at least sixteen inches long by a foot in diameter. A common stone would hardly carry across, but, after a number of fruitless attempts, one of the boys hit the nest with a flat piece of slate, and two seconds later the mules joined in a series of antics that would have made the fortune of any circus-proprietor. The old ran-

chero laughed till he screeched, and we had just secured our
animals, who were watching the evolutions with growing
interest, when the performance closed with a thundering
hurdle-race through the underbrush of the chaparral.

When the boys returned their progenitor broached a package of cigaritos, and the whole family then indulged in a
sociable Christmas smoke. They were *peones de rotura,*—
board-laborers working for their rent and a few shillings
a month,—too poor to indulge in *pulque* or garbanzas on
week-days, but evidently with no reason to envy the noon-
ing of a Northern factory-laborer with his ten dollars a
week and ten daily working-hours. He who thinks otherwise has never seen a Pittsburg iron-worker on a midwinter
day bolting his dinner in a corner of the rolling-mill, where
flying cinders and sooty drops mix with his pea-soup, and
the draught of three open doors with the breath of the
furnace, while his son or the boarding-house boy stands
shivering by, waiting for the dishes and his share of the
leathery pie-crust. *O Dios del Sur!*

Excess of caloric might cause as much discomfort as
excessive cold if it could not be so much more easily
counteracted. Even the after-dinner hour—generally the
warmest from within and without—may be passed right
pleasantly at such trifling expense as may be involved by
a trip to the next shade-trees. After a frugal dinner, resting on a shady eminence, without insane scruples against the
removal of superfluous garments, you may defy the dog-star
to do its worst. Such a siesta-camp found, what can exceed
the luxury of its dreamy repose?—though in the tropics
you have to dream with your eyes open. it is not easy to
slumber during the busiest working-hour of the organic
powers. Earth seems surcharged with vitality as the sky
with sunlight. You feel the pulsations of Nature's heart,

the breath of the Dea Genetrix: the essence of life quickens the soil, moves over and in the waters, and peoples the air with a thousand forms: the spirit of Vishnu is almost visibly present, the day-fairies may bring you visions, but they are visions that banish sleep.

After an hour or so we remounted, though the weather was still oppressively warm. Dark-gray clouds had risen from the east, but failed to overtake the sun, and we envied the parrots that returned in swarms from the fields to their homes in the depths of the virgin woods. A flight of macaws in a wooded valley on our left were called together by their leader and started off in double file, or rather by sets of twos, for high overhead the column divided pairwise, and the separate couples took a bee-line to their respective nests. It was a pretty sight, and their harsh screams sounded clear and melodious from the distance,—from an astonishing distance indeed, for the voice of the larger parrots is not less remarkable for its power than for its versatility: the crested macaws can summon their mates from across the broadest rivers of the American tropics.

"It reminds me of home," said the Cuban. "In the province of Bayamo they are our weather-prophets, and if they hurry home before sunset the farmers follow, because it is a sure sign of rain."

"I do not know about rain, but I reckon we'll have a storm before night," said the guide. "They have dry gales in this country that are worse than any thunderstorm: the wind doesn't seem to have so much force if there is water in the air."

"Did you see that lightning?"

"Yes: that decides it," said he: "we are in for a rainstorm now. Close up, gentlemen: I'm trying to get you to Charley Cortina's tower-house if I can: he has better accommodation than any ventero we could possibly reach to-night."

If animals cannot be credited with reason proper, it must be a sort of acquired instinct which enables them to appreciate their own share of interest in the rate of progress. Our mules went ahead at a spanking trot, and continued to improve their gait without other prompting than that of the muttering thunder and a chill gust of wind which suddenly cooled the air by twenty or thirty degrees. Splashing through a creek, we started a drove of *mayarros*, or dwarf peccaris, which had huddled together in the canebrake under the shelter of a fallen tree, and I noticed that one of the young pigs had its legs so entangled with pond-weeds and mud that it might have been easily captured. But there was no time for zoological adventures: a whirlwind of dust and leaves swept across the creek and over our heads when we reached the top of the opposite bank.

"Single file!" yelled the Pecador. "Keep up, caballeros, unless you're waterproof· not a minute to lose."

We galloped through a rocky defile and away over the chaparral in the direction of a banana-plantation at the foot of a wooded ridge.

"Is that Cortina's place?"

"No· the next below it,—the house at the farther end of the ridge."

"Too late!" cried the Cuban. "Look back there: it's coming like a flying deluge."

"We have to keep ahead of it. Wake 'em up, gents! *Alza!* Devil take the hindmost!"

"He won't take me, then," shouted the Cuban. "Let's see what they call riding in your country, Mr. Guide. Here goes! Santos de Cuba!"

He had the advantage of us, being slight-built and long-spurred, and the hydrophobic mule forged ahead at a rate which completely redeemed her character. There was no need of looking back: the oncoming storm roared in our rear like a waterfall, and a dust-cloud whirling leaves and twigs over our heads made us clutch our sombreros. The rancho was almost reached,—they had seen us, for we heard their cheers and the creak of the swinging gate,—but in the moment when we galloped through the corral the flying sea overtook us, and no wetter guests ever crossed the threshold of Carlos Cortina.

The "tower-house" had originally been built for a convent, and the walls were of enormous thickness, the material having been brought in the form of ready-hewn limestone blocks from the ruins of a neighboring teocalli; but I could not get rid of the impression that I *felt* as well as heard the storm-blasts which seemed to strike the house from all sides at once. After removing our wet mantles the family of the landlord pressed around us in silent awe, till we had to laugh in our own despite at the manœuvres of a little sapajou monkey who was trying to hide behind a hand-loom in the corner, and squealed and chattered in his attempts to squeeze his shoulders through. Daylight was almost eclipsed, but the air was fairly deluged with electric fire, and the voice of Jupiter Tonans rose to a continuous roar. There were eleven persons in the room, including two women and several children, but I do not think that any of them were *afraid:* the feeling of fear in such moments is kept in abeyance by a stronger emotion, an excitement which neither experience nor lightning-rods will help us to outgrow. It may take the form of devotional exaltation or of boisterous mirth, but only the opium-torpor of a Turk would be proof against crashes that shake the air behind a wall of bombproof masonry and flashes that can penetrate the veil of a cloudburst. Moreover, I suspect that the sensations of a deaf and blind person during a tropical thunderstorm would furnish some curious arguments in favor of Von Haller's conjecture that the organism of the human soul is an electro-magnetic apparatus

"That will cool the weather for the next two weeks, anyhow," said the landlord, when the worst was over; "but it comes a little too soon to suit me: my corn isn't quite ripe, and I am afraid there is not much left standing."

"That will disappoint your long-tailed neighbors, the apes," laughed the guide. "Better get your corn in as it is, or they will take it for a New Year's present, as they did last year."

"Oh, they are welcome," said the farmer. "I made them pay for all they got: I caught fourteen last summer and sold them all but three."

"Do you catch any in winter-time?"

"There will be a chance to-morrow if it clears up before morning, but the best time is the rainy season" (June to November). "If the woods are thoroughly soaked, they can't stand it any longer, and come out into the open fields with the first sunshine."

"You ship them to Campeche, I suppose?"

"A few, señor, but my foreign visitors pay me more than the regular traders. This is only eight miles from Uxmal, you know, and strangers pass almost every week. One of my neighbors has a regular curiosity-shop of birds and pets."

"What is the average price of your monkeys?"

"All the way from four reals to four dollars, sir · one American lady paid me four dollars for an old *mono rusteco*" (sapajou), "the wickedest brute I ever caught. Strangers somehow seem to prefer the full-grown ones,—maybe on account of their glossy fur,—but if they asked my advice I should tell them honestly that they throw their money away if they pay as much as four copper cents for the finest old monkey in Yucatan, unless they want to eat him or stuff him. If they hope to get any fun out of the brute, they are cheated· a badger or a boar peccari isn't half as contrary as an old monkey. As a rule, the funniness of a monkey ends with his second year."

The rain ceased toward morning, but the air was still humid and sultry, and our guide advised us to wait for a safer guarantee of fair weather, a change of wind or of temperature. While the farmer inspected his corn-fields we ascended a little mound behind the house to take a look at the ruins of a teocalli, or ancient altar-pyramid, which from the valley looked almost like a strongly-entrenched rock-fortress. I could not ascertain the former height of the pyramid, nor how often its ruins had been pillaged by modern builders, but, to judge by the dimensions of the present ruins, I believe that the original structure must have been the work of different generations, unless the mandate of a despot had assembled an army of architects. The mission of Sacrificios, or the "tower-house" (*casa torrada*), as the neighbors call it, was built in 1812 with the contributions collected by the Franciscan monks in the district of Valladolid; but the site chosen by its first projectors was sixteen English miles farther up the river, near the junction of the Rio Macoba with a perennial affluent. It seems that the workmen and their purveyors were in the habit of fetching their forage from the woodlands of the lower river-valley, and that on one of these expeditions a Mexican woodcutter discovered the teocalli of Sacrificios, a huge rubbish-mound entirely covered with a shroud of creepers and tanglewood. Finding the stones superior in size and finish to those his countrymen were chiselling with so much labor, he reported his find to the contractor, who at once came down, and, after a careful examination of the ruins, offered to execute his contract at one-third of the stipulated price if his employers would agree to change the site to the neighborhood of

THE RUINS OF SACRIFICIOS.

the teocalli. The Franciscans, seeing their way out of a financial embarrassment, consulted their superior, who, whispering he would ne'er consent, not only consented, but also recognized the miraculous character of the discovery, which is now claimed to have been the result of a vision revealing the locality of the strange quarry when the builders were straitened for the means of pursuing their pious work.

The teocalli itself is certainly a marvel of enterprise. The foundation-walls, consisting of a triple stratum of cyclopean blocks, cover an area of nearly half an acre, and would alone furnish the material for half a dozen churches, while the upper seven tiers of the superstructure are covered with ornaments which must have cost infinite labor if it is true that their sculptors were unacquainted with the use of iron implements. Between here and Uxmal the ground is almost covered with débris, and the "sacrificial mound" of the Rio Macoba may have been a suburban palace or fortified acropolis of the great city.

"Caught a monkey?" inquired our guide, when we met the farmer's family at breakfast.

"No, but we lost one," whimpered the little girl.

"Halloo, what's the matter? Did one of your pets get away?"

"Look here!" said the farmer, showing us the dead body of a little tamarin (*Midas rosalia*): "all the wild monkeys in Yucatan and all my dogs would I have given for this little fellow, and one of our pet squirrels bit him to death last night. *Parece que tuvo alma*—I'm sure he had a soul," said he: "my children never had a prettier playmate."

"Your squirrel did it, you say?"

"Yes, he burned his tail a couple of weeks ago, and last night the squirrel found that sore place and gnawed his tail clear up to the backbone,—bled him to death, I suppose. When my children found him this morning he was as limp as a rag, and died before I came back. It isn't my fault: I shouldn't have sold him for ten dollars. But just do look at those children: they wouldn't cry half as much if the curate of our parish had died."

"Never mind, Anita," said her mother: "your papa will catch you another one just like this."

"No, he never will," wailed Anita. "*O, mi querido, mi pobre chi'querido!*—my sweetheart, my poor little sweetheart!"

"Padrecito," said the boy, who had clutched his father's arm till he secured his attention,—"padrecito, mother says that you are going to skin that squirrel alive: when will you do it?"

"Yes, my boy,—as soon as we have buried poor Chico."

"Father," continued the boy, "will you let me rub him with pepper-sauce after you've skinned him?"

"He's right," laughed the Pecador: "you ought to get ten dollars' worth of satisfaction out of the brute that did it: are you going to kill him?"

"*Que sirve?*" ("cui bono?"), said he: "it's their nature, I suppose: squirrels are nothing but overgrown rats, anyhow."

Our kind host accompanied us to the upper end of his farm, from where we could reach our destination by a trail across the hill-pastures, the road through the river-bottom being somewhat miry after the heavy rain. The wind had veered to the northwest, and between the slowly-shifting clouds on the eastern horizon the sun glittered on a light-green plain intersected by still brighter, almost canary-yellow, stripes and lines, radiating up the river toward the dark-green hill-country at our feet. The bright lines marked the extent of the riparial palmetto-swamps, the home of countless varieties of water-birds and the favorite haunt of the roving Tabascanos, while the agricultural Maceguals stick to the upland valleys, where their crops are eked out by an unfailing harvest of spontaneous fruits. The banks of the Macoba are overhung with fig-trees and cabbage-palms, festooned with the coils of the *uva real*, whose small but sweet and very prolific yellow grapes alone would secure a homeless wanderer against starvation: farther up, butternut-palms, carob-trees, mangoes, and wild mulberries form evergreen and ever-teeming orchards, and the underbrush abounds with nuts, berries, and different wild-growing Leguminosæ, whose beans are often mixed with those of the cultivated varieties.

Of all non-indigenous fruit-trees, the biennial banana alone requires tillage and artificial propagation, but rewards its cultivator so abundantly that a populous village might here be supported with the same amount of labor and on the same acreage which in the North would hardly maintain a small family. A dinner of brown beans, maize cakes, milk, and bananas requires but few *entremets*,—grapes perhaps, a little honey or butter now and then, or an occasional bit of bacon; but of the four first-named staples the Yucatan farmer can secure a redundant supply by one hour of daily work, without using any of the labor-saving contrivances which have converted our large Eastern farms into so many steam-factories.

At the outskirts of a coppice of taxus-trees we came across a singular obstacle. A long wall of verdure it seemed, a perfectly straight hedge of brier and bush-ropes, but a closer inspection revealed a substratum of masonry, heavy and rough-hewn but well-cemented limestone blocks. A dome-like mass of foliage on a hill on our right was probably supported by a similar nucleus, and every now and then our animals stumbled over rubbish-heaps and scattered blocks covered with grass or a network of cordero-brambles. A good deal of building material seemed to have been quarried in the next neighborhood, for the rock-walls of a narrow valley a little farther down were hewn into terraces and polygons for a stretch of nearly half a mile.

As we pursued our trail along the shady banks of a little

creek our guide suddenly halted at the foot of a massive bridge-head, and we dismounted to lead our mules over a barricade of heaped-up débris: we had entered the suburbs of Uxmal. The forest seemed literally to rise from a buried city. Almost everywhere the ground was paved or strewn with square-hewn limestone blocks; leafy arbors and copses, standing about in detached groups, turned out to be rubbish-heaps with a film of vegetation; and when we haltered our mules under the canopy of a flowering tamarind we found that its roots had wrenched a sculptured corner-stone from the base of a buried terrace.

What might a dwelling-place of the living be where a city of the dead could robe itself in such a garb of joy? The platform of the crumbling terrace was covered with a flower-carpet of wildering geraniums, lianas and evergreen vines twined their garlands from wall to wall, and pendent tresses of tillandsia moss fluttered like banners from the lintel of a broken gateway. As the sun rose higher the noon-blooming heliconias shook the rain from their locks and opened the light-blue eyes of their feather-flowers, and when the north wind dissipated the clouds the sun himself blinked through the swaying screen of the liana tangle and coquetted with the dancing rivulet at our feet. Not a nook, not a recess, was tenantless: lizards peeped from the narrow loopholes, butterflies and humming-birds carried their morning salute to their favorite flowers or visited the shady arcades where a pair of squirrel-monkeys chattered roguishly in their hiding-place, and the leafy vault overhead resounded with the jubilee of the weaver-thrush.

How cheap is happiness in the tropics! and how expensive in the latitudes where light and warmth cease to be the free gifts of Nature! Our tongues have been attuned to hymns of thanksgiving and resignation, but how many thousand hearts in Europe and North America may repeat the lament of Lenau's exiled Circassian and his prayer to the sun,—

> Take me from this icy desert,
> Up to thee, eternal One!

We may point to our superior civilization, our steam-ploughs and sewing-machines, our petroleum stoves, gas-lit cities, benevolent societies and feather beds, but all that proves only that life has become more complex on the in-door plan, and that the absence of natural comforts has promoted the elaboration of some highly ingenious substitutes. Reduced to its essentials, however, the problem is just this: Has our net surplus of happiness been increased? Can we discount the gratuitous blessings of the South after subtracting the manufacturing expenses of our boasted succedanea? Or has our burden of woe been lightened enough to incline the balance in our favor? Are cold and hunger a less fruitful source of misery than indolence? Where is the reward of incessant toil if its produce is swallowed by those ever-clamorous creditors? Our system of ethics, a mixture of puritan and mercantile principles, makes us liable to forget that labor is a blessing only as a means to something better, not as the end of existence, and that the temptations of leisure may survive its golden opportunities. Ten hours of factory-work, often followed by a heavy share of domestic drudgery, leave not much chance for the gratification of an ugly habit, but certainly even less for the cultivation of a fine talent, for weeds may still thrive where nobler plants must hopelessly starve.

It cannot be denied that the higher latitudes have become the home of the superior races, but the theory which ascribes the shortcomings of our neighbors to unavoidable climatic influences cannot be reconciled with the stature and strength of the ancient Greeks and modern Abyssinians, nor with the relics of a thousand cities whose builders proved that enterprise and genius may flourish in a winter-less clime.

The present degeneracy of the noblest Southern nation is rather a consequence of the baleful physical vices which have fastened upon mankind like a canker, whose ravages can only be counteracted by a powerful prophylactic. This antidote has been found in a cold climate. Cold air is a tonic and antiseptic: like quinine and belladonna, a heavy frost acts as a febrifuge; it preserves animal tissues from decay, and enables us to indulge with comparative impunity in a variety of anti-natural habits for which our Southern neighbors have paid with their prestige and their pristine vigor. The bitterness of the cure may be the condition of its efficacy. But is the evil itself a necessary one? Our scientific journals lately adverted to the discovery of a California opium-eater who could "sober up" at ten minutes' notice by swallowing an heroic dose of arsenic; and more than three centuries ago Paracelsus found that the progress of a virulent, and till then incurable, disease could be arrested by the internal use of mercury. These remedies, too, may be infallible, and, on the whole, the lesser evil, but all that would hardly justify the assertion that sobriety and purity can only thrive on a basis of arsenic and quicksilver; and yet it is in a precisely analogous way that a cold climate counteracts a tendency to sloth and ignorance and mitigates the consequences of dietetic abuses.

To Nature-abiding nations and individuals the upland regions of the tropics would offer chances of a happiness superior to that of the frost-plagued latitudes, by just as much as sunlight is superior to coal-gas, and the botanic garden of Lima to the finest Northern conservatory.

21

CHAPTER X.

THE AMERICAN POMPEII.

Sleeping in a leafy vault,
In a winding-sheet of ivy —SHENSTONE.

" EVERY tomb is a cradle," says Jean Paul ; and his apothegm holds good wherever the organism of Nature exerts its functions in undisturbed harmony. Life is the heir of Death : every mouldering plant fertilizes an aftergrowth of its kind, and if the races of mankind succeeded each other as the trees of the forest, a superior spirit might view the decay of an oak and of a nation with equal unconcern.

But while the fading flowers of the old year may console us with the hope of a coming spring, our lament over the withered empires of the Old World has a deeper significance ; the dying nations of the East have involved their fields· and forests in an equal fate : the lands that know them no more have themselves withered, and no spring can restore the prime of an exhausted soil. From Eastern Persia to Western Morocco, Earth has thus perished together with her inhabitants· Vishnu has resigned his power to Shiva, and the Buddhistic Nirvan, the final departure of the Genius of Life, has already begun for some of the fairest countries ever brightened by the sun of the Juventus Mundi.

The western shores of the Atlantic, too, have seen the rise and decline of mighty empires· the ruins of Uxmal equal those of Nineveh in grandeur as well as in the hope-

326

lessness of their decay, but the soil of Yucatan has survived its tyrants. In the struggle between Chaos and
Cosmos the organic powers have here prevailed, and the
sylvan deities have resumed their ancient sway.

There is a well-defined ridge of Tertiary limestone formation which divides the table-lands of the eastern peninsula from the wooded lowlands of the west, and the ruins
of Uxmal, Chichen, Izamal, and Macoba have all been
discovered in the western timber-lands, but have nowhere
betrayed their existence by the diminished exuberance of
the vegetation. Their walls are hedged, interlocked, and
covered with trees, and while the Oriental archæologist
has to grope in the sand-drifts of burning deserts, his Transatlantic colleague can thus pursue his studies in the shade
of a forest-region whose living wonders may well divide
his attention with the marvels of the past. Eighty years
ago the district of Macoba and Belonchen was an unexplored wilderness. The Jesuit missionaries of Valladolid
had recorded an Indian tradition about the vestiges of a
giant city in the neighborhood of Merida, but their vague
descriptions were supposed to refer to the large teocalli
near the convent of Sacrificios, and the rediscovery of the
Casas Grandes seems to have been as complete a surprise
to the citizens of Merida as the exhumation of Pompeii to
the burghers of Nola and Castellamare.

The great treasure-trove of 1829 has often been ascribed
to the Baron Frédéric de Waldeck, though since the publi-
cation of his memoirs in 1837 his countrymen have never
claimed that honor. His subsequent explorations made
Uxmal the Mecca of American antiquarians, but the amus-
ing account of the original discovery, as given in the *Voyage
Pittoresque*, proves that in archæology, not less than in other
sciences, the better part of our knowledge is what Lessing

called a "museum of collected curiosities, discovered by
accident and independently of each other." On the evening of the 1st of November, 1828, Don Pancho Yegros, a
Yucatan planter, and his guest, Dr. Lewis Mitchel, a Scotch
surgeon of Sisal harbor, returned from a hunting-expedition
in the Sierra Marma, and, seeking shelter from the threatening weather, happened to come across an Indian woodchopper, who guided them to a *sacristia*, an old Indian
temple in the depths of the forest. They lighted a fire,
and, having noticed some curious sculptures in a sort of
peristyle, the Scotchman proceeded to inspect the interior
of the building. The masonry was covered with dust and
spider-webs, but the application of wet rags discovered a
triple row of bas-relief decorations running along the walls
horizontally and at equal intervals, and between the roof
and the upper lintel of the door the limestone slabs were
covered with small figures which seemed too irregular for
simple ornaments, and might be hieroglyphic symbols.
After daybreak the Scotchman rummaged a pile of débris
behind the temple, and unearthed the torso of a little image,
which he pocketed with an enthusiasm that puzzled the
Spanish planter as much as his Indian serf. The natives
were unable to give any satisfactory account of the building,
and, taking his leave, the doctor requested his host to interview the old Indian residents of the neighborhood in regard
to the problematic temple, and rode away with the promise
to renew his visit in the course of the year.

"Isn't it strange," said Don Yegros when he was alone
with his peon, "that we have lived here for a lifetime without suspecting that there was such a curiosity in our neighborhood? Why, that caballero tells me that some of his
countrymen would buy those pictured stones for their weight
in silver!"

"He gave me half a dollar, anyhow," chuckled the Indian. "He ought to take those countrymen of his to the north end of the sierra: in the chaparral of the Rio Macoba there is a square league of ground just covered with such empty old buildings."

The hacendado turned on his heel: "Are you deranged? A square league of such ruins! You do not mean buildings like that we slept in last night?"

"No, señor; very different buildings,—houses as high as yours, and forty times as long. One of them has more rooms in it than there are tiles on your roof, and long galleries with sculptured heads and figures."

Don Yegros stood speechless for a moment. "Mil demonios!" he burst out when the stolid countenance of his serf told him that the fellow was in sober earnest. "Why, in the name of your five senses, could you not tell us that a minute sooner? Did you not see how delighted the caballero was to find that one old broken statue?"

"He liked it, did he? Well, I didn't know that, señor. I found a much prettier one in that same place a few years ago, and took it to our village priest, but came very near getting a good hiding for it. He smashed it, and cursed it for an idolatrous monster and me for a monstrous idiot."

"Well, so you are. Get on that horse now, and I give you just twenty minutes to overtake the caballero and bring him back here. Why, man, you came very near missing the only opportunity you ever had of being of any use in the world."

The caballero and the opportunity were retrieved, and on the next day the peon led an exploring-party to the jungles of the Rio Macoba, where they had to make their way through all the obstacles of a pathless wilderness, but on the third day found themselves in the midst of a hana-

shrouded Pompeii, and entered different edifices whose dimensions so far exceeded the expectations of their archæological companion that he decided to return at once and carry the news to the foreign residents of Sisal. They had discovered the ruins of Uxmal, which rival those of Thebes and Persepolis in beauty and grandeur as well as in extent, and stand unequalled and unapproached among the architectural relics of our own continent. While volumes had been written about the clumsy burrows of the Mound-builders and the naked brick walls on the Rio Gila, this city of palaces had slumbered in its forest shroud, unexplored by any visitor save the prying catamount and the silent tribe of the tropical bats, and, but for the accident of the rainstorm on that November night of 1828, might thus have slumbered for ever, like the lost Atlantis in her ocean grave.

Soon after his return to Sisal, Dr. Mitchel was interviewed by a French traveller, the Baron Jean Frédéric de Waldeck, who had visited the West Indies, Panama, and Guatemala, and had been attracted to Yucatan by the rumor of the marvellous discovery. They started for the backwoods as soon as the doctor could disengage himself from his professional duties, Waldeck intimating his intention to weed and clear the ruins at his own expense. But a cursory inspection of the main *casas*, their great extent, their distance from each other and from the next inhabited town, and the intricacy and rankness of the all-covering and all-pervading jungle, convinced the French traveller that the work of restoration would overtask his private resources. He therefore contented himself with making a careful draught of the accessible buildings, and prepared a memorial to the Mexican government, which the doctor undertook to translate and forward with the recommendations of all the provincial magnates and officials whose interest could be enlisted by his personal influence. A number of foreign merchants and landed proprietors of Yucatan signed this petition, and entrusted it to Don Cesar Pedraza (a relation of the general and presidential candidate of the same name), who was about to visit the Mexican capital. But the Yucatecos had been unfortunate in the choice of their delegate: General Pedraza was defeated, and Don Cesar, by his zealous support of his kinsman, incurred the ill-will of the omnipotent Santa Anna, during whose long military dictatorship and subsequent presidency Mexico was to all purposes an absolute monarchy. Santa Anna retained his power by proving himself a patriot in some international transactions, but reserved to himself the privilege of deciding all domestic matters by favoritism. He deposed the governor of Yucatan, and in his place appointed a man whose partisan policy and unscrupulous interference with the municipal affairs of the peninsula produced a ferment of factions that kept all non-political questions in the background. The explorations of Stephens and Catherwood at last revived the sensation, and in the summer of 1845, Señor Lizadas, the mayor of Merida, was induced to send a civil engineer and some of his peons to Uxmal with a view of improving the wretched roads; but soon after the mayor was worsted in a political trial of strength with the new state autocrat, and had to take refuge in New Orleans, while his real estate was confiscated by the governor. The death of the latter functionary in 1849 enabled Lizadas to return and recover his property, but in the mean while the archæological excitement had subsided, and the mouldering ruins were left to their fate.

A year after the election of Benito Juarez the president's accomplished secretary, Lerdo de Tejada, visited Yucatan,

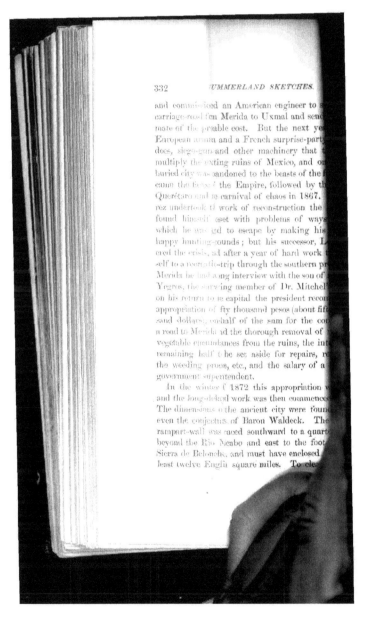

and commissioned an American engineer to s
carriage-road from Merida to Uxmal and send
mate of the probable cost. But the next ye
European armies and a French surprise-party
does, siege-guns and other machinery that t
multiply the existing ruins of Mexico, and on
buried city was abandoned to the beasts of the f
came the farce of the Empire, followed by th
Querétaro and its carnival of chaos in 1867.
rez undertook the work of reconstruction the
found himself beset with problems of ways
which he was glad to escape by making his
happy hunting-grounds; but his successor, L
ered the crisis, and after a year of hard work t
self to a recreation-trip through the southern pr
Merida he had a long interview with the son of a
Yegros, the surviving member of Dr. Mitchell'
on his return to the capital the president recom
appropriation of fifty thousand pesos (about fift
sand dollars), one-half of the sum for the con
n road to Merida and the thorough removal of
vegetable encumbrances from the ruins, the int
remaining half to be set aside for repairs, re
the weeding press, etc., and the salary of a
government superintendent.

In the winter of 1872 this appropriation w
and the long-delayed work was then commenced
The dimensions of the ancient city were found
even the conjectures of Baron Waldeck. The
rampart-wall was traced southward to a quarte
beyond the Rio Ncabo and east to the foot
Sierra de Belonche, and must have enclosed
least twelve English square miles. To clea

of its jungle-maze and the organic deposits of centuries
would have exhausted the scanty appropriation of the
trustees of the fund had to content themselves with clearing the main buildings and connecting them by avenues with
each other and with the carriage-road that is now opened
to San Lorenzo, where it connects with the old disused
highway to Merida. Even thus the undertaking can only
be completed by employing peons or Indian workmen
the neighboring planters volunteered to furnish gratis the
trustees only providing their food and the necessary tools.

For the same work of destruction and clearing which
the fire-deluge of Mount Vesuvius accomplished in a single
night has here been effected by the silent progress of the
real vegetation and decay in a manner which illustrates the
scientific axiom that in dynamic force and time are convertible factors. The mixture of ashes and pumice which
covers the City of Pompey is far easier to remove than the
tegumen of mould, gnarled roots, and tangled vines that
spread itself over the ruins of Uxmal. Like the rib of
a boa-constrictor, the flexible arms of the forest of the
cordero-vines have wound themselves around the beams
and projecting rocks; nay, forced their spreading into the
crevices of the thickest walls, sending out laterals
along the inner surface, so that often their grip can be
broken at the risk of breaking the building itself, some
times ... were found which had twenty root of the
... window sill after another is the
... completely around. If it
... has been supported close to the
... buildings it is very that
... by trees and vines that had
... and in the coming their
... its foundations. It is that

and commissioned an American engineer to survey a good carriage-road from Merida to Uxmal and send him an estimate of the probable cost. But the next year brought a European armada and a French surprise-party with torpedoes, siege-guns, and other machinery that threatened to multiply the existing ruins of Mexico, and once more the buried city was abandoned to the beasts of the forest. Then came the farce of the Empire, followed by the tragedy of Querétaro and the carnival of chaos in 1867. When Juarez undertook the work of reconstruction the poor Indian found himself beset with problems of ways and means which he was glad to escape by making his way to the happy hunting-grounds ; but his successor, Lerdo, weathered the crisis, and after a year of hard work treated himself to a recreation-trip through the southern provinces. At Merida he had a long interview with the son of Don Pancho Yegros, the surviving member of Dr. Mitchel's party, and on his return to the capital the president recommended an appropriation of fifty thousand pesos (about fifty-five thousand dollars), one-half of the sum for the construction of a road to Merida and the thorough removal of rubbish and vegetable encumbrances from the ruins, the interest of the remaining half to be set aside for repairs, repetitions of the weeding process, etc, and the salary of a mayoral, or government superintendent.

In the winter of 1872 this appropriation was granted, and the long-delayed work was then commenced in earnest. The dimensions of the ancient city were found to exceed even the conjectures of Baron Waldeck. The *muralla* or rampart-wall was traced southward to a quarter of a mile beyond the Rio Macabo and east to the foot-hills of the Sierra de Belonchen, and must have enclosed an area of at least twelve English square miles. To clear such a space

of its jungle-maze and the organic deposits of centuries
would have exhausted the scanty appropriation, and the
trustees of the fund had to content themselves with clearing the main buildings and connecting them by avenues with
each other and with the carriage-road that is now finished
to San Lorenzo, where it connects with the old military
highway to Merida. Even thus the undertaking could only
be completed by employing peons or Indian serfs, whom
the neighboring planters volunteered to furnish gratis, the
trustees only providing their food and the necessary tools.

For the same work of destruction and obstruction which
the fire-deluge of Mount Vesuvius accomplished in a single
night has here been effected by the silent progress of arboreal vegetation and decay in a manner which illustrates the
scientific axiom that in dynamics force and time are convertible factors. The mixture of ashes and porous lava which
covers the City of Pompey is far easier to remove than the
tegumen of mould, gnarled roots, and tanglewood that has
spread itself over the ruins of Uxmal. Like the coils of
a boa-constrictor, the flexible arms of the lianas and the
cordero-vines have wound themselves around the columns
and projecting rocks; nay, forced their sprouts through the
crevices of the thickest walls, sending out lateral shoots
along the inner surface, so that often their grip can only be
broken at the risk of breaking the building at the same
time. Trees were found which had incorporated themselves
with a detached pillar or window-sill after wrenching it
from its place, or by growing completely around it if it
proved immovable; and it has been supposed that the remarkable absence of smaller buildings is owing to this
cause. They were disintegrated by trees and vines that had
fastened themselves upon them and in the course of their
growth dislodged them from their foundations. Only the

enormous weight of the larger edifices could preserve them from the same fate. If much longer, would have been a different question, but the buildings which have so far stood their ground are now probably safe.

A year after the commencement of the work the carriage-road to San Lorenzo was completed, and the ruins can now be reached by private conveyance from Sisal in twenty-four hours, or by the semi-weekly stage *viâ* Merida in two days, the distance from the coast being about eighty-five miles.

About twelve miles southwest of Charley Cortina's "tower-house" we crossed a tributary of the Rio Macoba, and came in sight of a broad terrace that overlooks the river and the undulating woodlands beyond. Here Colonel Rochez, the mayoral, or government agent *en chef*, has collected all the detached statues, ornamented stones, and sculptured curiosities which his workmen unearthed in the course of their labors. They are grouped in pyramids and monumental piles of various shapes, rather with a view to picturesque effect, as it seems, than for the accommodation of antiquarian students, most of the hieroglyphic tablets being stacked up like slabs in a slate-quarry, with their inscriptions partly or entirely covered.

The road then enters the forest once more, and the rank intricacy of the cordero-thickets gave me an idea of the appearance of this region in Baron Waldeck's time, and the difficulty of uprooting square miles of such jungles.

"Is Captain Luiz at home?" inquired the Pecador, when we met a loafing peon at the lower end of the terrace.

"I don't know, but I can tell you where you may find the mayoral himself. He's hunting quails in a ravine behind the Nunnery. I'll show you the way, if you like."

"Never mind, I know the place. That fellow means the superintendent," exclaimed the Pecador,—"old Colonel

Rochez, who has been in charge of this place since they built the new road. But the real mayoral is his son, Captain Luiz: I believe he knows more about these buildings than any twenty men in Yucatan. Charley Cortina told me that he saw him the day before yesterday, so we shall find him at home, I guess."

"Captain Luiz Rochez? Wasn't he down in Campeche a few months ago?" inquired the lieutenant.

"Yes, he went down last May, trying to get a few more quarrymen, but the government would not foot the bill. The old colonel should have gone himself."

"They helped themselves to military titles all round, it seems?"

"No, they earned them honestly," said the lieutenant. "The old gent was in charge of Fort Miguel near Acapulco till they had to retire him on account of his deafness, and his son used to belong to the Second Artillery, and had the name of being the best engineer in the regiment. Up in Matamoras he got mixed up in the Escobedo rebellion, and they made him resign, I believe,—probably because he wouldn't bribe the court-martial. He was too much of a gentleman for the frontier service, anyhow. He would be in his right element here if the pay wasn't so confounded small."

"He has to share it with his father, I presume?"

"No, the government doesn't recognize him at all, they merely tolerate him because the old man needs an assistant. He generally shows the visitors around, and is the most obliging and modest fellow you ever saw, though his circumstances do not always permit him to decline a compensation."

"Just wait here," said the Pecador, when we reached one of the larger casas: "I'm going to the lodge to see what provisions they have on board. We can take our dinner here, and camp in the upper story: it's a great deal more comfortable than their narrow guest-rooms. The captain will soon be here," said he, when he returned with a basketful of yams and corn cakes: "he is cleaning a ditch down in the bottom, and they promised to send him up as soon as he comes home."

The ground-floor of our casa was a large hall, divided by a bar of débris from a sort of antechamber with a narrow window in the farther corner, where we lighted our fire on a platform of rubbish and broad flags. We had just toasted our maize cakes when a merry "Halloo!" in the front hall announced the arrival of the captain. "Don't let me disturb you, gentlemen," said he, when he clambered into our refectory: "you are disturbed enough by the smoke, I see Halloo, Don Nicolas," recognizing the guide. "Now, you have been travelling all over Yucatan, have you ever seen a trace of a chimney or fireplace about any of the old casas? I never did: they must have swallowed their meat raw in those times."

"Maybe they roasted their beef in the sun," said the Pecador. "Why, in the name of reason, don't you keep some ice on hand, Don Luiz? There would be some inducement to patronize your hotel."

"I'm sorry you didn't say so before," laughed the captain. "Our visitors are mostly Yankees, you see, and after all you told us about their smartness we never doubted that they were clever enough to make their own ice. Well, this afternoon you can't complain about the weather," said he, when we had finished our dessert: "so, if the gentlemen are ready, we can begin with the principal casas, and leave the suburbs until to-morrow: the bush is a little wet yet after last night's rain."

We left our baggage in the antechamber, and tethered our mules on the north side of the building in a sort of moat with plenty of grass and weeds. Seen from the distance, our casa resembled a Spanish inn with a Moorish courtyard below and a row of small bedrooms above, but in its original dimensions it seemed to have extended along the entire length of the moat, which is flanked with the vestiges of a foundation-wall for a distance of more than sixty yards beyond the present east end of the building. The woods behind the moat are intersected by a similar wall, which at different places rises to a height of twenty feet. "El Quartel—the Barracks—we call this building," said the captain: "the large hall below is supposed to be the drill-shed."

No other ruins were in sight, but on the summit of a rock-strewn acclivity the woods opened and revealed a grayish stone pile rising like a mountain rather than like a building from a wilderness of weeds and débris, but assuming more symmetrical outlines as the road approaches A quadrangular esplanade, with a range of stone steps, leads up to a narrow terrace that forms the foundation of a mound of cyclopean blocks, house-shaped, but craggy and cliff-like from the massiveness of the pillars and walls. The entire structure rising to a height of eighty-four feet, with a façade of three hundred and twenty and a circumference of eight hundred feet, it stands there with its open and desolate doors like an antediluvian skeleton—"La Casa del Gobernador, the most massive, though not the highest, of the main buildings," says our guide.

At Uxmal the Spaniards have illustrated that talent for nomenclature which has made them such useful pioneers in the river- and mountain-labyrinths of the New World. All the houses, temples, and caves, and even the more conspic-

uous statues, have their names, most of them singularly
appropriate as well as pretty. If Yucatan was a province
of prehistoric Mexico, and Uxmal the state capital, the
house on the double terrace must have been the residence
of the governor. These high portals with their carved columns, and these sculptured walls, were not built for a
granary or a fort, and the character of the bas-reliefs, as
well as the absence of altars and idols, makes it unlikely
that the edifice was a temple.

From the upper terrace to the third story the walls are
entirely covered with ornaments that might be described as
sculptured mosaic, each figure being formed by a combination of carved stones. These sculptures represent human
heads, colossal figures, fantastic birds and quadrupeds, and
every variety of arabesques, which, viewed at a certain
angle, give the walls the appearance of those rough-hewn
granite blocks our architects love to display over the entrance of a tunnel or massive gateway. The lower halls
are partly obstructed by a pile of débris, for the range of
stairs leading to the second floor has fallen down, and has
been replaced by a wooden ladder. The most interesting
rooms are on the second and third floors, which also connect
with outer galleries bordered by long balustrades of graceful
fretwork. According to the measurements of Señor De-
vegas, the walls of these two stories contain thirty-four
hundred yards—or nearly two English miles—of bas-relief,
most of them at a height of about four feet from the floor,
and running along the wall in an unbroken row, the lower
border being on a line with the lintels of the windows and
doors. These decorations are often coarse in execution and
defective in the details of design, but the total impression
is nevertheless strangely pleasing. There are long proces-
sions of men-at-arms, groups of animals and stars,—the

latter perhaps astrological symbols,—and countless faces (*portraits*, our guide called them) in profile, some of them distinguished by a turban-like head-dress. One of the more elaborate groups represents a warrior promenading on a row of prostrate bodies, probably a symbol of royal power if not a memorial of a martial triumph. Another shows a procession of mutilated men, one-legged, armless, or entirely dismembered, which our cicerone supposed to be a regiment of veterans returning from war, but which may possibly have had an allegorical significance. In one of the third-story rooms a portion of the floor is paved with a coarse mosaic representing a battle between light-armed and naked giants and warriors of smaller stature, but well equipped with a panoply of heavy arms. The faces and attitudes of the antagonists are well distinguished, and the whole conveys the impression of having been suggested by an actual occurrence, perhaps an encounter between the citizen-soldiers of the ancient empire and some savage tribe of the northern forests. It has been observed that the black marble which is used in the composition of these and other mosaics is not found anywhere in Yucatan, and must have been brought from Central Mexico, if not from Cuba.

Before the arrival of the present superintendent this building was infested with every possible variety of creepers and air-plants: in the basement their growth was somewhat checked by lack of sunshine, but in the upper stories they formed a continuous tapestry along the walls of every apartment, and vestiges of these expletive decorations still defy the pruning-hook of the mayoral. The arm of an idol here and there or the head of a long-snouted animal is wreathed with leaves like a thyrsus-staff, and many of the coarse arabesques around the larger *retratos* are mingled with the delicate folioles of a twining grenadilla. With a sort of vegetable instinct, most of these intruders have pierced the walls at places where the convolution of their tendrils is favored by a pilaster or the protuberances of a bas-relief.

The next turn of the road leads to the *plaza*, or market-square, a partly-cleared field of about sixty acres, offering a view of the three largest and most interesting buildings in Uxmal,—the Casa de las Monjas, the Palomal, and the Casa del Enano. The largest of these—and, indeed, the largest architectural relic of our continent—is the Casa de las Monjas, the "House of the Nuns," so called from the vast number of little cell-like apartments. There are eighty-seven larger and half a hundred smaller rooms, besides extensive corridors and several halls, distributed over a three-story building of four wings, which enclose what may have been a spacious courtyard, but now resembles a neglected garden.

Entering from the north, you pass through a gateway supported by pillars of enormous thickness, and an inner vestibule that communicates with a broad gallery or interior veranda, stone-paved and inviting by the grotto-like coolness of its shady recesses. The builders of this city were not acquainted with the keystone arch, but formed their vaults by overlapping stones, held in place by the weight of the superstructure and covered with a large slab or with lintels of wood, the latter being found over every door and window whose horizontal diameter exceeds two feet. The wood used for these lintels is of iron toughness and texture, and has been identified with a species of lignum-vitæ that is found in the mountains of Guatemala, but nowhere in Yucatan or Eastern Mexico. From the middle of the first flight of steps upward the walls are decorated with glaring pictures, checkered and polychromatic like a collection of

SOUTH WALL OF CASA DE LAS MONJAS.

butterflies, though a pale carmine and a brilliant golden yellow predominate. Frescoes the mayoral calls them, but the process of their production seems to have involved a preliminary plastering of the walls with a grayish-brown

22

substance that makes an effective foil for the brighter tints, and the employment of a very durable varnish that would explain the freshness and the metallic lustre of some of the colors. On the second floor the cells begin, and monopolize the two larger wings of that story. Few of them are provided with more than one aperture, either a door communicating with the corridor or a window opening upon the outer gallery, their average size being five yards square by four high. Many cells in the second story are paved with polished and variegated marble slabs, while the walls opposite the entrance are covered with pictures; and if the dwelling was a nunnery the convent rules cannot have been very ascetic, the character of these retratos being decidedly secular, —so much so, indeed, that some of the artists must have belonged to what poor Southey called the "Satanic School." The windows are festooned with rock-ivy and grenadilla-vines with small red pipe-flowers, and in one of the lower rooms an abeto-bush, a species of juniper, has forced its way through the masonry of the floor and of a sort of stone bench near the window, rising from the flags like a Christmas-tree from a table.

All the cornices and window-sills of these countless chambers, all the balustrades of the long galleries and the balconies overhanging the court, are ornamented with bas-relief figures, colored stuccoes, and sculptured mosaic, carved with an unrivalled richness and variety of detail; and if it is true that a portion of the material was brought from a great distance, the treasures of a wealthy empire must have been lavished on the Casa de las Monjas. Señor Escalante, an intelligent Mexican architect, estimates that even with all the raw material on hand the present cost of such a building would exceed four million piastres, and thinks that the carvings of some of the larger pillars would employ a hardworking statuary for six months. Bats are now the only tenants of this sculptured Coliseum, since a colony of *monos chicos*, or Mexican raccoons, that had established themselves in the basement, were ejected by order of the mayoral.

THE PALOMAL.

In a grove of mango-trees that were spared on account of their edible fruit, and hardly fifty yards from the Nunnery, stands the Palomal, or "Dove-cote," a large but plain and artless edifice that received its name from the number of little niches in the masonry of the inner walls which the ready imagination of the natives compared to pigeon-holes. Baron Waldeck believed that the Palomal was a prison, but its proximity to a royal palace makes it more likely that it was a guard-house and the cellular apartments the soldiers' dormitories.

Near the front gate of the Palomal stands—or rather leans—an obelisk, a large sculptured pillar which the wood-cutters discovered in the midst of a thicket of rhexia thorns. South and southwest of the Pigeon-house the plain is covered with continuous woods, clumps of wax-palms waving over dense thickets of figs and euphorbias that obliterate the undulations of the soil and almost overarch the valley of the Rio Macoba. To a native of the Old World the luxuriance of this vegetation in the neighborhood of such ruins appears strangely anomalous, like tufts of flowers rising from a snowbank or a fountain from the desert sand. Moreover, the forests of Uxmal do not exhibit the characteristics of a spontaneous second growth—dwarfed trees and sun-scorched weeds. many of the tree-clumps are as gigantic and their arcades as leafy as if shade-loving birds had been their only inhabitants since the birth of the Western continent

As we passed through the mango-coppice an obstreperous bird of the shrike species, that had followed us from the Nunnery, perched on a bough in front of us, as if resolved to attract our attention, and chattered away with a voice that expressed indignation as plainly as the barking of an enraged cur.

"There he is again!" said the Pecador. "I threw a stone at this same chap when I was here last March, and I do believe he has been screaming ever since."

"He seems to have his nest in that thicket."

"No, he does not want strangers to come near these buildings at all," said the captain · "he will follow you from bush to bush if you don't drive him away. El Pregonero (the town-crier) our Indians call him."

Proceeding southward and upward, we reach the platform of a little hill, and are brought face to face with a dome-like pile of colossal dimensions, the Casa del Enano, or "House of the Dwarf," so called from the narrowness of the sally-port, which is, in

THE TOWN-CRIER.

fact, a mere loophole in what originally may have been the second story, the basement having been buried by avalanches of débris that have tumbled from the decaying walls. A tower encircled by galleries that contract toward the top is the nucleus of this pile, and leads to a circular platform of about forty yards in circumference. The strength of this central tower has supported the building, but the galleries with their substructures have collapsed all around, and give to the whole the appearance of a conical mound covered with a wilderness of broken fragments and weeds. Goats, and even cows, frequent the slopes of this artificial hill, and make their way to the very top, where mountain-breezes and patches of rank wall-grass reward them for the somewhat arduous ascent.

The interior of the edifice forms a striking contrast to this rustic outside. After passing (on all-fours) through the loophole above mentioned the visitor finds himself in the vestibule of the tower-hall, which he enters through a portal of pillar-like buttresses. This hall seems formerly to have been lighted from above, but the wall on the south side is now full of cracks and holes, which serve as so many windows, but have admitted rain as well as sunshine, as attested by a considerable pool at the lower end of the sloping floor. The wall on the west side rises like a terrace or a range of colossal stairs, tier above tier, receding a yard and a half after every three yards of elevation. The upper tier is a shapeless mass of ruins, connected with the ceiling and the opposite walls by a network of liana-coils, some of which have become detached with the crumbling stones and hang across the hall like tight-ropes in a circus-tent. But farther down the vertical surfaces of the terrace are covered with hieroglyphics, while the intermediate levels afford seats for a large assembly of "idols," as the Spaniards call them indiscriminately, though the plurality of these shapes seems to have been suggested by the exigencies of symmetry, since they reappear at equal intervals from a common centre, and may have been nothing but architectural extravaganzas, like the caryatides and griffins of our Gothic chapels. The human—or rather anthropoid—shapes *were* idols, to judge by their central positions and heroic proportions, and some of them are as composite, though not quite as monstrous, as the divinities of a Hindoo pagoda.

On a special pedestal about four feet above the floor sits a four-armed giant with a disproportionately large but not altogether repulsive face, and with a corselet that resembles the scaly hide of a crocodile. Two of his arms are akimbo: the other pair are extended, with the palms of the hands down, as if in the act of delivering a benediction. Just above him, on the third terrace, stands the semi-torso of a youth with a coronet of spikes or rays upon his head and a sort of rosary wound about his waist. Both his arms are broken off at the elbow, but seem to have been lifted above his head or to have supported a shield, like a similar but

THE HOUSE OF THE DWARF.

smaller statue farther up. The figure is supposed to be a symbol of the Chasca, or evening star, whose statues in the old Peruvian temples were distinguished by a halo of vertical rays. In the menagerie of animals and animal fragments there are six elephants' heads, distributed in the corners of three successive tiers. Whatever they are intended to represent, the curled and tapering trunks and pendent ears are decidedly elephantine, and even the small piggish eyes are characteristic of pachyderms, though it ought to be mentioned that the tusks are uniformly omitted. These heads have caused a good deal of curious speculation, since even the illiterate Yucatecos know that only imported elephants have ever displayed their trunks on this side of the Atlantic. Did the fauna of prehistoric Mexico include elephants, or had the builders of this city preserved traditions of a Transatlantic fatherland,—India, Siam, or Southern Africa? Or may it be possible that ante-Columbian visitors from the East had carried elephants, or the pictures or descriptions of such animals, to the Western World? *Quien sabe?* But it would certainly be curious if unassisted fancy had produced such *congruous* combinations.

The hieroglyphics that alternate with the sculptured rows are subdivided by vertical mouldings at irregular intervals, forming longer or shorter quadrangles that seem to enclose separate inscriptions. Many of these mouldings are ornamented with a sort of arabesque, while the elaborate characters are strongly suggestive of an important meaning. Different recent visitors have copied such inscriptions *in extenso*, but it is to be feared that their labors have been in vain: the key to that picturesque alphabet has been lost forever.

The ghost-ridden natives give the casas a wide berth, but the House of the Dwarf is an object of their especial dread. Mezequenho, the Good Spirit, was never properly worshipped by the citizens of Uxmal, they say; and when the boundary between his patience and his wrath was passed he turned the entire population into stone and confined them in this building. But after sunset the petrified assembly revives, and woe to the wight that passes the Casa del Enano in a moonless night! The north side of the building looks, indeed, as fantastic as any castle in Fairydom: a lofty dome, crowned with a tuft of vegetation not unlike a colossal cactus or a gigantic skull with a wisp of hair standing on end and bristling in the breeze, while the shroud of creepers forms a compact mass of foliage from the middle terrace—*i.e.*, from a height of sixty-five feet—to the ground, recalling the legend of Dornroschen's Burg circumvallated with a rampart of wildering roses.

Southwest of the Casa del Enano there are different smaller buildings, too rude and artless or too far advanced in decay to merit a separate description, though I might mention the Casa de la Vieja, the "House of the Old Woman," an ivy-mantled, snug little cottage with a balcony and a single alcove; and the Casa Cerrada, or "Closed House," a cubic mass of masonry without any opening whatever,—a watch-tower, perhaps, or a mausoleum.

Besides these buildings the excavations have brought to light a considerable number of detached statues, terraces, paved courtyards, etc., and some miscellaneous objects whose significance is as problematic as that of the hieroglyphics. There are an amphitheatre and an artificial lake, both excavated from the solid rock; a "tennis-court" or gymnasium, paved and encircled by a low wall, and a nameless rotunda with fragments of carved columns. On an artificial mound northeast of the Casa Cerrada stands a double-headed sphinx, twelve feet long and five feet high, and a little farther back a six-sided nondescript cut from a single block and with a polished surface about eight feet square. Some American merchants from Sisal had the bad taste to christen it the "Altar of Abraham," and the mayoral, in commemoration of their visit, now calls it the "Altar of Abraham Lincoln," which is certainly worse; but Lincoln is popular in Mexico.

I have already referred to the open-air museum on the river-terrace, where the superintendent has amassed a ship-load of idols and sculptured tablets. He boasts that he has hieroglyphic slabs enough now to roof the largest building in Yucatan, and the excavations which are still progressing will probably increase his collection.

Neither the descent of man nor the purpose of the Pyramids is shrouded in deeper mystery than the origin of these ruins. All we know with certainty is this. that they antedate the advent of Columbus by a period which reaches far beyond the oldest records and traditions of the American aborigines, for that Uxmal was not built by the Aztecs is positively demonstrated by architectural and archæological evidence, and indirectly by the entire absence of local tradition

Señor Simon Escalante, of Puebla, who has devoted a lifetime to the study of Mexican antiquities, adduces a long list of technical arguments against the alleged identity of the structure, sculpture, and system of hieroglyphics of these buildings with those of the Peruvians and North Mexican temples, of which I can quote only a few, and perhaps not the most conclusive ones. The Casa del Gobernador, the Nunnery, and the Dome (House of the Dwarf) contain columns, entablatures, and stuccoes which are found nowhere else in America Relicta, and a careful comparison of the hieroglyphic systems of Uxmal and Central Mexico has established the fact that they bear no more resemblance to each other than either bears to those of Luxor and Nineveh. Besides, all the Indian temples and palaces from Peru to the Rio Gila are dwarfed in comparison with the gigantic piles of the Yucatan city. The Nunnery alone would furnish cut stones enough to reconstruct all the castles of the old Mexican capital and all her temples, which rarely exceeded forty yards in length, and never contained more than two stories, if we except the teocallis or sacrificial mounds, which were simply terraced mud-piles with a superstructure of stone slabs or bricks.

It seems also certain that the founders of Uxmal were familiar with the manufacture and use of metal implements, for their stonework does not present the chopped appearance of the Mexican masonry, cut with chisels of flint and obsidian; and to produce the elaborate cornices and mosaics in the Governor's House with such brittle tools would, as the Puebla antiquarian expresses it, "snap the sinews of human patience."

Some of the foundation-walls and terraces in West Uxmal were covered with a stratum of vegetable mould which could hardly have been formed in less than a millennium, even if we allow for the rapidity of organic development and decay in a tropical coast-region, while trees with the self-registered record of their age in their texture have grown from rubbish-mounds where they must have taken root before the Spaniards had gained a foothold in America or the Visigoths in Spain.

The argument derived from the absence of historical records has been met with the remark that the Old World too has ruins the record of whose origin has been lost, not in the cloudland of the Dark Ages, but in the confusion of wars and conquests of comparatively recent date. But it must not be forgotten that all such ruins are the primitive relics of a primitive race, like Stonehenge, the *Hunengraber* of Westphalia, or the cairns of Ireland and Western Normandy, while the monuments of more civilized nations have transmitted, even by oral traditions, a record of their construction and destruction which can only be obliterated by a succession of ages. The traditions of Mexico date back to remote centuries of the Christian era, but about a vast and wealthy city in Western Yucatan they are as silent as the annals of the Conquistadores. The ruins themselves have never betrayed their secret.

Before the sun went down we mounted the Casa del Enano and rummaged the pile of broken statues on the upper terrace till the chill of the evening air admonished us to return to the Barracks.

"No wonder your Indians believe in ghosts," said the lieutenant, when we passed a little mound in the open woods.

THE OLDEST INHABITANT.

"Look up there! — a spectre stalking around in broad daylight."

On the mound grazed a horse,—the remains of a horse, I should say, the component parts of the animal's body being reduced to a framework of bones and a very thin tegumen of hide and hair,—an equine skeleton endowed with the faculty of locomotion.

"Yes, that's one of our antiquarian curiosities," said the captain. "Nobody knows where he comes from, but we suspect him of being the identical steed that ran away from Balboa in the battle of Chiapas, though my father holds that he must be one of the Mohammedan horses that were rewarded with immortality for having carried the Prophet. We call him 'the oldest inhabitant,' and he was certainly grazing in Uxmal before any white man cooked his dinner in the casas. There he goes. Precisely at the same time every night he walks to his stable in the Palomal, and stays there till sunrise, leaning against the wall with his eyes half shut. He sleeps in the daytime too: I have found him leaning against a tree and pricking up his ears in his dreams. I wonder what he hears? He might tell us something about Uxmal if he could talk."

"Do you ever feed him?"

"Oh, he finds all the feed he wants,—he generally stays around the western casas,—but it puzzles us all to explain where he gets his water from. We never saw him at the creek: he must know the whereabouts of a spring which nobody else has discovered yet."

Returning to the Quartel, we found a good supply of firewood in one of the upper rooms, where a broken alcove had been fashioned into a sort of chimney, and the captain promised to get us a few extra blankets, as the cool night wind threatened to degenerate into a regular *borasso*, or "norther," which here often follows upon a heavy rain It has been said that the strain of a harp ranks first among the acoustic aids to inspiration, but it is more certain that, to a Northlander's ear at least, no other sound in the infinite scale of Nature and art is more promotive of domestic comfort than the music of a good crackling wood-fire. As soon as the recess of our alcove resounded with that hyperborean anthem we felt at home, and soon all earthly cares were merged in the pleasant occupation of renewing the supply of fuel from time to time.

The mayoral sent us a basketful of cakes and plantains, excusing himself with the state of the weather and of his rheumatic knee, but Captain Luiz returned in person, and, having met our mozo in the basement, complimented us on our success in overcoming the national prejudice of that youth. " As a rule, their superstition is incurable," said he. " When we went to work on the western casas our laborers would rather forego their dinner and their siesta than enter the buildings after dark. Their ghost-horror overcomes every other kind of fear: they would sooner make a circuit through a panther-jungle than take a short cut through the haunted ruins."

" That seems to account for their reticence. Don't you think they have known something about this place before its so-called discovery by the whites ?"

" I am quite sure of it. They have known it all along, and would have kept the secret for another century or two. And even without any superstitious motive."

" Why, what other reason could they have to conceal it ?"

" I don't know ; but the matter is this : you and I would certainly see twenty reasons for *not* concealing it, but if an Indian could see any of them is a different question. You know, perhaps, what word our old official records used in referring to the Indians : *gente sin razon,*—creatures devoid of reason. Their character may have changed since the Conquest, but so much is certain : some human attributes seems to have become extinct in their natures : desire of knowledge, for instance, and sympathy with the intellectual pursuits of others. If a Yucatan Indian should discover Paradise or the Fountain of Eternal Youth, or if a confiding spirit had betrayed the secret of futurity, he would neither say a word about it nor take any personal interest in the matter. The wants of these people are purely animal,— food and drink and a liberal share of rest. If they have any ideas above that, they certainly do not express them in words. You may have noticed that yourself: could you ever interest them in your botanical collections?"

"Only in the digestible varieties: they do not care much for scientific curiosities."

"Not one straw. I had a curious illustration of that a year ago, when I was out badger-hunting with one of our peons one evening. Two miles southwest of the Nunnery there is an artificial lake about a furlong across and some forty feet deep, and just when we passed it we heard a loud splash in the pond right behind us, as if somebody had struck the water with the broadside of a heavy oar. Alligators are unknown in this part of the State, and no large fish were ever seen in that pond; and to this day I have not the least idea what it was or possibly could have been; but my astonishment was still greater when I looked at my Indian: the brute had not even turned his head, but trudged on with the unconcern of the most stupid quadruped, for a dog would at least have stopped and pricked his ears."

"It's a wonder how the ancestors of such animals could build a city like this."

"It puzzled me confoundedly," said the captain, "but I have now reasons to suspect that they were no relations of theirs at all. They belonged to a different race."

"Toltecs? or what is your private theory?"

"I am no scholar, señor: I can only tell you how the Indians themselves have led me to my conclusion. There are no large ruins in the western suburbs of the 'town,' as our peons call it,—nothing but low walls and débris of rough-hewn stones,—and we ascertained that among the old Indians of the neighboring settlements this part of Uxmal goes by the name of the At'acegual, the 'Indian Town,' but the eastern portion they call the 'Main City'—El Huasacmal,—and that's whence the word *Uxmal* is derived.

Who inhabited that ' main city' is more than I can tell, for it seems that the ancestors of our Indios had to live in a pariah suburb. M'acegual is the native word for a Mayo Indian. Up in the Sierra de Macoba, where white men have hardly ever been seen, there is a plateau they call the *Campo de Rota*, the ' Field of Defeat;' and in districts where our priests do not watch them they celebrate a festival about the end of September under the name of the ' Week of Deliverance.' So far as I know, they cannot pretend to have been delivered from us or the Spaniards in that week. And as you came up the river from Don Cortina's place you may have noticed the large quarry on the right-hand side of the cañon. That quarry goes by a name which our peons tell us means *la Matanza*, the ' man-killery,' as if they had been worked near to death there, cutting stone,—probably for the same foreign gentlemen who inhabited the ' main city.' "

" Don't you think your excavations will bring something to light that may solve the puzzle ?"

"I hardly think so. The holes and cellars have been rummaged pretty thoroughly. We found a large skeleton two years ago, and some English gentlemen told us it might help to settle the race-question ; but it has been in Sisal these last ten months, and it does not appear that they can make anything of it, except that the bones seem larger than those of any living Yucateco. There has been a good deal of private digging going on here, our neighbors tell me, but most of the explorers were treasure-hunters, and that business has declined for want of encouragement. One poor devil thought his fortune was made when he found a big earthenware box in the cellar of the Palomal, but when he got it open it proved to be full of skulls and knuckle-bones, mixed with sand and a sort of yellow brickdust. Our

Indians speak of a time when their forefathers used to dig up iron swords and spear-heads from the débris, and have a dim tradition that once—long before the Spaniards came

A DISAPPOINTED TREASURE-HUNTER.

—a body of armed men landed at Cape Penasco, twenty miles south of Campeche, marched to Uxmal by following the ridge of the mountains, and removed a great mass of

23

plunder from one of the buildings where it had lain concealed under the stone slabs of the floor."

"If you understand their language or have a Spanish-speaking peon, you ought to collect such traditions."

"I do, but few of them are worth repeating. There is no lack of legends, of course: for instance, the tradition of the Indian hunter who crossed the Rio Macoba before sunrise one morning, and heard a sound of merry music when he approached the Casa de las Monjas, and, crouching behind a tree, saw a number of young men step from the ruins before long and pass within a few yards of his tree with garlands on their necks and guitar-like instruments in their hands, as if they were returning from a nocturnal fandango; but the starlight was too dim to see where they went to. Indian ghosts are more sensitive than ours: they cannot stand moonlight any more than sunshine. Have you ever heard of the *rebosada?*"

"Some female spook, I suppose?"

"Yes, it means the veiled woman, the lady with the hood, —a sort of female Bluebeard who entices unwary young men to out-of-the-way places and massacres them after a very short flirtation. In the Cerro de Sacrificios, twelve miles east from here, the Indians say that one of her intended victims was saved by the timely rising of the moon. He recognized her by her gleaming teeth, but instead of betraying any fear he flattered her in the most amiable way, and told her so many diverting stories that she missed her chronological calculations. They were walking up hill arm in arm, due west by good fortune, he stealing an occasional look at the sky, while he managed to keep her from turning her head till they reached the summit, when he suddenly stopped and pointed to the east. 'Look, mi amante,' said he, 'who comes there with a white cap!'

She turned, saw the rising moon, and vanished with a horrible shriek."

The captain rose and walked toward the window. "That reminds me I ought to vanish myself," said he: "the moon is up, and I guess I can find my way home without a lantern. The sky is quite clear: it's going to be cold tonight."

"Yes," said the mozo, "we had better keep our fire going. Wait: I'm going to fetch that big log we left in the basement where we cooked our dinner."

"It's your own fault, captain," laughed the Pecador. "that ghost-story of yours will cost you a pretty lot of firewood, don't you see? Our poor Indian wants an excuse for keeping up a light all night, so your spooks can't get the better of him."

We were not the first travellers who had camped in this palace of unknown kings, or whose witch-expelling smoke had ascended through the chimney: in the alcove of an adjoining room we found a large heap of wood-ashes and broken bottles the next morning, and between the hiero-glyphic inscriptions the stone tablets on the south wall of the Quartel bore the less interesting but more legible signa-tures of the Messrs. Smith, Brown, and Schultze. Around some of the tablets the cement seemed to have been chopped off with a hatchet, but if some inquisitive barbarian had tried to remove them his attempt had been foiled by their thickness and the resistance of the surrounding masonry. On the east side the third story of the building has been made accessible by means of iron spikes driven into the wall at handy intervals, and in a corner of the basement we found the remains of a rude scaffold which a visitor from Sisal had constructed for the purpose of photographing the inscription over the front portal. Some English officers who had rusticated here for a couple of weeks went to the trouble of copying the entire façade of the Casa de las Monjas, a sculptured chronicle of many chapters; but I contented myself with making a drawing of the best pre-

OBELISK OF UXMAL.

served side of the above-mentioned limestone obelisk, which is almost covered with emblems and iconographs.

The Indians stick to the belief that the inscriptions will ultimately be deciphered and reveal the hiding-place of the *tesoro del regote*—the treasure of the Great King—that lies buried somewhere in a stone chest, and may perhaps be resurrected by a learned Indian, a mail-carrier, or a parish clerk, though they have a sore misgiving that the erudite foreigners will be beforehand with them.

But it is extremely probable that neither red-skin nor pale-face will ever disturb the royal treasury, for the ablest American archæologists and philologists have resigned themselves to the conviction that the hieroglyphics of Uxmal will remain what they are now,—a book with seven seals. Even if another Champollion should discover a key to the alphabet, he would be confronted by a further and more insuperable difficulty, for, like the parrot of the Orinoco mentioned in Humboldt's travels, these inscriptions speak the language of an extinct tribe,— a language that has outlived its interpreters. The buildings themselves, indeed, are symbols of a more manifest significance, and proclaim in a language which cannot be misunderstood that Eastern Mexico was not always a land of wild woods and thatched wigwams; but of the builders not even the *nominis umbra* is left. Like the rock-skeletons of an earlier world, the walls of their houses have remained, but all that is perishable about the works and the memory of a nation—their name, their fame, their language and every trace of their influence—has been obliterated forever. The havoc of war and the blight which the decay of a large city entails on the surrounding country have left no vestige in the neighborhood of their ruins; a forest-vegetation which seems to date its origin from the dawn of creation covers their battle-grounds, their highways, and their forsaken fields: the malady of civilization has been thoroughly cured. The ghosts, too, have been laid, the avenging spirits that haunt the burial-places of murdered Eastern nations: there are no robbers in Yucatan; the harmless natives seem to belong to one of those elder races which, like the autochthones of Egypt and India, have bent before successive storms of conquest and survived them all. Their assailants have fulfilled their doom in mutual destruction, and the abandoned ruins have been reconciled with Nature, in whose hands a tomb becomes a temple of peace.

CHAPTER XI.

THE BACKWOODS OF GUATEMALA.

Days that passed by like hours, but whose remembrance
Will pall our city joys for many years
                                CLEMENS BRENTANO· *Alpen-Reise.*

L'art de chasse-ennui,—the "art of pastime,"—I take
it, has been more liberally patronized, and consequently
more assiduously cultivated, than any other, but the costly
amusements of our gayest cities can never emulate the gratuitous diversions which Nature provides for her favored
guests. "I was brought up in the fashionable quarters of
a large capital," says Victor Jacquemont, "but from early
boyhood I could not get rid of the impression that the life
men were intended for must have been different from ours,
—less dull especially. Before I left Europe I could not
account for this idea, but among the tropical wonders of
the Nerbudda I felt that I had been right."

I became conscious of a similar feeling on the hunting-
grounds of the lower Rio Grande, and again, seven years
later, when I crossed the primeval forests of Eastern Guatemala in midwinter, which here corresponds to the spring-
time of our Northern woodlands. Eastern Guatemala is
the American Siam, a zoological park, the botanic garden-
spot of our tropics,—a land whose marine climate and rich
black soil can vie with the happiest regions of the Sunda
Archipelago. Especially the *alturas* or mountain-forests

362

of the department of Vera Paz, between Yucatan and the main chain of the Sierra Negra, cannot have been more luxuriant when Avila and Pedrarias landed in the Bay of Belize. Southern Mexico may rival this region in the marvels of its primeval vegetation, but no land on earth in the number and variety of its birds and flying insects. The hill-country of Vera Paz is Nature's museum of living birds and butterflies, as the upper valley of the Zambesi is the great preserve of the four-footed *feræ naturæ*.

In the last year of my sojourn in Spanish America I visited the *alturas* as the commissioner of certain Belgian colonists who intended the settlement of a public domain in the Sierra Negra de Vera Paz. At the urgent recommendation of the French consul in Guatemala I had induced them to engage the services of a veteran frontiersman, the ex-mayoral or mining-superintendent, Don Nicolas Ruan, who had been obliged to resign in expiation of his *inpatriotismo* ("unpatriotism"), like many others, who, with or without an active interest in politics, had been guilty of the indiscretion of holding office under Maximilian. A likewise rather unnational foible for scientific experiments and books had prevented him from hoarding the wages of his sin, and for the last eight years he had eked out a frugal living on a little banana-farm in the frontier State of Chiapas, whence he had frequently visited the mining-districts of Northern Guatemala on the chance of earning a few dollars as a surveyor or mineralogist. His topographical memory might have saved me the expense of an Indian guide, and, in spite of his advanced years, he proved a stout pedestrian and most entertaining travelling-companion. In the village of San Remo, where the Chiapas *camino real* terminates at a rope-ferry, Don Nicolas met me with a large boar-hound and a mestizo peon who had shared his fortune in all its vicissitudes, and on the following morning we crossed the frontier near the cascades of the Rio Dolores and entered the virgin woods of Vera Paz. Guatemala has no tierra caliente proper, no lowland jungles, for on both shores the cliffs of the plateau reach to the very edge of the sea, and the airy hill-forests contrast agreeably with the stagnating swamps of Eastern Yucatan; still, the exuberance of the vegetation is fairly astounding: the varieties of palm-trees alone are considerably more numerous than all the arboreal species of the New England woods taken together. It often made me laugh to imagine the bewilderment of an omniscient Northern botanist in these tangle-woods; and, begging Professor Linné's pardon, I hold that the still prevailing system of botanic classification by staminal distinctions would be admirably calculated to increase this confusion. The plan of classing quadrupeds after the shape of their tails, though it would group cows with lions and horses with ant-bears, could hardly lead to more perplexing results. A member of the just-mentioned great family of palms, for instance, can always be identified by unmistakable outward characteristics, but the division by stamens and peculiarities of inflorescence would dismember and scatter the same family among the grasses, brassicas, coniferæ, and sixteen or twenty other species that differ as widely as a pine-tree does from a cabbage.

Our trail followed the windings of the Rio Corso, a small affluent of the Dolores, and as long as we kept the creek in sight the canopy of leaves overhead was almost unbroken, —a continuous screen of tangled lianas, through which the sunlight came mellowed as through a roof of opaque green glass. But after two hours of climbing up and down over fallen trees and through rocky ravines and fern-thickets, the valley contracted into a glen, and we had to breast a hillside whose slippery slate-cliffs would have tripped even the goat-footed Sierra Madre mules. Seeing that the woods opened as we ascended, we made our way to the very top of the ridge, and obtained a fair view of the surrounding country on three sides, the lookout in the west being barred by the wooded knolls of the ridge, a spur of the slate-mountains that flank the upper valley of the Rio Dolores.

The ravines at our feet were hidden by the foliage of their giant trees, and from our height we beheld the obverse of the screen, the upper and sunny side of the leafy vault that overshadows the valleys of Vera Paz far and near. It was in midwinter, the flower-time of the lower tropics, three months after the end of the rainy season, and in the sun-gilt foliage the various tints of green were mingled with an equal number of different flower-hues, white and light blue predominating, with other colors scattered here and there like butterflies on a meadow of snowdrops and violets. In the southwest the ocean of golden green was bounded by the heights of the Sierra de San Luiz,—a blue range with that hazy outline peculiar to wood-covered mountains,—while the hill-country in the east sloped toward the Val de Madera (the "timber-valley"), a deep woody glen expanding in the northeast, where the Lake of Peten glittered between the tree-tops of its forty islands.* A greater elevation would have revealed a glimpse of the Bay of Honduras between the headlands of the eastern coast-range, but we saw only an unbroken contour of wooded hills. The department of Vera Paz is the backwoods State of Guatemala, neglected, or rather spared, by the

---

* Lake Peten (*el lago de quarenta islas*) is about sixty miles in circumference. On the largest of its islands stands the old convent-town of Flores, now abandoned to the Mission Indians.

Spanish colonists, who mostly confined their settlements to the gold-bearing valleys of the western sierras.

Birds of all kinds chased each other through the tree-tops or darted across the ravines, but in regard to the fauna of a tropical woodland the ear is a better criterion than the eye. In the littoral pineries of North Carolina I have often wondered at the utter stillness of their gloomy depths, which for half-hours together remained unbroken by any sound save the rustling of a squirrel or the occasional moan of a ringdove. In Florida and Southern Texas the pauses of the diurnal bird-concerts rarely exceed five minutes, in Eastern Mexico hardly twenty seconds, and south of the fifteenth parallel their music may vary from a ringing diapason to a chirping monotone, but is never entirely interrupted while the sun remains above the horizon. On the Rio Corso the multitudinous twitter of small songsters formed a sort of accompaniment to the shrill melodies of the weaver-thrush and the fitful counterbass of a croaking iguana, while the antiphones of screaming parrots and shrieking sapajous came at various intervals from different distances, and often suddenly from trees where not the stirring of a leaf had betrayed the presence of any living thing. Here I heard for the first time the plaintive cry of the spider-monkeys, a pitiful howl with singular flute-like variations.

"I have sometimes heard them in Chiapas" (Southern Mexico), remarked the mayoral, "but only from a far distance: they are absurdly shy, and fly at the sight of the smallest Indian boy as if they had seen a panther."

"You may have studied the habits of other monkeys," said I: "what woods or trees are their favorite haunts?"

"They prefer the sunny side of the foot-hills," said the mayoral, "but there is no such thing as counting upon their appearance at any certain place or time, as you would stalk deer at a saltlick or hogs in a canebrake. Monkeys build no nests, and they are migratory: they may suddenly appear in swarms in districts where they have not been seen for years, and there is no kind of food that can be relied upon to attract them to any particular place, with the exception perhaps of fig-tamarinds and ripe mulberries at a time when other fruit is scarce. It would be easier to say with assurance where you *cannot* find them: they wander to and fro between the settled mountain-valleys and the coast-jungles, trying to give hunters and panthers an equally wide berth."

On the western slope of the ridge we lost our trail among the slate-cliffs, but the ground was tolerably free from underbrush, and before sundown we reached the shore of the Rio Moscon, a tributary of the Lago de Peten, and our valley-road to the plateau of the Sierra Negra. We halted under a clump of magnolia-trees, for a dancing swarm of twilight gnats admonished us to get our hammocks ready, as we could not have reached any building before midnight nor leave the river bottom without going out of our way. A stout *canameño* (or travelling hammock) of Sisal hemp weighs about five pounds, and with an air-pillow or folded shawl and a woollen blanket makes a bed that secures you against the dampness of the ground, and, if you will take the trouble to hang it high enough, against all the gnats of the tierras calientes. Magnolia-, mango-, and walnut-trees make the best roosts, being tough and free from thorns, and after the traveller has overcome the nervousness which will probably interrupt his slumbers for the first few nights, the only objection to the use of a canameño is the trouble of finding trees which are at once high enough and not too difficult of ascent. An elevation of twenty feet in the

EXCELSIOR.

alturas and of thirty in the lowlands is the minimum, but even in the reeking swamps of the coast-jungles a roost-height of fifty feet constitutes an absolute excelsior to all the insect-plagues of the lower world.

After dividing the blankets between our two aërial cradles, the mayoral descended for his gun and travelling-bag.

" *Quiere subir?* Hadn't you better join us up there?" he asked my guide, who was but ill provided with bedding of any kind.

The Indio grinned and shook his head. "I'm a bad hand at climbing," he said, "and would rather trust to my feet *si seria novedad*" (if anything should happen).

He had set his heart on reaching an Indian village that night, and did by no means approve of our camp in the river-jungle. The night, however, was passed without *novedad*, except that I lost a package of topographical charts from under my pillow in a way which I have never been able to account for. The mayoral being above suspicion, and the Indians below, I had to devote my imprecations to a swarm of hypothetical tree-rats, of whose squeaking in the branches my guide had heard or dreamed something between midnight and morning.

When we resumed our march the ground was covered with a "grass-fog" (*nube yerbal*), as my companion called it,—a dense white mist that shrouded the undergrowth up to a height of two or three feet, while the upper air was clear enough to reflect the sunbeams from the dew-drenched foliage overhead. At a distance of ten paces our guide seemed to wade up to his knees in a lake of milk-white matter, and a squirrel which leaped to the ground at our approach disappeared at once, like a frog in a turbid creek. We stopped for breakfast at the beach of the Rio Moscon, not far from the mouth of a creek where the ripple of the current and a bridle-path winding up the steep bank indicated a ford.

"That's the San Tomas trail," said the mayoral, "the interoceanic road from San Tomas to Michatoya on the Pacific coast. Do you see that gap in the spur of the ridge over there? If ever Guatemalans become a commercial people, this same trail will be the route of a transcontinental railroad: the saddle of the gap where it crosses the Sierra Negra is only twelve hundred feet above tide-water, and almost in a bee-line between the Bay of Honduras and then best Pacific port."

The gap, in a ridge of faint blue hills in the western sky, seemed about on a level with the horizon, but toward the south the mountains rose in all the majesty of the Sierra Madre, and among the bold summits of the central chain we recognized the twin-peak of Amilpas, whose western horn is the highest active volcano (thirteen thousand eight hundred feet) between Ecuador and the valley of Anahuac.

In proportion to his strength, a dog is a far more courageous animal than his master, at whose bidding he will charge a bull or a bear regardless of consequences, yet even the bravest dog is apt to recognize the resistless superiority of certain enemies. When we passed a cane-jungle at the mouth of the creek, Don Ruan's big boar-hound Leoncito came rushing out of the bushes, *ventre à terre*, with his tail drawn in, and, after retreating behind his master, looked back at the jungle with a sort of shudder bristling his shaggy coat.

" What was it? a panther?"

" No, no," laughed the señor: " you wouldn't see this old boy making room for a panther, or a jaguar either, in that respectful way. He has seen a snake, a *vivora parda*" (species of moccasin), " I suppose. You would hear him all over a square league of ground if he had met a panther, but to a snake he knocks under without any ' back talk,' as a man would to a ghost or a bombshell."

Beyond the creek our trail improved to a broad beaten path, and toward noon we reached a village of the Casca

Indians on a high bluff above the Rio Moscon, which here enclosed different islands, on whose flat shores a number of pits and little sand-piles attested the recent visit of a

VILLAGE OF THE CASCA INDIANS.

turtle-egg hunter. There were about sixteen lodges, but ten squaws or five stout men could have removed the entire camp in half an hour. The huts were mere *tiendas*, open tents of bombax matting, and one framework lodge of poles, with a roof of concentric wattles partly covered with flat bundles of swamp-grass and bulrushes. There is something in the expression of the lower facial features—the mouth, the maxillary bones, and the chin—which at first sight distinguishes the carnivorous Indio from his vegetarian cousin; and the face of a young squaw in the first tent told me at once that the Casca Indians belong to the hunting-tribes of Eastern Guatemala, the hunting and fishing forest-nomads, who may pick a few berries from the wild-currant bushes or a windfall from under the nut-bearing trees, but prefer the uncertain prizes of the chase to the abundant rewards of agriculture,—in the tropics, at least, a hardly natural bias, and somewhat akin, methinks, to the moral perversity of gamblers and tramps. They had not removed the rubbish from behind their tiendas, and disdained to drain a large puddle in the centre of what might be called their market-square, though a short ditch would have discharged the water over the bluff, and though an old pitfall in rear of the camp proved that they were not unprovided with ditching implements. From the ridge-pole of the main lodge depended the remains of a peccari and a string of wild pigeons,—shot with bamboo arrows and bows of bignonia-wood, the mayoral assured me, and the patriarch of the village was engaged in the manufacture of hunting-snares from the fibrous bast of an unknown plant, the strings being greenish-yellow and apparently tough enough to hold a peccari. A live harpy-eagle in a kind of hen-coop near the tent had one of his talons quite entangled with strings of that sort, which must have resisted the edge of his powerful beak. I took up a piece of the green bast and tried to tear it between my fingers. "No wonder the poor devil could not break it," said I.

Pointing to the eagle, the old man crooked his five fingers into the shape of a claw, and drawing them across and lengthways over the wrist of his other hand, gave me to understand that the king of Central American birds had not been captured with impunity.

In spite of their prognathous profiles, the Casca Indians cannot boast of the grim misanthropic visages of our North-

ern red-skins, and have the reputation of treating their squaws with a good deal of indulgence.

IN THE TOILS.

Their pappooses too, in their intercourse with their male seniors, behaved like privileged personages, and took liberties which a Sioux warrior would have resented with an impressive kick. One toddling little muchacho followed

24

me all over the camp, and watched my face with an
expression of mingled curiosity and amusement when
I bent over the cage of the harpy. In a remark about
the difficulty of keeping such pets alive I used the
word *alimento* (food), and the modulation of the four
syllables so tickled the fancy of my little companion that
he repeated them again and again, accompanying each
successful attempt with a burst of merry laughter. But
when we continued our march the same infant clung to
my shawl with a question which our guide interpreted as
an inquiry after the amount of my loose coppers,—a request
for backsheesh, in fact!

"How old would you take that little monkey to be?"
I asked, after a moderate disbursement—"three or four
years?"

"Hardly three," said the mayoral: "wonderfully pre-
cocious kids, are they not? They are up to a lot of snuff
before a white man's child can walk on its hind legs. A
couple of years ago I was out hunting a few leagues west
of my place, and came across a stray pappoose,—just four
years old, as I afterward found to a certainty. When she
spied me first she started to run, but stopped when she saw
that I should overtake her anyhow. 'Oh, mi señor,' she
snivelled, 'do you like fried plantains or yams with bacon
fat and chipped onions?' 'Don't I, now!' I said, wondering what she would be at. '*Pues tendra usted muchos*'
(then you will get lots of them), she said, 'if you will
please take me to my mother's place. I got off the right
road: it's all my brother's fault;' and then went on to explain how she came to lose her way, and that her mother
lived down on the creek near the Elena country-road; but
all after inquiring after my dietetic predilections. A child
of four years!"

Imagine a lost babe in the woods prefacing its tearful appeal with such a question!

"I tell you what it is," continued the mayoral, "I suspect that the smartness of very young animals stands in inverse ratio to their future intelligence. Have you ever noticed the nimbleness of young pigs and the clumsiness of puppies? The same with children: with the sagacity of the average young Indian any white boy of the same age would pass for a prodigy; but the tables get turned after twelve or fourteen years, and in comparison with a long-headed and long-bearded old Caucasian the wisest Indian is only a clever boy. The smaller the brain the quicker its development A young hog-tapir of ten months is out and out as intelligent as the senior sachem of its tribe"

Two miles west of the village we met a squaw with a large basketful of sweet acorns, the edible fruit of the *Quercus ilex*, which flourishes in evergreen groves on both sides of the river. Either the mast or the hollow trunks which characterize the old trees of this species had assembled a variety of parrots and macaws, whose screams would have excited the envy of the proudest English rookery-owner. The great purple macaw, the *macayo real* of Central America, is certainly the phœnix, the polychromatic wonder-bird, of the New World, hardly rivalled by the humming-birds and the gayest gallinaceous roosters. I have never seen the star-spangled peacock in his native jungles, but I saw him on the wing in a Swiss poultry-park, flaunting his iridescent plumage in a blaze of sunlight: and still I hold that Juno's favorite would have lost his prestige if the goddess could have seen the royal macaw sweeping like a meteor through the dark arcades of a tropical forest.

By leaving the river a mile or so to the left we passed dry-shod through a series of lateral valleys, each with its highest slope to the west, for when we halted on an open plateau we saw the bluff far below, and had now for the first time a bird's-eye view of the Lago de Peten in its full extent. We had reached the alturas, or upland woods, in the very centre of Vera Paz,—thirty miles, by the mayoral's estimate, from the next largest settlement. As compared with the lowland vegetation, the varieties of palms had diminished, but not the number of fruit-bearing trees : the air was saturated with the honey-smell of ripe and rotting chirimoyas, a species of wild plums, and the carob-beans ("St. John's food"), tamarinds, and mimosas displayed bunches of green pods that must have flowered before the end of the rainy season.

"Wasn't I right?" said the mayoral. "I told you yesterday that monkeys make their head-quarters on the sunny side of the foot-hills. They are at their old game again : those tamarinds are just swarming with sapajous : hear them!—Hallo!" said he, "look there! Old Lucas" (the peon) "has hoisted his blue peter. I guess he is after a wild-cat : he promised his squaw to get her a catskin or two."

The taciturn old peon had hung back since we entered the high timber, still-hunting, as it seemed ; but, looking back, we saw him dash through the thicket at a lively rate, stop short and clap his old trabucco to his cheek, aiming almost straight overhead. A short snap, but no smoke,— the crazy flintlock had not even ignited the pan-powder,— and the Indian grabbed his gun as if he had a good mind to break it against the next tree.

"What is it?" the mayoral sang out : "a cat?"

"No!—*fratres delgados*" ("Brothers Long-legs"—*i.e.*,

spider-monkeys), shouted the peon—"about seven of them!
El Demonio take this seven-times-accursed old shooting-
iron of mine!"

We started at a double-quick, cocking our guns as we
ran, but too late: the long-legged brethren had justified
their nickname and reached the tree-tops on the other side
of a broad ravine, going through the liana-tangle at a rate
of a furlong per minute, hand over hand, with a swing of
five yards at each grab. The English language has no
single word for superlative nimbleness, but the spider-
monkey (*Lagothrix paniscus*) is nimble to a degree which
makes one smile at the readiness with which that word is
applied to such creatures as rats and raccoons. If a spider-
monkey could be trained like an East Indian hunting-pan-
ther, I believe that his owner could safely back him to
catch twenty squirrels in as many minutes.

"Don't waste your powder," said the mayoral: "better
try the *monos*" (sapajous) "if you have a long-range barrel.
Unless I am much mistaken, I heard some baby-squealing
over there: it's their breeding season, you know."

The fig-tamarinds formed a continuous arbor along the
crest of the ridge, tree joined to tree by bush-ropes and the
thorny mistletoe (*Viscum rubrum*), with the accumulated
brambles of many years' growth. As we approached, the
chattering of the monos receded· they had evidently espied
us, though we were yet unable to judge even of their ap-
proximate whereabouts, except by the occasional shaking
of a branch or the sudden flight of a nest-bird from the
tree-tops. Still, we could see that the whole troop was
moving in the same general direction, and, hoping to profit
by the confusion of a panic, we concluded to head them off
and let our Indians disorder their retreat with a shower of
clubs. But the sapajous proved that they could combine

circumspection with speed, and in spite of an audible rush through the mistletoe-brambles we did not get sight enough for a snap shot till the sly scramblers reached an hiatus in their covered way, a gap in the roof of the long arbor occasioned by the fall of a dead giant tamarind. All was quiet for a minute, but the rattle of clubs came nearer and nearer, and presently a bold blockade-runner cleared the chasm with a flying leap and disappeared in the network of the opposite branches. By and by faces and hands peeped from their leafy hiding-places, and the reviving chatter showed that the success of their leader had restored the confidence of the fugitives. A middle-sized mono left his lurking-place and clambered boldly up a dangling liana into a higher branch: two veterans followed, and close on their heels a nursing mona, trying to keep her bantling out of sight by squeezing herself through on the safe side of her predecessors. Our guns rose together, and at the first report the mona doubled herself up like a person in a fit of cramps, and at the second flung herself back with a convulsive leap into the lower branches, where a rustling scramble and the simultaneous shaking of several vines showed the numerical strength of the remaining troop.

While we strained our eyes to discover the whereabouts of our victim, I spied another mona, with a much larger baby, slipping noiselessly behind the next largest branch, through one of whose forks her brown head reappeared a minute after, looking exactly like a spongy protuberance or a loose piece of bark. But if I had doubted the first testimony of my senses, a slight movement of the apparent excrescence reassured me; so, crouching down, I rested my gun-barrel on the knob of my walking-stick and took a cautious aim at the saddle of the fork. With and *like* the

flash the head disappeared, but the commotion in the
branches now sounded like the struggle of a dying animal
beating its body against a twig, till the leafy screen parted

LOVE AFTER DEATH.

and one of our monas came down with a heavy thud;
which of them I am unable to say, for the baby, which still
clung to her neck and eyed us in a reproachful way, seemed
somehow of a medium size between the first and the second
we had seen with their living dams. I should have liked
to keep it for a pet, and my guide had already made a nest

for it in his bundle of sundries, when an examination of its limbs showed a double fracture of its left forearm ; so we permitted our dog to put it out of its misery.   As soon as we shouldered our guns the rest of the troop broke out *en masse*, showering down leaves and excrement in their head-long flight ; but, seeing there would be no pursuit, they stopped in the next high trees to vent their feelings in a chattering indignation-meeting.

A panther-cat jumps four or five feet farther than any monkey of the same size, but no other animal rivals the quadrumana in the ease of, the absence of any visible effort in, their rapid movements.   Still more astonishing is the quickness of their eye and what I might call the retentive-ness of their *visual memory*.   At a single glance a flying monkey seems able to precalculate the direction and the length of the next dozen jumps to a fraction of an inch, and then dash ahead through branches and tangled vines at a height of perhaps eighty feet from the ground, yet with his head turned back and his eyes fixed on his pur-suer.   And this in forests abounding with spinescent trees and creepers which neither man nor monkey could grasp without lacerating his hands !   To the three things which are too wonderful, while the fourth is too queer, for human comprehension (Proverbs xxx. 18) King Solomon should have added the way of a monkey through a liana-tangle.

We found several pieces of mica on the western declivity of the ridge, and the mayoral seemed inclined to return and prospect the upper cliffs, but our guide was getting fidgety. " *Nos vamos a chingar ·* we are going to catch it before night," he said.   " Look at the sky back there, as murky as pitch-smoke, and the caprimulgas swarming like swallows."

We regained the valley by following a *rambla*, or dry ravine, and found the Indian's apprehensions confirmed.

Before we reached the river-shore crescendo thunder-echoes boomed from the glens of the Dolores range, and the purring night-hawks (*Caprimulgas*) had turned out in swarms, as if the day were waning. An awkward place to weather a tropical rainstorm,—wilderness all around, except on a range of hills on the other side of the river, where the upper slopes had been partly cleared. On one of these clearings I thought I discerned the white walls of a stone-built rancho or limekiln. The river seemed shallow enough to be easily forded: could we reach that building before night?

"The matter is this," said the mayoral, after a topographical council with the two Indians: "your guide wants to know if you would prefer a sure drenching to the possibility of getting into a mosquito-trap? As a sleeping-place the rancho would be preferable, but it is fully three leagues from here, and there is an old logwood-chopper's camp on this side of the river not more than a mile ahead."

An ominous moaning in the tree-tops biased our consultation: the next shelter seemed the best. The shores of the principal rivers of Guatemala and Southern Mexico are dotted with the camps of the *leñeros* or logwood-men, the most useful pioneers of the backwoods States,—path-makers rather than desert-makers, since, unlike our professional lumberers, they confine their attacks to a single species of trees—trees which are neither the finest, nor, aside from their chromatic properties, the most useful, of the abounding tierra caliente. Their *casuchas*, or temporary huts, are of the rudest description, having neither windows nor that *sine qua non* of a habitable Northern log-shanty, a fireplace; but the woodcraft of the builders is generally attested by a weather-tight roof. In the camp on the upper Moscon we had the choice between four well-roofed casuchas, additionally sheltered by a canopy of mighty cecropia-trees, and not much the worse for having been abandoned six years ago, such trifling inconveniences as transparent walls and a rickety floor being probably original defects.

While we made a bonfire of the dry leaves and chips which covered the bottom of our chosen casucha we became aware of the fact that the forest around us had turned dark, —darker than a London reading-room during a fog,— though by my watch the next two hours seemed yet to be entitled to a fair share of daylight; and when, finally, the rain came down in sheets and cataracts, a person suddenly awakened from a long slumber would have been unable to say if the faint shimmer between the riverward tree-tops emanated from the sun or from a waning moon.

The fury of the rain abated after a sudden shifting of the wind, but the untimely twilight continued for half an hour: our dog barked furiously at the foot of a little gum-tree not more than forty yards from our hut, but we tried in vain to distinguish more than the dim outlines of an animated object in the upper branches of the tree. It looked too round for an iguana, too small for a bear, and much too sluggish for a monkey or wild-cat.

"There are two or three of them," said the peon, after walking close up to the tree through the drizzling rain,— "raccoons or young bears I should say, and in no hurry to leave, by the way they are crawling around. They keep close together: you might bring them down with a single shot."

"Kill them, but not bring them down," said the señor. "I would bet my gun that I know what they are,—a brown *tarda*" (sloth) "with her young ones. The black variety is not nearly so sluggish, and no raccoon or bear in the world would stand that amount of noise without getting out of the way. If brown sloths find a tree that suits them, they stick to it, dead or alive; for if you shoot them the carcass hangs on by its hooked claws till the feet rot away."

The wind turned chilly, and just before sunset the western sky cleared, and brightened the woods with a reddish light. We made ourselves comfortable for the night, and identified our silent neighbors. Don Nicolas was right: they were a family of brown sloths, crawling slowly along the branches, —slowly and placidly, like insects rather than like arboreal mammals, which as a rule are the liveliest creatures of Nature. I believe there is no doubt that wild animals enjoy rain, a warm rain especially: in a tropical woodland a good shower after a sultry day awakens the same grunting and screeching acclaims that greet the rising sun or the discovery of a bonanza of palatable food. To the naked savage too the glowing sunshine is perhaps a comfortable warm-air bath, and a cloudburst an agreeable shower-bath. To the children of Nature, I suspect, *naturalia non sunt sœva* any more than *turpia*.

While we suspended our hammocks under the eaves of the roof my Indian guide spread his thin blanket between the threshold and the root of our protecting tree, preferring the chilly wind to the broken floor. The only piece of level plank had been occupied by the old peon, who was already snoring, with his poncho on a leather pouch for a pillow, and no covering at all.

"It is curious what a hardy education will do for a man," said Don Nicolas. "That old chap would rather sleep on a pile of cobblestones or in a hollow tree than go half a mile out of his way for the finest feather bed in America. You have seen him walk barefoot through the jungle, and he used to do the same in winter-time up in the Durango mountains, with four inches of snow on the ground. Your priests and city people may affect to pity the ‘ poor Indians,’ but if the *duendes*” (the fate-fairies) “ offered to grant me one wish, and only one, I should be much tempted to choose perfect health in preference to any other kind of perfection.”

The night was moist but still, and we could plainly hear the squealing of a troop of peccaris in the neighboring jungle,—long-drawn squeals, closely resembling the quavering *nocturno* of a group of recumbent barn-yard hogs. From a greater distance we heard occasionally the low wailing cry of a *mono espectro*, or night-monkey, a small quadrumanous animal allied to the lemures, and very rarely seen in daytime.

One great advantage of a woodland over a treeless country is the purity of its rivers and creeks, an all-present vegetation acting as a filter and purifying the running water before it reaches the larger streams. Travellers in the United States often wonder at the contrast of the blue Susquehanna and the clear Ohio to the turbid waters of the West. The Mississippi Valley forms the dividing-line between the great East American sylvanias and the treeless Central States, as we should call them, for the true West, California and Oregon, can vie with West Virginia in arboreal wealth and the purity of the streams. The rains of that winter night would have flooded a Kansas river with a swill-deluge of fluid mud, but the Rio Moscon looked as limpid and almost as shallow as on the preceding afternoon: the dense vegetation of the surrounding hills had absorbed the water like a sponge, to deal it out in driblets of never-failing springs.

Six miles above our last camping-ground the river forked: we followed the southwestern arm, which issues directly from the cañons of the Sierra Negra, while its tributary curves around the eastern spur of the main range. We

now had to breast pretty steep up-grades, and before long
the increasing altitude began to tell upon the vegetation:
the palms shrank to palmettos, and the blue-green euphorbia
groves were succeeded by copses of cypress- and juniper-
trees and stately *pinabetes*, or mountain-larches. *Piñales*, or
pineries, the Spaniards call these hill-forests, as we would
speak of a "strawberry-patch" in the mountains, where a
few strawberry-plants are scattered among hundreds of other
herbs and grasses. Unmixed pine woods are hardly ever
seen south of the twenty-fifth parallel, for even in the
heights of the tierra fria the stunted fir-bushes are mingled
with rhododendrons and rock-birches.

On the eastern slope of our ridge the acacias and tamarinds were still in full bloom, and on the opposite bank of
a steep cañon we saw a veritable arboreal nosegay, a clump
of feather-mimosas, whose sweet-smelling white and lilac
flowers had attracted a cloud of butterflies, which, seen
across the gorge, seemed to swarm like bees around a new
hive. Only a painter could do justice to the brilliant lepi-
dopteral insects which frequent the sunny sides of this terrace-land · I saw some sphinges and a rare variety of the
genus *Colia* which sorely tempted me to encamp on the spot
and devote a day to entomology. The *Papilio phœbus*,
especially, seems to find a congenial home on the flowery
leas of these uplands, as does a milk-white *Vanessa* with a
border of flame-colored rings and dots; also a dark-green
humming-bird moth, which here appears long before twilight, and, darting from bush to bush or hovering with
quickly-vibrating wings, looks exactly like the *Trochilus
colubris*, or emerald colibri, of Southern Mexico.

Soon after entering the piñal we met a solitary wanderer,
a little Indian fox-hound, whose master was chopping wood
somewhere up in the sierra, leaving his poor cur to take his

breakfast out of such opossums or nest-birds as he might
fall in with on his lonely rambles. A chip of dried beef
attached the hungry stranger to our company, and, after
conciliating Leoncito by several reverend prostrations, he
followed us at a distance and began to range the thickets
along our line of march. Hunting-dogs stimulate each
other. Leoncito joined in the search. Before long the fox-
hound gave tongue, and two minutes later we heard a bay:
they seemed to have treed their game at the first heat or
run upon a peccary sow with a litter of pigs to defend.
The bay seemed stationary; so, handing our share of the
cargo to the Indians, we cocked our shot-guns and entered
the thicket at a trot. There we had them. What could it
be? The dogs were standing round a low bush, their game
hidden by the lower branches and a few tufts of bamboo-
grass not more than fourteen inches high. Could they have
raised all this din about an opossum or a coiled-up armadillo? But no getting sight of us, Leoncito made a rush
forward, but as quickly sprang back. A long claw had
darted out at him like a stiletto: the customer he had to
deal with was evidently averse to familiarities.

"Hallo! a *hormiguero*,—an ant-bear!" said Don Nicolas.
"Did you see his fangs? Take care! stand over on this
side."

It was a curious sight: a young ant-bear (*Myrmecophaga
gigas*), about the size and weight of a full-grown panther,
lay flat on his back, guarding his body with his poised
claws, each toe armed with a fang as long as a boar's tusk
and as sharp as a penknife, his head slightly raised and his
eye, gleaming like bright steel, restraining its wink for fear
of losing the slightest movement of the adversary. With
the same glittering eye, expressive of the same determina-
tion to make the most of his one chance, I have seen a

swordsman with poised sabre watching the advance of a knife-armed foe: at close quarters the sabre would be useless, but its first stroke may be fatal, both parties knowing this, and fully aware that the first mistake will decide the game. The legs of the ant-bear are too stiff to be turned inward or upward with much effect, but a sidelong stroke of those awkward paws will rip a dog from throat to tail

AN ANT-BEAR AT BAY.

or gash a man's leg to the bone in spite of gaiters and cowhide boots.

Don Nicolas at last whistled his dog off, and the ant-bear, suddenly getting sight of us, regained his feet and started to run; but danger now threatened him from too many sides, and from the first unguarded point the fox-hound leaped upon him with a sudden spring, and had him by

the neck at the first grip; and, cheered by his master's halloo, Leoncito in the next moment grabbed him from the
other side and pinned his head to the ground.   He brought
his hind feet into play and Leoncito came in for a few ugly
scratches, but between them the dogs had him foul: his
desperate efforts to turn on his back were unavailing.   The
fox-hound at last got an under grip on his throat, and now
for the first time the hitherto mute hormiguero raised his
voice,—a rasping grunt, rising quickly into ear- and soul-
harrowing shrieks, more piercing than the shrillest screech
of a wet slate scraped with a blunt caseknife.   I felt sorry
for the poor devil, but there was no help for him: the dogs
were covered with blood, and could not be whistled off now
without exposing them to the full vengeance of those long
hooks that clawed the ground with impatient rage.

" *Malgasto es pecado*" ("All waste is sinful"), said the
thrifty Mexican when I raised my gun, "but you are right:
let us be merciful;" and approaching his victim from behind
with his long hunting-knife, he showed him what hunters
call "mercy" by cutting his throat from ear to ear.

During our absence our Indians had been more usefully
employed in routing out a nest of dwarf rattlesnakes which
they had discovered at the wayside.   The *gusano infernal*,
or "hell-worm," is not much longer than some of the
largest tropical caterpillars,—from ten to twelve inches,
about sixteen inches as the maximum,—in color not unlike
the yellow Texas rattlesnake, which it also resembles in its
general appearance, its *harmless* end being decorated with
two or three horny capsules which produce a faint rattling
sound.   But this epitome of the *Crotalus horridus* rivals its
big relative in the deadliness of its venom, and its very puni-
ness makes it the most dreaded reptile of Central America.
In grass or stunted herbs, where the Northern rattlesnake

would betray itself at a distance of twenty yards, its tropical congener finds a safe hiding-place, and its rattle is generally too feeble to be of much use as a warning signal.
The old peon had discovered a large conventicle of the imps
under a ledge of slate-rock, and mashed eight of them with
the butt of his blunderbuss,—repulsive little creatures,
writhing in the sand like overgrown leeches.

"By rare good luck they are very sluggish brutes," said
the mayoral : "they will not strike unless you are about to
tread on them ; but if you do—and they will do nothing
to prevent it—off they go like a spring-gun, and a man
may think himself lucky if he gets off with twenty-four
hours' fever and a week's headache after exhausting all
remedies. Children mostly die, and nothing can save a dog,
so far as I know."

"What remedies do you apply ?"

"Bleeding and heroic doses of *persico*" (bitter-peach
brandy), "repeated alternately till you swoon. The Indians use an abominable decoction of a stuff that tastes
like a mixture of tobacco and quinine, and throws you into
a delirium of gastric fever ; and an old wretch of a half-
breed medicine-man of my acquaintance used to bleed his
patients by slitting their ears, on the theory that a man will
not die as long as you can keep his brain clear."

The nostrum used by the Guatemala natives I afterward
ascertained to be an infusion of *Papaver nanum*, or bastard
poppy, a plant that frequents the open glades of the western
sierras and is sometimes cultivated for its intoxicating properties. The *rationale* of all snake-remedies, by the by, seems
to be founded on the circumstance that two diseases cannot
coexist in the human body, and the effects of most poisons
can be prevented by a swifter toxic agent. On the same
principle, a sore eye may be cured by inducing an artificial

25

inflammation on the upper part of the neck, and the seeds of consumption, though their fruit is death, will for years prevent the development of any other disease.

An hour after midday we passed the Portello de Esmarcada, a gap in the eastern or lower chain of the Sierra Negra, and, standing on the brink of the western slope, we beheld our next objective point, the Lago de Tortugas, a triangular highland tarn which forms the source of the main fork of the Rio Moscon. The valley between the two main chains of the sierra, with their magnificent terraces, is traversed by the dividing-line between the departments of Vera Paz and Chiquimulga, and is dotted with little lakes, and on the western slope with villages and haciendas, whose clearings, viewed from this height, looked like bright-green lawns in a frame of pine forests. At the head of the Lago de Tortugas stands the little village of the same name, whose nucleus is formed by a rendezvous of turtle-egg hunters, who make this point their head-quarters, whence they visit the rivers and smaller lakes of the valley if the report of their scouts has announced a *bonanza de huevos*.

"If your countrymen are good ditchers they can pay their land-rent in turtle-eggs," observed the señor: "the agents of the Guatemalan government will take a hundred fresh eggs, in lieu of a *peso fuerte*" (one dollar and a quarter), "in payment of all dues and taxes, or buy them at any time at three-fourths of that rate. Scientific mining too would pay almost anywhere in the main range: if I were not so completely out of cash I would build a quicksilver-furnace about ten miles northeast of your reservation. The lead ores of the old Izatlan mines would pay sixty dollars to the ton if they were correctly handled."

Following the windings of the Val de Tortugas in a southerly direction, the lake dawns gradually upon your view through an opening screen of magnolias and cork-oaks, but, standing upon the brink of its steep shores, a scene uniting so much loveliness to such grandeur would still be a surprise even to a senior member of the London Traveller's Club,—the charms of Pennsylvania and Piedmont combined, Eric Bay framed with Alps and Apennines, or Lago Ticino wreathed with the fine forests whose loss the Italian lakes have mourned for the last eighteen centuries. A deep-blue lake, about twenty miles in circumference and fed by innumerable rivulets, which come down on the western or sierra side in a series of tiny waterfalls, forming as many shady bays on the south shore,—a lake that will yet be a favorite resort of pleasure- and health-seekers, but whose clear waters have never yet been furrowed by the keel of a sailboat or even by a prosaic ferry : the shiftless natives prefer a circuit of several miles to the trouble of constructing a transit-boat, and their wretched dug-outs hug the shore and never leave their landing in rough weather.

About six miles south of the outlet (the head of the Rio Moscon) we reached the first houses, an Indian farm-hovel and a little *tendajo* or cross-road store kept by a mestizo " merchant," as he styled himself. We halted at the shop, but found the door locked, and, looking around, discovered a long wooden horn dangling from the porch, and above it a board with the following inscription in rather phonetic Spanish : " If Sr. Matias the merchant is not at home, apply to the next neighbor or *wind the horn.*"

" Don Matias is out in the sierra grouse-hunting," explained the next neighbor : " you'll have to give him a good blast or two."

For the fun of the thing I tried the primitive telephone, a tube of taxus-wood six feet long, with a knuckle-bone for a mouthpiece, but all my efforts resulted in an inglorious grunt, a gurgling splutter. I might as well have tried to get music out of a bean-shooter.

"Never mind," laughed the mayoral: "I only wanted to buy a few pounds of sugar, but I guess we can get enough at Don Gascar's pulque-shop, where we are going to stop to-night."

Imagine a storekeeper of a New England valley requesting his customers to summon him with a cowhorn, perhaps from the hunting-grounds of the upper White Mountains!

The village, with its miserable shanties embowered in walnut groves and copses of blooming cecropias, proved that arboreal vegetation can ennoble almost any architecture, while its absence will leave an aching void in a city of palaces. Let travellers compare our Savannah with Turkish Damascus: here a garden-city in a wilderness of swamps, there a wilderness of whitewashed sepulchres in a garden-land.

"Oh, Juan!" the mayoral hailed one of the house-boys when we had deposited our luggage in a back room of the pulque-shop, "do you think you could find old Martin,— old Martin Santiago, you know?"

"I guess I could, sir."

"Well, then, run like a good lad and tell him to come over here: I want to treat him and introduce him to this gentleman."

"Santiago? Who is he? a local celebrity?"

"Not exactly: local marvels are rarely appreciated by the natives, you know; but he is a great curiosity, nevertheless. Have you ever heard of a man cutting a third set of teeth?"

"I heard of it, but I did not believe it."

"Well, you will have to believe it now. This old man was sweeping and scrubbing floors in the San José custom-house for more than twelve years, and there are hundreds of persons who can testify that he hadn't a tooth in his mouth when he left there; but after roughing it for a couple of years in his native *pueblo*, where he had to chew parched corn bread and acorns, his jaws revived: he cast his old snags and got a new set,—as pretty as any dentist could make him,—after being plagued with gum-aches like a teething child for several months. Three years ago he went down to San José with a load of eggs, and happened to meet Dr. Ortez, the quarantine physician, who had seen him nearly every day in his toothless condition, and didn't know if he could believe his own eyes when he noticed the anamorphosis. But, being a man of methodical business habits, he gave the old fellow an appointment, invited two dozen mutual acquaintances, and made them sign an affidavit to the above facts."

We were just going to supper when Juancito returned. "Here he is now," he whispered, drawing me back behind the door.

Mr. Santiago had entered the adjoining bar-room,—a brawny old Indio, well built, but with a baboonish cast of countenance and with an animal fire in his hollow eyes which, like a ray flashing through vacant night, only served to make darkness visible.

After a short conversation with the bartender he strolled into our room and announced himself with a grunt, raising his hand in an awkward imitation of a military salute.

"How are you, Don Martin? Sit down. What is your present occupation, señor?"

"Occupation?"

"How are you getting on, I mean? what are you working at?"

"Curing plantains, señor. I am boarding with Mr Herrera,—Juan Herrera's brother, you know."

"Just think of that!" said Don Nicolas,—"doing farm-work like a young man! He is nearly seventy years old now."

"Indeed! You are looking remarkably hearty for your age: what is your diet, Don Martin? What do you generally eat, I mean?"

"I generally get corn bread and beans, señor,—wheat bread on Sunday."

The mayoral made me examine his teeth, and I found his lower jaw and all his incisors perfectly sound, two of the upper molars being slightly carious. His front teeth were white and even, like a young girl's, and disproportionately small compared with his defective molars.

"Do you eat any meat?" I asked.

"Yes, señor. But no—" with a sudden gleam of suspicion—" not to-day—oh no, not on Friday, señor." I might be a masked priest, for all he knew.

"Do you like pulque?"

"*Si, señor*," his countenance brightening: the bishop himself would not traverse such an impeachment.

"Do you take any—aguardiente?"

"Yes, señor. You know" (half-apologetically) "a man needs *zafarse de su memoria*—wants to get rid of his memory—once in a while."

Get rid of his memory! After all, that is the only valid excuse a man can plead for admitting the "enemy that steals away his brains;" but where did a savage learn that humiliating truth? Could it be that the happiness of that golden age which mankind may "learn to forego, but never to forget," was founded upon habits from which the ignorant children of the wilderness have strayed as far as the sickly city-dwellers, only in a different direction?

CHAPTER XII.

THE VIRGIN WOODS OF THE SIERRA NEGRA.

Is this my birthland? Has this echo wakened
Dim recollections of a former home?—LENAU.

THE English language has no indigenous word for that
curious psychic phenomenon which Jean Paul calls the
"dualistic mystery" (*das Geheimniss des Dualismus*), and
which he describes as "a revival by an actual event of a
reminiscence of unknown origin." In our pilgrimage
through life most (perhaps all) of us have met with adventures which somehow surprised us with the consciousness
that the same train of incidents, in the same succession and
under the same circumstances, had somewhere crossed our
path before; not in a dream nor in a fit of second sight,—
that would have left a different impression,—but in real life,
as it would seem, only a long time ago,—so long ago, indeed,
that we could hardly bridge the interval without some compromise with the doctrine of metempsychosis. "'Tis a
transmitted experience," says the German pantheist,—"an
incident in the life of one of our forefathers, the recollection
of which has been awakened by a similar occurrence (like
a sleeper starting at the sound of his own name) after having lain dormant in our soul together with millions of inherited ideas, opinions, talents, and inclinations,—all the
result of ancestral experience. Each human brain is stamped
with the records of all preceding generations."

On the same principle we may perhaps explain the strange suggestiveness of certain landscapes, which remind us of nothing we can possibly have seen before, except, maybe, with the eyes of an ancestor,—with eyes which could still read the language in which Nature writes her secrets and her promises. A country which would repel the modern agriculturist by its ruggedness and the city-dweller by its solitude might thus prove attractive to those older instincts by which even a cockney may now and then recognize the original home of his species, as stall-born chamois are said to be lured away by the sight of the Alpine highlands. In the mountains of Central America there are regions which seem peculiarly adapted to all the requirements of a primitive home, having a comfortable climate, natural shelter-places, and an abundant supply of man- and monkey-food, besides a variety of plants whose bast and seed-cotton might be used for rude textile fabrics. The *alturas,* or wooded uplands, of Eastern Guatemala abound especially with productions of that kind; and if the American Indians are real autochthones the rivers of the Sierra Negra de Vera Paz may have been the Pisons and Gihons of the Western Paradise.

The government lands between the Val de Tortugas and the sources of the Rio Motagua comprised some highland pastures and an abandoned lead-mine, with a few acres of cleared ground, but the main part of the reservation lay between the Val de Motagua and the Rio Polochique, in the very heart of the timber region, where no agricultural settlements had ever been attempted. Before committing my countrymen to a definite contract I wanted to verify the report of the land-office by personal inspection of the resources and market-facilities of this region, and, if possible, get the government to assist us in the construction of a wagon-road to Macultepec, where the camino real to the capital crosses the valley of the Rio Moscon.

We left Tortugas an hour before sunrise on the third of February,—in the midwinter week, here corresponding to the early spring of Southern Texas or the end of May in the Northern Alleghanies. Only the moonlight kept watch in the vineyards of the little village, but the crests of the sierra were already tinted with a reflection of the morning-clouds, and a flock of tarn-geese rose screaming from the mist of the lower lake.

" We are going to have a warm day, caballeros," observed my carrier. " Look at those red mountains up there: that's San Florian's weather-signal,—he's heating his *dest'-aguardiente*" (fire-water still).

" Never mind," said the mayoral: " we shall be in the upper sierra before he gets his machinery a-working. Do you see that white streak, Don Felix,—that long streak of mist south of the sierra? That's the valley of the Rio Motagua. If your countrymen could get as far as the Macultepec ferry, they would have a good country-road to Port Isabel, with twenty markets instead of one · the Honduras bergantins call there, and a weekly steamer to Sisal and New Orleans. Port Isabel is only thirty-five miles from the ferry."

" Couldn't we go there and be back before the end of this week?"

" Yes, if they do not delay us in the sierra. We might try to stop at Gil Mateo's ranch to-night: if you should find him at home he could give you as much information as all the natives of the Indian village."

The upper slopes of the Val de Tortugas are very sparsely settled. Near Plan del Monte we passed a few Indian huts, with a patch of garden-land and a field whose proprietor was pulling out cornstalks by the root. Farther up, the trail entered a thicket of catalpa and iron-wood trees, that seemed to mark the upper boundary of the agricultural region. The vegetation of these slopes on the whole resembled that of the Moscon Valley, but when we began the ascent of the main chain the dryer air and the dry, aromatic herbage of the ravines reminded me of the rainless highlands of Southern California. There was but little dew on the grass, and the morning air was perfectly free from any taint of swamp-mist; the rivulets were as clear as plate glass, and the leaves rustled under our feet as if they had been dried in a hop-loft.

It is hard to decide if red-skins and pale-faces had a separate "centre of creation," but I hold that our original home or homes were in the woodlands of a tropical mountain-region. In spite of the infinite diversity of our domestic habits, all normally-constituted human beings, I believe, still prefer a wooded to a treeless country, a dry to a swampy soil, and a temperature which on the whole maintains itself above the freezing-point. Conjointly, these conditions can be fulfilled only by the mountain-forests of the lower tropics, at the same time the favorite home of the palms, figs, mangos, and larger Nuciferæ, in itself a significant circumstance, for that sweet tree-fruits were our original food is one of the few points on which Moses and Darwin agree. Our *Ur-vater*, whether demi-gorilla or demi-god, was probably a *montanus;* ancient and modern mountain-countries, Syria, Greece, Italy, Switzerland, Scotland, and Circassia (Virginia, her F. F.'s would add), have always produced a superior breed of men ; and the "garden planted eastward in Eden," between the head-waters of four great rivers, can hardly have been a lowland plantation. For railroads, ship-canals, and machine-farming purposes the prairie States offer certainly superior advantages, but if our manifold sins should result in another deluge, and an American Noah had to select a homestead for recommencing business with limited resources, his first choice would probably be the highlands of Vera Paz, his second the palm-region of Western Tehuantepec or the whortleberry and chestnut woods of Northern Alabama. In the upper valleys of the Sierra Negra a man could sleep in the open air the year round under a common plaid · according to all accounts, the variations of the temperature seem almost limited to the diurnal changes, its annual range being from a monthly average of eighty degrees in June to sixty-five in November.

The surface-rock, a trachytic feld-par, is honeycombed with clefts and caverns where a homeless squatter could find abundant shelter from October to Christmas, the rainy season being here confined to those six weeks. Near the pass of Los Cumbres I saw a series of caves that seemed to have sheltered benighted wanderers,—prospecting miners perhaps, or a *tropa* of muleteers,—as the ground around there was strewn with charred sticks and corncobs. I entered one of them, and found the bottom perfectly dry, with no trace of moisture on the walls, but a profusion of gray and reddish lichens. Even near the watercourses we could take short cuts through the woods wherever we pleased. they were as clean and dry as an Austrian mountain-park artificially drained and weeded. And yet we were treading on virgin soil, as primitive a wilderness as any between Peru and Oregon. From the glens on our left rose the true primeval forest of Central America,—bulky caucho-trees with smooth bark and leathery foliage, lignum-vitæ giants, Torreya pines, yellow-wood, tulip-trees with large woolly leaves,—all crowding each other on the sunny sides

THE HIGHLANDS OF VERA PAZ.

and making room on the northern slopes for the hardier
myrtles and laurel-trees.   The Torreya pines swarmed with
a small and short-tailed variety of the genus *Parus* (tomtits),
and on the same trees I noticed several bird-spider nets,
one of them with a diameter of more than six feet, without
including the long brace-threads that ran out like forestays
to the extremity of the surrounding branches.   To judge
from the tenacity of their filaments, I should think that
they would make a good substitute for coarse silk.   I had
no means of measuring the strength of the single threads,
but I found that the main body of the web stopped a
number of wild lemons (about the size of a pigeon-egg)

which I flung against the centre with all my might and
from a distance of hardly fifteen yards. The animal itself
has a peculiar talent for keeping out of sight: I remember
that I once rummaged for half an hour around a leafless
catalpa-bush before I detected the eight-legged weaver that
had nearly covered the tree with his viscid tissues.

The weather-saint verified his augurium, after all. The
morning was rather warm for the midwinter week, and the
mayoral unbuckled a little gourd from his hunting-pouch
and clambered down into a bushy ravine to get a drink of
water. "Stop a moment," he called up from the bottom:
"there must be a wild-turkey nest down here: the dog
flushed a hen from almost under my feet Do you hear
her? I know what that cackling means."

While we waited my Indian took a seat on a wayside
rock, but suddenly jumped up and into the middle of the
road, "Mira! mira! mi capitan: que animalote!—Look up
there! what a monster of a beast!" he cried, pointing to a
big caucho-tree at the brink of the ravine. It was a *boa
de pollos* ("a chicken-boa"), winding her sluggish length
through the upper branches of the tree, and evidently ill at
ease at seeing herself discovered. I cocked my gun, and she
reared as if she contemplated an escapade into a neighboring
and somewhat higher tree, but retracted her neck, and,
hugging the main stem of the caucho, managed to conceal
the bulk of her body on the safe side. Her head was still
in view, but oscillating in a way that made me a little mis-
trustful of my aim, the height of the tree-top being about
sixty feet, as near as I could judge. Having no ramrod-
screw handy, I put a load of buckshot on top of a bullet-
charge, and, allowing for the elevation, aimed a little above
her eye, which seemed to watch us sideways, still rather
doubtful about our intentions. When the smoke cleared

away the head of the serpent hung back as if her neck had
been crushed by an axe-stroke, while her coils contracted
slowly and firmly.   But in the next moment the convul-
sions commenced : independently, as it seemed, of any cere-
bral promptings, her tail laid about with a vigor that filled
the air with flying twigs and leaves, and, suddenly reversing
its coils, the body slipped off and came plumping to the
ground amidst the uproarious shouts of the two Indians
" Esta hembra, y llena de huevos (it's a she, and full of
eggs), I bet," cried the peon.   " Wait till I get Don Ruan's
hunting-knife.   I'll lay a dollar that we get a hatful of
eggs out of her."

He was actually going to cut her up, but at my request
the mayoral vetoed the disgusting operation.   The boa was
about sixteen feet long, and very prettily speckled with
black and orange-brown spots   Her neck was riddled with
shots that seemed to have broken the vertebræ in several
places, but when we finally marched our Indians off she
was still writhing in the grass, and, as the peon assured me,
would not die before the next ghost-hour (11-12 P.M.),
when *El Demonio* would call around for her soul.

The true *Boa constrictor* is found only in the coast-forests :
in the mountains the name is applied to four or five species
of smaller tree-snakes, and even to a python which frequents the canebrakes of the upper lakes.   Lynxes, panthers,
and cinnamon bears are occasionally seen in the alturas, but
they are getting scarce in the neighborhood of the settlements : the enemies and rivals of man cannot maintain
themselves in the comparatively open forests of the upper
sierra.   Yet with one exception : the *hormigas* (ants and
termites) still hold their own, and scorn to recognize the
sovereignty of the self-styled viceregent of the Creator.
The " strength-in-union" principle is indeed strikingly illus-

BOA-SHOOTING.

trated by the achievements of those leagued Liliputians who dread no foe in Brobdingnag, and prey upon man as he preys upon all other creatures. Ants cannot be starved out, for they can subsist on decaying organic substances of any kind, vegetable as well as animal; you cannot kill them out, for their name is legion of legions; you cannot exterminate them, like mosquitoes, by draining the lagoons, for they will thrive on dry ground as well as in the swamps; and if you cut the trees down they will move into your house. The ant-bear is their only dangerous foe, but his activity can only check over-multiplication: the total number of all species of ants has been estimated as fifty thousand times larger than that of all vertebrate animals taken together. They have their colonies on the ground, underground, and in the rocks; and one variety of termites, the *mat'abejas*, or bee-killer ants, build their nests in the tree-tops, and if they really feed exclusively on honey, bee-culture must be difficult in Guatemala, for we saw mat'abeja-nests which I at first mistook for monstrous clusters of mistletoe, as they covered all the upper branches of good-sized cauchos and magnolias.

Our path had gradually turned from southwest to south, and about 2 P.M. we crossed a deep glen, the upper cañon of the Rio Motagua, opening a vista toward the eastern valleys through a wild chaos of rocks and pine-forests. Clambering up the southern slope, we caught a glimpse of a waterfall that seemed to come from the cloudland of the upper sierra, and, after tumbling in a cascade over the rocks of the first forty or fifty feet, fell straight into the apparently bottomless abyss below. We had a steep ascent of sixteen or eighteen hundred feet, but when we got up, perspiring as if just out of a Turkish bath-house, I could not resist the temptation to follow the brink over boulders and brambly clefts till I got a front view of the falls. It was a veritable *staub-bach*,—a large creek dissolved into a shower of spray before it arrived at the bottom of the cañon. The water reached the main stream by a number of rills between loose mossy rocks, but the descent of the rain-cataract seemed to create a strong current of air, for a mountain-ash ten or twelve yards below the junction swayed as if moved by a fitful gale, though the trees farther down stood rigidly erect.

About four miles below the falls our trail approached the cañon once more, and we found that the glen had widened into a broad valley, with stretches of level ground on both sides of the river, some of them wide enough for a little farm, and exposing a thick stratum of black mould where the river had washed the sward from its banks. All this valley was included in the reservation: we were still four or five leagues above the lower boundary. At the next turn of our trail the forest had been partly cleared: we passed a stack of cordwood, scattered fence-rails, and other indications of a neighboring settlement. Half an hour before we had heard a cow-bell, and now heard it again only a short distance ahead.

"That's Gil Mateo's ranch," said the mayoral. "I believe I heard his dogs too, so I hope we shall find him at home."

"Does he know you?"

"Yes: I stopped here several times. He's a *trasgresor*" (trespasser, wild squatter), "and a rough sort of a customer, but I would advise your countrymen to keep on his good side: he'll not bother them, I guess, and can be right useful if he chooses. By birth he is a Catalan, and has been in California during the gold years, but he's pretty well acquainted in this neighborhood,—has lived here ten or twelve years, I believe."

"Listen! there's somebody coming," said the peon.

Two boys galloped across the road, but drew rein at the halloo of the mayoral, and eyed us with evident surprise.

26

They looked like twin-brothers, eleven or twelve years of age, fair specimens of the *muchacho gachupin*,—acclimatized and Indianized young Spaniards. One was mounted on a stout donkey, the other on an equally thick-headed sierra pony.

"Why, Pablito! don't you know me?" the mayoral called out.

Pablito stared.

"Oh, I know him now," cried his brother. "Yes, that's Don Ruan: I recognized him as soon as I saw his big dog."

"Glad to meet you, boys," said the mayoral, after a general handshaking: "is your father at home?"

"He was home for dinner," said Pablito, "and he isn't very far off now. He's boiling maple-sugar down the river, about three miles from our place: you can see the smoke from our porch. I am sorry we didn't know you were coming, but we'll try to get back as quick as possible."

"Where are you going, boys?"

"Going to Señor Coban's place to borrow a bear-trap."

"Señor Coban in Val Secco? Wouldn't this road be the shorter way?"

"Yes, I know," said Pablito, "but the ford is very bad, my father says; so we are going to take the old Indian trail over the Torreya gap, if we can find it. But come on, hermanito, or we sha'n't get back before midnight."

"Yes, we want to be back in time for the dog-fight," laughed his brother; "don't forget what you promised us, señor. Adios meanwhile."

They wheeled round and galloped away with merry cheers into the thick of the pathless forest.

"Poor devils!" said the mayoral, "they have never had shoes on their feet since their father made this clearing.

In your native country they wouldn't take them to be white men's children, would they, Don Felix?"

I said nothing. I believe I envied them. They were both unkempt, barefoot, and almost barelegged, and had perhaps never seen the inside of a school-house; but, transplanted to an Illinois country town, with substantial farms, railroad facilities, and Christian colleges, those same boys would have pined away with homesickness and ennui. Dull times—in the domestic rather than a financial sense—drive thousands of our country boys from their homes to the wilds of the Great West or to the more bewildering wilderness of a great city: they seek *circenses* more than *panes*, fun rather than fortune. Our young metropolitans satisfy that craving after a fashion of their own, but it is cheaper and out-and-out safer to let your boys explore the mysteries of the wildest sierra than the *mystères de Paris*.

"We can save ourselves the roundabout way," said Don Ruan. "I can see the smoke now. I guess I know where he is: there is a maple-grove close to the cañon, about three miles from here."

"He is a Spaniard, you say: is he an intelligent fellow?"

"His manners are a little off color, but he can give you a deal of useful information: he has tried all kinds of gardening on a small scale, and is likely to know what crops pay best. And it's worth while knowing how he has managed to hold his ground against the Guachinos" (the hostile Indians of the Honduras border). "If a single family could do that, a colony of old frontiersmen with rifles and pistols needn't have any apprehensions on that account."

We left the path, and picked our way through the woods by guess and instinct till we got back to the bank of the river-valley. Between the pines and arbor-vitæs we saw a good many maple-trees, with leaves that looked a little smaller than those of the genuine "bird's-eye maple," but resembling the *Acer saccharinum* in their general appearance. Most of the larger trees had been tapped, and the little log troughs and elderwood siphons at the "sugar-camp" showed that Don Mateo had learned the business in the United States. The smoke rose from a crevice in the solid rock, where a copper kettle had been suspended over a smouldering wood-fire. Heaps of billets and kindling-wood lay around, and near one of the larger piles an axe and a hat, but where was Don Mateo himself?

"Just look at that Indian *casucha* he has built!" laughed the mayoral. "A half-savage, isn't he? Yes, he is in there, sure enough, just like a bear in his winter-quarters. Step over here, will you?"

At the very brink of the cañon a fallen pine-tree had formed a natural arbor, and by the simple process of lopping the lower branches and interlacing them with those on top the casucha had been made weather-tight, and commodious enough for half a dozen recumbent lodgers. The floor was covered with a litter of chips and pine-needles, and in this litter Don Mateo lay on his back,—a half-savage, indeed. His face, hands, and naked arms were smeared with a mixture of soot and maple-honey, and the color of his old leather breeches resembled that of his naked feet. He was napping, or trying to.

The mayoral handed me his gun, clambered over a pile of kindling-wood, and hailed him: "Buenas tardes, Don Gil."

The don turned on his elbow, stared at his visitors and then at each one of us separately, before he spoke a word. "Halloo! come in," said he at last.

"Is this your private country-seat?" asked the mayoral.

Another pause. "I do not know if it is my own or not,"

said the squatter. " I guess those men are the new settlers you told me about, the colonists who are going to kick me out ?"

A HUNTER'S CASTLE.

" Who said so?" replied Don Ruan. "This gentleman here is their agent, and he tells me they will thank God for having one white man for their neighbor. There are smart carpenters among them, Don Gil, and they will help you to fix your house up comfortably."

" I'm sure I won't ask them to bother themselves on my

account," said the squatter: "I can do my own housebuilding and housekeeping."

"Yes, it seems so," said I, "and we want you to show us how to do it, Don Mateo. There are eighteen families of them, and we will make it worth while for you to help us. We want to put up some temporary shelter-places before the beginning of the rainy season. You may find some old chums among them if you have been in California," I added.

He looked up and eyed me in a curious way: "Been in the *Altas?*" (Upper California.) "How are times there now?"

"All settled up, amigo,—full of Chinamen and land-speculators: no chance there now for an independent man. You picked out a much better country. But let me ask you one question. How did you contrive to manage the Indians? That's more than the government troops can do."

"God help your colonists if they are going to rely on the government troops!" said the Catalan. "Look here, sir," taking up an old rifle. "that's what I rely upon."

"Halloo! let me see. Why, that's a genuine American squirrel-gun: what will you take for it?"

"More than you would like to pay, captain: that gun is meat and bread to me. Look over there," said he, pointing to the opposite bank of the valley: "do you see that ravine across the river? I killed a buck there yesterday morning, and right from where I stand now. Could you do that with such shooting-machines as you can buy in this part of the world?"

"No: you are right. Is there much game in this neighborhood?"

"Plenty of grouse, and some peccaris farther down. Deer

are getting scarce, but that's just what I was talking about: if a man can rely on his gun, he needn't make a hog of himself and shoot a hen-grouse on her nest or a peccari-sow with pigs, as our Indians do. I caught one of them cutting spare-ribs out of a peccari with ten unborn pigs last month. Well, sir, I would have given his own pork a dressing if I could have run him down. On the marquis of Figuera's estate in my native country they would have shot such a fellow like a mad wolf. Just let me know if your colonists want a gamekeeper: I'm their man. I mean, if they are going to back me up if I should happen to cripple a pot-hunter or two."

Don Marco described the climate as very equable: he had never seen snow in the lower sierra, and the summer months were rarely disagreeably warm. Two crops of corn and wheat and perennial string-beans could be raised in the river bottoms, and the sunny sides would make promiscuous orchards, to judge from the great number of spontaneous tree-fruits. Viticulture might be very successful, he believed, but good wine would hardly find a market in Guatemala; and he advised me strongly to survey a wagon-road to the *boca* (Port Isabel), where several foreign traders would be glad to take commissions at liberal rates.

We decided to bivouac at the sugar-camp and continue our journey at daybreak to Macultepec, where the Port Isabel road could be reached by a rope-ferry over the Rio Motagua.

"We are rather short of provisions," said the Catalan, "but I will send you all we can spare: you can pay the boy or settle after you come back. Please don't let the fire go out. Oh, I nearly forgot," said he: "you will have some visitors to-night. There is a camp of Indian turtle-hunters about three miles from here, and they come up every night to get the sugar-scrapings: it saves me the trouble of cleaning the kettle myself."

After supper we crawled into the casucha, and slept peacefully till about an hour after midnight, when I was awakened by the low growling of the dog at my neighbor's feet.

"What's up?" said the mayoral.—"Oh, I see," he whispered: "Yes, here are the Indians,—licking the treacle out of Mateo's kettle, I bet. Listen! What in the name of reason are they doing? Singing, praying, or what?"

I raised my head, and thought I saw six or eight of them squatting in a circle around the sugar-kettle, but the flickering fire gradually resolved all these shapes into piles of chips and firewood,—all but one. right in front of the kettle crouched an old hag, a solitary old squaw, warming her bony hands over the embers and crooning a melody that had perhaps been composed in a tent-village of the Mongolian steppes.

I made the mayoral get up and take a look at the apparition. "She's the wigwam-cook, I guess, belonging to a tribe of wandering Guachinos," said he. "I shouldn't wonder if Don Gil lets them have something besides scrapings: they are very apt to blackmail a solitary farmer, like our Mexican bandits, who go around begging with a cocked musketoon in their fist."

"The Guachinos have no fire-arms, have they?"

"No, but they manage to get even with their enemies somehow or other. In Napaluco they nearly killed the lieutenant of the Mexican garrison with poisoned tobacco. They are as vindictive as gypsies,—hold human life very cheap, and commit murder or suicide on the slightest provocation. Our soldiers rather admire them for it, being themselves such arrant cowards that they respect courage in any form."

" The Guachinos are mostly heathens, I suppose?"

" Yes, but baptism doesn't tame them very much. One of my neighbors up in Chiapas had a baptized Guachino boy on his hacienda who threatened to commit homicide or suicide whenever they put him to any hard work or crossed him in one of his peculiar whims. They had him about two years, when he took it into his head to make red-hot love to the haciendado's daughter, who was too good-natured or too much of a coquette to cut his acquaintance in an off-hand way till her father sent for the priest, the only person who had any influence on the young demon. They were going to find him a good place in Soconusco, in order to get him out of the way. The priest told him that they would have kicked him out of the hacienda without any ceremony if he hadn't been a convert, and then, appealing to the fellow's common sense, told him that his suit was perfectly hopeless, and that he would find a good home in Soconusco, where kind friends and a new occupation would by and by cure him of his passion. The boy made no reply, but hung his head. 'Am I not right?' asked the priest when they parted. 'Yes,' says Master Guachino, ' but *me sanaré mas pronto*—I shall prefer a shorter cure.' The next morning they found the body of their late convert in the woodshed of the sugar-mill."

We decamped in the twilight of a cloudless morning, went a mile to the right to get clear of the manifold windings of the Motagua, and then steered due east over a descending plateau of park-like groves and mountain-meadows. The eastern slope of the Sierra Negra being exposed to the Atlantic trade-winds, the vegetation absorbs moisture enough from the atmosphere to preserve all its freshness in the rainless season. The grass was mixed with flowering stone-clover and bindweed (*Convolvulus tamus*), and alive with chirping grasshoppers, busy bumblebees and still busier ichneumon-wasps, the murderous enemy of all tropical caterpillars. The conifers here alternate with catalpas and wild china-trees, beeches and walnuts, and in the lower valleys the variety of nut-bearing trees is almost infinite. The farmers of Vera Paz gather the mast of a small kind of wild chestnut, grind it and bake it into bread and cakes of a peculiar pleasing flavor, resembling a certain sort of almond pastry. The slopes are intersected by numerous ravines, running mostly parallel with the Motagua Valley, and occasionally widening into grassy dells where a Swiss goatherd could forget his Alpenland. Here flourish the mezquite and the madroña or strawberry-tree of the Southern Cordilleras, and amidst broom-corn and rosemary the wild pineapple ripens its sweet-scented fruit. Combined with the atmosphere of this aromatic herbage, a high temperature can be not only tolerable, but strangely agreeable: in a flowery glen where we rested for the benefit of our carriers my pocket-thermometer indicated 92° Fahrenheit, and the sun stood almost directly overhead, but its glow felt so pleasant that I began to comprehend how the Roman epicureans could build special *solaria*—glass-covered cottages—for the purpose of bathing in sunshine.

During the whole forenoon we enjoyed the panorama of the snow-capped sierras of Chiapas and Tabasco, standing like turreted cloud-castles on the northern horizon, till we reached the depths of the Val de Motagua, where the view and the noonday sun were hidden by the canopy of the ancient pine-woods which had accompanied the river from its source in the rocks of the alturas. Under many of the larger trees the ground was covered with gnawed fir-cones, and now and then we caught sight of a squirrel-monkey or two dodging behind the stems after the fashion of the Northern fox-squirrel. The American squirrel-monkey (*Jacchus sciureus*) forms the connecting link between the rodents and quadrumana: its hands terminate in claws instead of blunt-nailed fingers, and its food consists chiefly of nuts and oily seeds, but its movements and general appearance suggest a close relationship with the tamarin and other small American monkeys. It generally has two young ones at a time, —strange, fluffy little kittens, that cling to their mother without hindering her movements in the least degree, and during a rapid flight clasp her neck in a way that seems to incorporate the three bodies into one.

When we came once more in sight of the Rio Motagua we found that the mountain-torrent had widened into a respectable river, bordered with ground-palms, fan-shaped canes, and gigantic mulberry-trees whose lower branches were festooned with long tresses of maidenhair (*Adiantum*) dangling from projecting limbs or trailing in the water like fish-nets. We reached the rope-ferry at the same time with a company of *pantaneros* (literally, "moormen"), gum-gatherers, and logwood-cutters, who had been at work in the river-swamps, and were now on their route to Port Isabel and New Orleans. Since the great dyewood forests of Campeche have been depleted these men, like our California gold-hunters after the exhaustion of the placer-mines, wander about in troops, generally under the auspices of a *patron* or speculator, who makes it his business to ferret out bonanzas of gum- and logwood-trees, and engages a gang of pantaneros either at fixed wages or with the promise of a *tantième* of the uncertain profits. In dull seasons the patron boards his men on credit, generally in Vera Cruz or New Orleans, or some other Gulf-port with regular steamboat facilities, in order to tackle the next bonanza without loss of time. As a matter of course, the average pantanero is in a chronic state of indebtedness; but *quien sabe?* A lucky season and a fair dividend may fill his pockets, and with health, hope, and smoking-tobacco he is the merriest muchacho in Spanish America. Every man of this party was a walking curiosity-shop, loaded with Indian trinkets, dried humming-birds, living monkeys, etc., for the New Orleans market, and besides their spades and axes most of them carried heavy Mexican musketoons Their commissariat was somewhat reduced, but their leader intended to replenish their provender-bags at the Zapateria, a wayside tavern about a league ahead, where he advised us to put up for the night.

The Zapateria, or cobbler-shop—so called from a subsidiary trade of the first proprietor—proved to be a stage-coach dépôt, at a triple cross-road, and, with its outbuildings and enclosed corrals, flanked the first good-looking farm we had seen since our departure from Chiapas. The river was conveniently near, and at the time of our arrival the entire male population of the farm seemed to be engaged in watering cattle and horses. Leoncito, our four-legged *avant-courier*, entered the open gate without ceremony, but came flying back, followed by a chorus of dog-voices that would have done credit to the three-headed gatekeeper of Tartarus. We clubbed our guns, expecting a disastrous sally, but nobody came: the dogs were chained up in the horse-stable, —three Aragon wolf-dogs, the most ferocious brutes that ever claimed descent from the genus *Canis*. When we passed their den they crouched down like jaguars, and then leaped forward with a fury that made the timbers of the stable creak, uttering yells that differed from the bark of a common dog as the bellowing of a sea-lion differs from the yelp of the seal.

The *posadero* was in luck that night. The evening stage

brought two merchants from Guatemala City who were going to a horse-fair in Macultepec, and before dark the Port Isabel party was reinforced by a detachment of soldiers, who had been on special duty on the Indian frontier and were now returning to their barracks at the head of the boca. As first-comers, we had our pick among the various sleeping accommodations, but after an ocular and olfactory examination of the interior dormitories I preferred a couch on the open porch, to the glad surprise of the merchants, who dreaded the "night-chill" with that meteorological fastidiousness of the New Spaniard which is only equalled by his entomological indifference.

They alluded in vague terms to the ubiquity of the third Egyptian plague when I met them at breakfast the next morning, but seemed to regret their choice chiefly on account of having missed a rare piece of fun.

In that half-hour of cool ethereal twilight which precedes a tropical sunrise I was awakened by a sound of hurried footsteps on the paved corral, and, looking up, saw a number of half-dressed men running in the direction of the stable at the top of their speed. "What's up?" I asked my neighbor, who seemed to have been awake for some time,—"a horse stolen?"

"No, no: *un tropo de monos rastecos*—a troop of cebou-monkeys—stealing maize," he replied. "One of the soldiers on his way to the spring has spied them in the big cornfield, and the proprietor is going to unchain his hound."

While he spoke hound, master, and soldiers had passed us in silent haste, and, snatching up my shot-gun, I left my baggage in charge of the Indian and ran out in my stocking-feet.

Before we reached the gate the monos had taken the alarm, and on a level field a cebou-monkey can get over the ground at a lively rate: but the distance to the high timber was nearly a mile, and, once started upon the fresh scent, the Aragon wehr-wolf gained upon them so rapidly that even bets were offered upon the chance of any of them escaping with their lives, when one unlucky mona made a scapegoat of herself by jumping upon a tree-stump hardly eight feet high and in full sight of the hound. He saw her, and at once changed his course to the left oblique, unconscious, as it seemed, of having a larger number quite as much at his mercy.

When he headed for the stump the consternation of the mona was both ludicrous and pitiful: she jumped backward and forward, looked up and down and sideways with indescribable grimaces in her efforts to devise ways and means of escape, clutched her head as if to stimulate her five wits into a quicker solution of the problem, and finally clasped the stump tightly, while the recollection of her sins seemed to affect her like a sudden cathartic; but in the next moment Nemesis overtook her in the form of a flying hound. Cerberus missed his grip, but, bearing her down by the impetus of his leap, caught her almost before she reached the ground, and a stifled screech announced the consummation of the vicarious atonement.

The distance from the cross-roads to Port Isabel is about twenty miles. Going east and steadily down-hill, we had a quick trip, still further shortened by the infectious merriment of our travelling-companions. On the railroad from Vera Cruz to the city of Mexico the smoking-car is at the same time the singing- and whooping-car, for neither the presence of ladies nor the fear of immediate ejection will keep the natives quiet while the train is in motion. They enjoy peregrination as we do our fireside comforts: only in the Germanic languages "at home" and "at ease"

ENFANT PERDU.

are synonymous terms. The Anglo-Saxon, though a great emigrant, is at heart domestic, while the Spaniard is by nature excursive. The Englishman, one might say, emigrates for the purpose of reaching a new home,—the Spaniard, in order to get away from his old one.

The programme of our musical entertainment included Indian war-songs, sacred and national hymns, mediæval ballads, and erotic impromptus: an American farmer would have taken us for a gang of migratory minstrels. The only quiet man in the party was the second sergeant, a big, strapping fellow with a deep bass voice, who contented himself with keeping the even tenor of his way, while the gait of the *sargento primero* was somewhat the worse for his frequent calls at the wayside pulque-shops.

The silent philosopher turned out to be a native of Temesvar in Southern Hungary, who had come over with

Maximilian and served in the third artillery of the imperial regulars till his battery was captured at Oaxaca, where they kept him at work in the public streets on two pounds of corn bread and four ounces of bacon a day. After the restoration he donned the bottle-green uniform of the republican army, gradually advanced to his present rank, and was now "as well off as any Austrian chaplain," he assured me,—"four dollars a week, nothing to do and plenty to eat,"—a man who had solved the problem of life to his satisfaction.

"What takes you to Port Isabel?" I asked; "going to wait for a Mexican steamer?"

"No, we are stationed there," he said: "since the Yucatan compromise our government keeps a garrison at the boca."

The northeastern corner of Guatemala is now under the protectorate of the Mexican government, after having for twenty years been the scene of an Indian and international rough-and-tumble fight which made it a most unprofitable possession to the smaller republic. The hostile Indians, like our Comanches and Apaches, used to escape across the convenient frontier whenever their depredations had started the government troops on their trail, and by the treaty of 1862, Port Isabel was to be free to a certain class of Mexican vessels, with the proviso that the Mexican government should furnish auxiliary troops whenever the advance of the hostiles threatened the safety of the harbor. The result was a tragedy of errors, a muddle of protests and counter-protests, marches and countermarches, till 1869, when the governor of Yucatan offered to garrison and improve Port Isabel at the expense of his State on condition that the privileges of the harbor should be extended to Mexican vessels of all classes. The Guatemalan government was

PORT ISABEL.

sensible enough to accept the compromise, and has ever since continued to derive a handsome revenue from a seaport whose protection and repairs have not cost it a cent for the last ten years.

Port Isabel (Itzabal or Atzabal the Caribbeans called the ruins of an ancient city on this coast) will never be of much importance as a commercial seaport, on account of the craggy reef that almost closes the harbor at ebb-tide, but the seaward prospect of its surroundings repeats on the grandest scale the peculiar scenic charms of Perth and Trieste, the town being situated at the head of the Bay of

27

Honduras, which, seen from afar, resembles a mighty river with terraced shores and mountainous headlands.

How is it that distances are so deceptive in the atmosphere of the Spanish Main and the southern Gulf coast? Standing on the brink of the steep plateau west of Port Isabel, the buildings of Fort Gonzales, viewed across a valley of ten miles in diameter, can be distinguished as plainly as the cottages and garden-walls at your feet : the officers' quarters with their row of shade-trees, the boat-house, the scarps and counterscarps of the bastion, are all crowded together on the tip of a promontory, but as sharply outlined as the picture in the spectrum of a telescope. The white walls reflect their light without glittering ; the shades are dark, but not *obscure ;* the atmosphere itself seems to act like a periscopic lens, unless its absolute freedom from smoke and dust should account for its wonderful transparency. That is what our neighbors mean when they speak of "el sol de México,"—the Mexican sun,—whose glories are reserved for their favored country, which vouchsafes such perennial summers to no other land, and whose light lingers on their sierras after it has retreated in disgust from the foggy swamps of the hyperboreans. Just now it gilded the crests of the South Mexican Alps, which tower above all the highlands of Honduras and Vera Paz.

The ruins of Itzabal are about six miles northeast of the seaport, but the modern village offers few objects of interest, and, as the moormen were anxious to reach their boat before sundown, we followed them to the wharf, where we treated our military escort at an open-air pulqueria, while the pantaneros reported at the agency of the Mexican steamer. The soldiers then formed in double file and marched off to the fort, and, after quartering our Indians at the next posada, we accompanied the moormen to the landing.

The steamer was moored about a mile and a half from the mainland, at the Barra del Padre, the "Parson's Reef," an ugly rock, but a golden gate to a swarm of ferrymen, who convey freight and passengers in boats of every desired rig and size, steam-tugs being unknown in the Bay of Honduras. The thrifty moormen selected a rowboat of a kind that can be hired at half-price if the passengers agree to man the oars; the steamer had already hoisted her *partida*-flag, and, as there was a chance of finding an American newspaper on board, we permitted ourselves to be lugged along. Seen from a distance, the Barra del Padre looks like a narrow chain of rocks with intervals that might be improved into a roadstead, but its submarine extent is unfortunately more considerable: between the mainland and the reef an archipelago of craggy islets becomes visible at low water, and every now and then our boat grated audibly against the *serrucho* (cross-cut saw) of a subaqueous ledge.

"No hay cuidado—no danger," laughed our pilot: "the serruchos are all worn out,—the big boats have broken their teeth."

But it struck me that the Bay of Honduras must be strangely afflicted with what our sailors call iron-bound coasts if the Mexicans could not find a better harbor of their own. Their territory borders the bay for more than a hundred miles, but Port Isabel nearly monopolizes the trade of Belize and Eastern Yucatan.

The ridge of the Parson's Reef is about four feet above low-water mark, but storm-floods have frequently submerged it, and, with the exception of the lighthouse, the buildings form a floating village, being mere wharfboat sheds that rise and fall with the tide. A Mexican gunboat and an English clipper were anchored alongside of the steamer, besides a considerable number of smaller vessels at the

lower quay and in the offing. There were sailors of various
nationalities squatting about the wharf in small knots, eating, angling, and gambling. Two minutes after landing
us and securing his boat our pilot was engaged in a game
of sixpenny monte with a Spanish sailor and a mestizo
'longshoreman.

"You'd better help us to get our traps on board," observed the leader of the moormen: "they are ringing their
bell now."

"Campana del burro!" grunted the Spaniard, "don't
bother this man: don't you see he's dealing? You have
got time enough and to spare."

"She leaves at six o'clock, sharp," explained the pilot,—
"at sundown, amigo: you will know it when they fire their
evening gun at the fortin."

The Fortin de Gonzales stands at the extremity of a
steep promontory, on the site of a larger fortress with an
arsenal and military storehouses which were destroyed by
the last Spanish garrison. The new buildings are only
used as barracks, now garrisoned by Mexican troops, but
on the roof of the guard-house the flags of Mexico and
Guatemala fluttered side by side. Our friends seemed to
have reached their quarters in the mean while, and I
thought I recognized the fat sergeant among a group of
soldiers who waved their *bandanas* from the parapet of the
battery.

At last the boatswain's whistle summoned "All hands
for'ard!"—*tropa adelante!*—the honest pantaneros wished
us "long life and a thousand such merry days," and the
ferryman solicited our patronage for the return-trip. The
reader will probably join the home-bound party, but before
the tender casts off her hawser let him take one more look
at the inland hills and the airy summits of the Sierra de

San Tomas, where the sun of Mexico has lighted the watch-fires that will gleam like gold when the last twilight of the valleys has faded into night. In what other land on earth will you see such a sunset, or such lights and shades reflected from every cleft and every rock of those soaring heights athwart a distance of forty English miles, or that dark-green ridge of the coast range, where the pine-trees stand so clearly defined against the northern sky that one might listen for the murmuring of the sea-wind in their matted branches?

But it is time to part. Yes, there goes the gun at the battery, and as the steamer swings slowly round the soldiers on the parapet throw up their caps and send a ringing shout across the water: "Adios, amigos!" while the moormen fire off their trabuccos and wave their hats from the forecastle.

Then, gentle reader, let us join in the answering cheer, "Adios á México!" shake hands with your guide, and take your farewell of the glorious sun.

THE END.

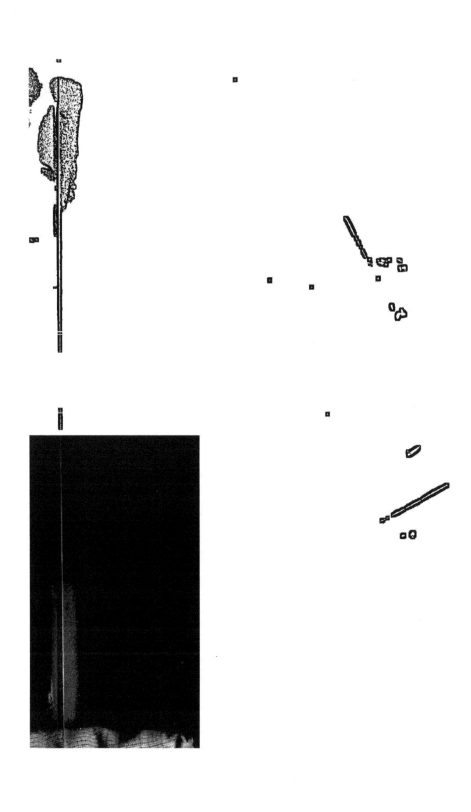